Digital Business Models

Annabeth Aagaard
Editor

Digital Business Models

Driving Transformation and Innovation

palgrave
macmillan

Editor
Annabeth Aagaard
Aarhus University
Risskov, Denmark

ISBN 978-3-319-96901-5 ISBN 978-3-319-96902-2 (eBook)
https://doi.org/10.1007/978-3-319-96902-2

Library of Congress Control Number: 2018959874

This Palgrave Macmillan imprint is published by the registered company Springer Nature Switzerland AG
The registered company address is: Gewerbestrasse 11, 6330 Cham, Switzerland

About the Book

By Editor-in-Chief

Annabeth Aagaard
Centre Director, Associate Professor, PhD
Aarhus University, Denmark

The Internet of Things (IoT) is expected to generate $14 trillion in revenue in the next decade from 2010–2020 (Bort 2013), and with the integration of IoT and digitalization, companies suddenly have access to Big Data to be explored in developing existing and new businesses, processes, networks, and ecosystems. Even though IoT technologies have been available for more than ten years, managers are still in need of innovative business models to monetize IoT-enabled markets. Digital transformation is affecting every business sector, and as investor capital, top talent, and customers shift toward network-centric organizations, the performance gap between early and late adopters is widening. New, scalable, digitally networked business models—for example those of Amazon, Google, Uber, and Airbnb—are impacting on growth, scale, and profit potential for companies in every industry (Libert et al. 2016).

The timing and requests for publications on digital business models (DBMs) have never been better. The first wave of books on digital transformation and case-based go-to guidelines aimed at managers and investors has left a void and calls for a new wave of research-based publications on DBMs and digital business development aimed at universities, lecturers, and students. The aim of this book is therefore to help fill this void and to present one of the first research- and case-based textbooks on DBMs targeting international universities and learning organizations and their lecturers/professors and students.

A key contribution of this book is to explore models, theories, and company practices to contribute to our knowledge of how companies, organizations, and networks can design, implement, and apply DBMs, as this is stressed as an insufficiently researched area by a number of authors (Westerman et al. 2014; Raskino and Waller 2015; Rogers 2016; Berendsen and Beckett 2017). Another contribution of this book is to view DBMs in different contexts, as digitalization can take on different forms and be integrated in a number of ways with very different objectives, potentials, and outputs depending on the specific context. Finally, a further main objective and contribution is to investigate the theoretical concepts of DBMs to enable further development and research among academic communities and hopefully to inspire existing companies and start-ups to explore and seize digital opportunities while prospering from digital networks, processes, and platforms in building new and better business models for the future.

While this volume focuses on the potentials of DBMs from a theoretical and research-based approach, the question is also highly relevant for practitioners, as the effective adoption of DBMs needs to be actively managed to create customer value, networks while creating new markets, businesses, and optimizations. The book therefore also seeks to explain and explore how companies build their organizations, strategies, processes, and networks to ensure successful design, integration, and management of new DBMs throughout the value chain and ecosystem of the company and organization.

The majority of the existing literature emphasizes digital transformation and the technical aspects of digitalization, and does not pay attention to DBMs and digital business development. *Digital Business Models—Driving Transformation and Innovation* explores the identification development and application of DBMs from a theoretical and empirical angle to benefit academia and students as well as industry and organizations. Thus, the publication of this book will be one of the first international and comprehensive contributions to the field of DBMs and DBM innovations. We hope it will help elevate and further develop the discussion, research streams, and practices relevant to DBMs, and wish you happy reading!

References

Bort, J. 2013. Cisco's John Chambers Has Found a New $14 Trillion Market. Retrieved May 12, 2015, from: http://www.businessinsider.com/ciscos-john-chambers-has-found-a-new-14-trillion-market-2013-5

Berendsen, G., and R.C. Beckett. 2017. Blending Digitalization and Services in Business Model Innovation. In *Conference Paper. 18th International CINet Conference*, Potsdam, Germany, September 10–12, 2017.

Libert, B., M. Beck, and J. Wind. 2016. How to Navigate a Digital Transformation. *Harvard Business Review*, June 22.

Raskino, M., and G. Waller. 2015. *Digital to the Core: Remastering Leadership for Your Industry, Your Enterprise, and Yourself.* Brookline: Taylor and Francis.

Rogers, D.L. 2016. *The Digital Transformation Playbook: Rethink Your Business for the Digital Age*. New York: Columbia Business School Publishing.

Westerman, G., D. Bonnet, and A. McAfee. 2014. *Leading Digital – Turning Technology into Business Transformation*. Boston: HBR Press.

Contents

Notes on Contributors

Annabeth Aagaard is an Associate Professor at Aarhus University in Denmark, where she teaches and researches in strategic business development, digital and sustainable business models, and open innovation. She is the Centre Director of Centre for Business Development that bridges research between digital technologies and business development. Furthermore, she is the CEO and owner of a consultancy company, KnowledgeHouse, which has designed and implemented strategies and management strategies among top 100 companies in Scandinavia. She has 20 years of experience working in these fields drawing on her experiences in the academic, public, and private sectors, where she was formerly a manager and management specialist. She has published nine textbooks and management handbooks, and numerous scientific and public articles on management, business models, innovation, and sustainability in scientific journals, including *Journal of Product Innovation Management*, *Creativity & Innovation Management*, and the *Scandinavian Journal of Management*. She is currently working on a book on Sustainable Business models for Palgrave Macmillan and is working on two national industry-sponsored projects on digital business models and two Internet of Things projects, IoT crawler and a NGI move (Next Generation Internet) sponsored by the European Commission.

Anja Bechmann is an Associate Professor, Center Director at DATALAB—Center for Digital Social Research & Research Fellow at Aarhus Institute of Advanced Studies at Aarhus University in Denmark. Her research examines data traces in digital spaces focusing currently on social media (Facebook and

Instagram) and topics such as democracy, social cohesion, privacy, accountability, anti-discrimination, next generation Internet, machine learning, artificial intelligence and ethics. She has been appointed a member of the ATV Digital Sages, Council for Digital Security and the EU Commission High Level group on Disinformation and she serves as cochair of the ethics working group for the international Association of Internet Researchers.

Michail J. Beliatis is a multi-disciplinary academic in the Center for Business Development at Aarhus University, where he is involved with research and teaching on Internet of Things, Advanced Digital Product Development and Technological Entrepreneurship. He has a great deal of experience on research innovation and development for nanotechnology, printed plastic electronics, IoT electronic products and industrial automations. He has worked in many large-scale national and international projects in these areas.

Emilia Evequoz is a legal expert and researcher actively participating in several European research projects. She is a member of the international Board of Experts on Data Protection of EuroPrivacy. Previously, she worked with the Data Protection Authority of Valais in Switzerland. Evéquoz is a Certified International Privacy Professional CIPP/E. She acquired her academic education in law in Poland and Switzerland. She is a graduate of Master studies at the University of Szczecin, Poland and the University of Neuchatel, Switzerland. Evéquoz also studied Transnational Law at the University of Geneva and at the Graduate Institute in Geneva and has a Certificate of Advanced Studies in International Arbitration from the University of Luzern.

Ana Maria Pacheco Huamani is the Head of Research at Archimede Solutions. She is leading and coordinating the participation of the company in several international research projects, including several H2020 research projects, with a focus on data protection and cybersecurity. She coordinated the development and specification of the EuroPrivacy certification scheme on GDPR and data protection compliance (www.europrivacy.org). After graduating in Political Science at the University of Geneva, she continued her academic education in the domain of Human Resources Management and in Management Control with a focus on control and audit methodologies. She has acquired over 20 years of experience in top management functions. She is a founding member and board member of an international foundation and coordinated several international events and conferences. She also worked in cooperation with the Peruvian Ministry of Foreign Affairs as Consultative Council Member for the Geneva Consulate.

Jeffrey Johnson is an associate professor at the Jon M. Huntsman School (Utah State University) in the Management Information Systems Department. His teaching and research interests include data security, data management, e-commerce, information technology entrepreneurship, and innovation. He is the faculty advisor for the student chapter of the Association for Information Systems (AIS) at Utah State University. He has three patents issued and one pending, and publications in several refereed journals.

Kirsi Kotilainen is a doctoral student in a double degree program at Tampere University of Technology, Finland, and at the University of Lausanne, Switzerland. She is also working in the Finnish consortium focusing on the Finnish electricity transition (EL-TRAN). She is also a visiting PhD researcher at the Energy Policy Research Group at the University of Cambridge. Her research interests are on energy transition, changing consumer role in the energy industry, innovations and new business models in energy and the development of energy policies. Before starting her academic career, she was working for over 15 years in international business development and strategy roles in high-tech industry focusing on, for example, new technology commercialisation and building business ecosystems.

Srdjan Krčo is a co-founder and CEO of DunavNET, a company designing turnkey IOT solutions for smart cities, agriculture and manufacturing. He has over 20 years of experience working with large multinational companies and international collaborative research and innovation projects. Krčo is one of the founding members of the International IoT Forum and is actively participating in IoT-EPI (IoT European Platforms Initiative) and AIOTI (Alliance for IoT Innovation) activities. In 2007, Krčo won the Innovation Engineer of the Year award in Ireland. He has over 15 patents and more than 70 papers at international conferences and journals to his name. Krčo holds an associate professor position at FEFA (Faculty for Economy and Financial Administration) where he works with students on business aspects of IoT and digital transformation. He is a frequent speaker at international events addressing IoT and its applications. Krčo is a Senior IEEE member was recently awarded MVP (most valuable professional) status for IoT activities by Microsoft.

Miloš Lončar is a digital transformation specialist focusing on business transformation/enablement of new business models and digital ecosystems. Currently, he works as an IoT solutions professional in the Microsoft Global Black Belt Team. In that role, Lončar is helping solution specialists to address business aspects of strategic IoT projects in the Western Europe region. Further to that, he evangelises Microsoft IoT platform to broader audiences during key events, workshops and conferences and supports business development of top Microsoft partners who have mastered IoT and digital transformation. He is an Innovation and Exploitation Advisory Board member of H2020 project TagItSmart and a visiting lecturer at FEFA (Faculty for Economy and Financial Administration) where he focuses on business implications of IoT as a crucial enabler of digital transformation. He has an engineering background, holds an Executive MBA from Sheffield University (UK) and is a PhD candidate in the area of management.

Mats Magnusson is Professor of Product Innovation Engineering at KTH Royal Institute of Technology in Stockholm and Permanent Visiting Professor at LUISS School of Business and Management in Rome, He has previously also been Visiting Professor at Aalborg University and the University of Bologna, and a visiting researcher at Ritsumeikan University. Moreover, he is President of the Continuous Innovation Network and a senior advisor of the Creativity and Innovation Management journal. Mats has a PhD in Innovation Engineering and Management and an MSc in Industrial Engineering and Management from Chalmers University of Technology, as well as a BA in Japanese from the University of Gothenburg. His research, teaching and consultancy activities concern strategic and organizational aspects of innovation, and he has published extensively on these topics in, for example, *Organization Studies*, *Research Policy*, *Journal of Product Innovation Management*, *MIT Sloan Management Review* and *Long Range Planning*.

Saku J. Mäkinen is Vice Dean for Research and Professor of Industrial Management at the Tampere University of Technology (TUT), Finland. He has previously been with CERN, Geneva (2014–2016), the Columbia University, New York (2011–12), National University of Singapore (2000–2002) and Australian Graduate School of Management, University of New South Wales, Sydney (1996). Mäkinen works in the intersection of technology and innovation management (TIM) and strategic management, mostly in close collaboration with industry. His research has appeared in leading international journals including *Technological Forecasting and Social Change*, *Journal of Product Innovation Management*, *Technovation*, *IEEE Transactions on Engineering Management*, *Journal of Cleaner Production*, *Resources, Conservation and Recycling* and *Advances in Strategic Management*. He serves in editorial roles including editor-in-chief, *CERN IdeaSquare Journal of Experimental Innovation* since 2015, Department Editor (Emerging Technologies) *IEEE Transactions on Engineering Management* since 2018, Associate editor, *IJITM (Int. J. Innovation and Technology Management)* since 2011 and Member, editorial board, *Technological Forecasting & Social Change* since 2015.

Frank McGroarty is Professor of Computational Finance and Investment Analytics, and Director of the Centre for Digital Finance at the University of Southampton, UK. His research mainly resides in the intersection of Business and Computer Science and is primarily motivated by real-world commercial and policy issues. Prior to joining the University of Southampton, Frank spent 13 years working as a fund manager in London.

David Paper is a Professor at the Jon M. Huntsman School (Utah State University) in the Management Information Systems Department. He has several refereed publications appearing in journals such as *Organizational Research Methods*, *Communications of the ACM*, *Information & Management*, *Decision Support Systems*, *Journal of Information Technology Cases and Applications*, *Communications of the AIS*, *Long Range Planning*, *Creativity and Innovation*, *Accounting Management and Information Technologies*, *Journal of Managerial Issues*, *Business Process Management Journal*, and *Journal of Computer Information Systems*. He has worked for Texas Instruments, DLS Inc., and the Phoenix Small Business Administration. He has performed consulting work for IBM, AT&T, Octel Communications Corporation, Utah Department of Transportation, and the Space Dynamics Laboratory. His teaching and research interests include data science, process management, database management, e-commerce, business process reengineering, and organizational transformation.

Mirko Presser is an Associate Professor and Centre Deputy Director of the Centre for Business Development at Aarhus University, where he researches and teaches in digital technologies, technological business development, innovation and sustainability. He has more than 15 years of experience in research and innovation, where he has worked in industry and academia on large-scale international projects within Internet of Things (IoT), data analytics and 5G. He is the vice president of the IoT Forum and one of the most influential IoT experts in Europe.

Ulla A. Saari is a Postdoctoral Researcher at the Center for Innovation and Technology Research (CITER), the Laboratory of Industrial and Information Management at the Tampere University of Technology (TUT), Finland. She holds a DrTech degree in Industrial Engineering and Management from TUT and a MA in Languages and Social Sciences from the University of Helsinki. Her current research topics include sustainability, eco-friendliness, stakeholder management, entrepreneurship and business ecosystems. She has 20 years' experience in the high-tech industry in various senior manager level roles in international organizations.

Johan Simonsson is Director Service Offer at Husqvarna Construction Products. He holds a Master of Science in Electronic Business Systems and Technologies from Golden Gate University in San Francisco and is currently also an Industrial PhD student at Product Innovation Engineering at KTH Royal Institute of Technology in Stockholm, focusing on digital business model innovation.

Patrik Ström is Associate Professor of Economic Geography, Centre for International Business Studies, Department of Business Administration, University of Gothenburg. He holds a PhD in Business Administration from Roskilde University and Econ. Dr. in Economic Geography from the University of Gothenburg. His research has focused on the internationalization and competitiveness of the knowledge-intensive service industry in Europe and Asia. Ström is the president of the European Association for Research on Services (RESER). He was also member of the EU Commission High Level Group on Business Services.

Zsolt Ugray is an Associate Professor of MIS in the Jon M. Huntsman School of Business at Utah State University. His publications have appeared in journals such as *Informs Journal on Computing, Optimization Methods and Software, Review of Business Information Systems, Journal of Information Technology Cases and Applications, International Journal of E-Business Research*, and *Interacting with Computers*. Before entering academia, he worked in the semiconductor industry for several years. His research and teaching interests include business analytics, data science, data mining, optimization methods, and heuristics.

Jussi Valta is a doctoral student in Industrial Engineering and Management at Tampere University of Technology, Finland. His research is focused in systemic innovations, path dependences and organisation of new energy systems, namely microgrids. He is also interested in energy policies and regulatory frameworks and his MSc thesis studied policies on energy prosumers. Besides his academic career, he has worked in sales in mining technology and construction material industries.

Rob van Kranenburg is the founder of #IoT Council. He works as Ecosystem Manager for the EU projects Tagitsmart and Next Generation Internet. He wrote *The Internet of Things. A Critique of Ambient Technology and the All-seeing Network of RFID* (Network Notebooks 02, Institute of Network Cultures). He is co-founder of bricolabs. Together with Christian Nold he wrote *Situated Technologies Pamphlets 8: The Internet of People for a Post-Oil World.* Kranenburg is co-editor of *Enabling Things to Talk Designing IoT solutions with the IoT Architectural Reference Model* (Springer Open Access).

Robert Wentrup is cofounder of the company Internago, which works with internationalization, and has a background with Business Sweden—the Swedish Trade and Invest Council in France and Morocco. His PhD focused on internationalization for online firms and the geographical perspectives on the online economy. He is a research fellow and a guest lecturer at the Centre for International Business Studies in the Department of Business Administration, University of Gothenburg in Sweden. His research draws from the disciplines of Internet and economic geography, international business, and development studies. He has worked several years as a consultant in Accenture's technology practice and is also member of the board for the non-governmental organization AAID, the Association of Accountability and Internet Democracy.

Xiangxuan Xu is a postdoctoral research fellow at the Centre for International Business Studies, School of Business, Economics and Law, University of Gothenburg. Her research focuses on spatial patterns of the digital economy and their policy implications. Her current research project is funded by the Adlerbertska Foundations, and studies sustainable manufacturing in the digital era from a regional industrial evolution perspective. Her doctoral dissertation was on IoT, "The Internet of Things: Projects-Places-Policies," and explored the spatial mechanisms underlying IoT implementations in an integrated digital/physical and local/global framework. She was previously an analyst in the mobile telecommunications industry and project manager within the European Union Framework Programme BSR Stars.

Qi Zhang is an Associate Professor with the Department of Engineering, Aarhus University, Denmark. Besides her academic experiences, she has had various industrial experiences. Her research interests include IoT, 5G, mission critical communication, network coding and compressive sensing. She is serving as an Editor for *EURASIP Journal on Wireless Communications and Networking*. She was a Co-Chair of the Co-operative and Cognitive Mobile Networks (CoCoNet) Workshop in the ICC conference 2010–2015 and was a TPC Co-Chair of BodyNets 2015.

Sébastien Ziegler is a founder and the Director General of Mandat International. He is President of the IoT Forum, Vice Chair of the IEEE ComSoc Subcommittee on the IoT, and Rapporteur on Emerging Technologies for the IoT and for smart cities at the ITU (SG20). Sébastien has a PhD in Management with a specialization in Information Systems at the Faculty of Economy and Management of the University of Geneva. He graduated in International Relations at the Graduate Institute of International Studies, followed by a Master in Environment, a MBA in international administration (HEC Geneva), and complementary executive courses at Harvard Business School in Boston, Stanford University, UC Berkeley and EPFL. He is also an expert in data protection accredited for EuroPrivacy, EuroPriSe and ISO 27001 certifications. Sébastien founded several foundations, SMEs, and organizations. Sébastien Ziegler initiated several international research projects in the area of ICT, with a focus on the Internet of Things, IPv6, and privacy. He is currently coordinating and associated to several ongoing European research projects and is co-directing the Master in Advanced Studies on the Internet of Things at the University of Geneva. With a multi-disciplinary academic profile, combining international law, science, and economics, he is a relentless promoter of research, innovation, and international cooperation. He also supported the creation of several organizations, foundations, and companies.

Xenia Ziouvelou is a Senior Research Fellow at the University of Southampton, UK. Her research focuses on innovation and technological transformation and the way that they revolutionise business, law and policy. Prior to her current role, Ziouvelou has worked in various roles in academia and industry in the fields of strategy, innovation and technology transfer.

List of Figures

List of Tables

1

The Concept and Frameworks of Digital Business Models

Annabeth Aagaard

1 Introduction

The increasing digitalization of businesses and society in general has triggered a veritable explosion in the amount of so-called Big Data made available and to be adopted and explored in the development of business. As stressed by Arthur (2011), digitalization is creating a second economy that is vast, automatic and invisible—thereby bringing about the greatest societal upheaval since the Industrial Revolution. Data has become massive and has moved from monthly, to weekly, to daily and hourly with regard to a large number of transactions made by millions of customers and entities across the ecosystems of organizations. Some studies estimate an increase in annually created, replicated and consumed data from around 1200 exabytes in 2010 to 40,000 in 2020 (Gantz and Reinsel 2012). Big Data is defined in terms of data volume (Manyika et al. 2011) and as high-volume, high-velocity and

A. Aagaard (✉)
Department of Business Development & Technology, Aarhus University, Herning, Denmark
e-mail: aaa@btech.au.dk

A. Aagaard (ed.), *Digital Business Models*,
https://doi.org/10.1007/978-3-319-96902-2_1

high-variety information assets that demand cost-effective, innovative forms of information processing for enhanced insight and decision-making. There is growing awareness that this view is limited, however, as other factors are also important in discussing it, including the uncertainty of the data; its *veracity*, referring to the reliability of a certain data type (Schroeck et al. 2012). Such data can be applied by companies to target customers more effectively, to make better pricing decisions and demand predictions, and to optimize assortments, production and logistics. Thus, Big Data is employed for user-centric, knowledge-driven product development (Johanson et al. 2014).

The use of digital technologies and digitalization in innovation is central for digital business model innovation (DBMI) and the disruptive business innovation tendencies of this decade (2010s)—and likely also for decades to come. Consequently, Nambisan et al. (2017, p. 224) conceptualize digital innovation as "the creation of (and consequent change in) market offerings, business processes, or models that result from the use of digital technologies." Consequently, digital innovation management refers to the "practices, processes, and principles that underlie the effective orchestration of digital innovation." Digitalization affects entire ecosystems, their business models (BMs) and the underlying business functions of a company's value chain. By digitalizing business functions, data can be provided to enhance and develop each of these functions—and thereby the entire value chain.

In practice, this is seen in the dramatic shift in focus toward marketing online, on social media and via mobile marketing, and a waning focus on traditional advertising. Stronger interactions are created and data is continuously collected from existing and potential customers through social networks. The online environment renders assortment and pricing decisions easier and much more flexible. Logistics and logistics streams are key to competitive delivery and services, and the marketing and logistic functions therefore need to cooperate more effectively to deliver superior customer value—and at a lower and more competitive cost. Standards have been developed to represent different forms of data (text, numbers, pictures and video) facilitating communication via Bluetooth and the Internet, which has led to the evolution of new products and services, all of which has further contributed to the commodification of data.

With intelligent devices becoming interconnected in "the Internet of Things" (IoT), new developments have created associated infrastructure and an expanding knowledge base. These innovative combinations are reflected in enterprise digital business models (DBMs) (Kiel et al. 2016). Holler et al. (2014) propose an information-driven value chain for IoT consisting of four inputs (devices/sensors, open data, operations support system/business support system (OSS/BSS) and corporate databases), as depicted in Fig. 1.1. Each of these four inputs undergoes value addition through production/manufacturing, processing, packaging and further through distribution and marketing as a finished product. Figure 1.1 depicts how the raw data is collected through different types of sensors, actuators, open data, operating/business systems and corporate databases, and how the data then undergoes processing and packaging through a wireless fixed network prior to becoming useful information. As stressed by Chan (2015), the variety, velocity and volume of the acquired Big Data infrastructure

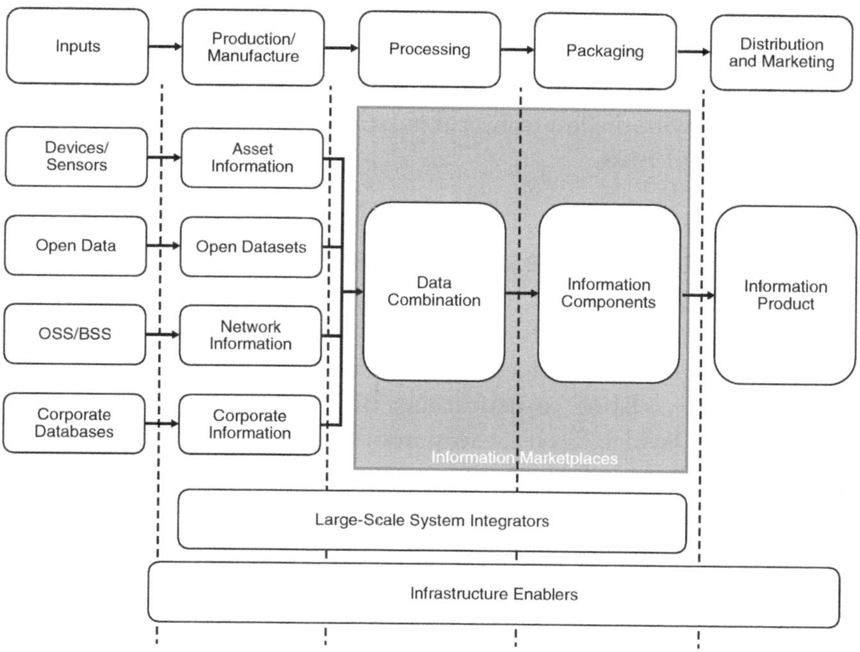

Fig. 1.1 Information-driven value chain for IoT. (Source: Holler et al. (2014))

enablers and a large-scale system integrator are required. Consequently, different players have to overcome the interoperability issue to ensure optimal value creation and performance across the information-driven value chain.

DBMI explores how companies adopt and deploy digital technologies and BMs to improve performance quantifiably. DBMI is thus considered to be a growth engine in the area of vertical and horizontal industry. IoT provides key leverage in digitalization and in providing data for digital BM development. The definition of IoT largely depends on the target audience and reflects the different types of IoT applications. However, according to Lee et al. (2017), four main categories of definitions describing IoT can be found in the literature: (1) IoT as intelligent objects, (2) IoT as an extension of the Internet, (3) IoT as a global network infrastructure and (4) IoT as an interaction of information. Throughout this chapter, IoT is defined as a global infrastructure linking physical and virtual objects through the exploitation of data capture and communication (EU FP7 Project CASAGRAS 2009). This clarifies how IoT is more than a set of technologies comprising IoT when "glued" together; it also involves the entire ecosystem in which IoT is present. In this chapter, we are concerned with the less technical properties of IoT and their meaning in the context of BMs.

2 Digital Business Models

BMs seek to make sense of how businesses go about their work, and they are presented with different levels of abstraction in the literature. However, a key challenge relating to performing BM studies relates to the issue addressed by David J. Teece, who states that "the concept of a business model lacks theoretical grounding in economics or in business studies" (Teece 2010, p. 174). BMs and business model innovation (BMI) have received extensive attention from academics and practitioners alike (Amit and Zott 2001; Chesbrough and Rosenbloom 2002; Markides and Charitou 2004; Teece 2010; Zott et al. 2011; Markides 2013; Spieth et al. 2014) and have been the subject of an ever-growing number of academic and practitioner-oriented studies. Several authors make attempts at defining the BM concept, including Afuah and Tucci (2001), who explain a BM as the means by which a business "creates, delivers and captures value" in a relationship with a network of exchange partners. According to Dodgson et al. (2013), the term "business model" is used either to commercialize new technology or ideas or as a source of innovation to the BM itself, which can lead to a competitive advantage.

While the extensive stream of work on BM innovation has generated many important insights (see Spieth et al. 2014), our understanding of BMs remains fragmented, as stressed by Zott et al. (2011). One thing all of the authors in this field seem to agree on is that a BM is a model of how a business does business (Taran 2011). However, while there is consensus on the meaning of "doing business," namely creating and delivering value to achieve a sustainable business position, there is less agreement on the "model" part. For Magretta (2002), a BM is a narrative that describes the customer, the customer value, the revenue collection of the model and the delivery of this value. Another level of abstraction by Gassmann et al. (2014) describes the BM as an archetype of 55 different BM building blocks that can be combined in various ways to accommodate the BM in which the business operates. Traditional BMs are thus designed on a firm-centric basis. Owing to the nature of the IoT ecosystem, in which firms must collaborate with competitors and across industries, however, it is easy to see why traditional BMs are inadequate. Moreover, rapidly changing market environments in technology-related industries mean that companies must swiftly adjust to market challenges to succeed and remain competitive.

When reviewing the literature on the DBM concept, it becomes clear that it primarily consists of practitioner papers, white papers and/or writings often initiated and carried out by consultancy companies. However, more recent BM research shows a growing interest in the digital transformation of businesses and stresses (Big) Data as a driver for BMI. Nevertheless, the DBM and DBMI research streams remain in the early stages. Veit et al. (2014) thus address the BM concept as a "missing link" between business strategy, processes and information technology (IT) and propose three application streams: (1) BMs in IT industries (a product orientation), (2) IT-enabled BMs (a process orientation) and (3) IT support for developing and managing BMs (a toolkit orientation).

In continuation, El Sawy and Pereira (2013) emphasize how, over time, the role of IT in business has changed from a connectivity view (IT as a communication channel) through an immersion view (IT as an operating environment) to a fusion view (IT as fabric), where modular digital platforms can be adapted and interconnected in different ways. The authors suggest that digital business ecosystems enable the possibility of combining capabilities across boundaries into innovative new offerings and solutions to create and capture value.

According to Bradley et al. (2015, p. 8), DBMs can be grouped into three categories:

1) Cost value (price transparency, consumption-based pricing, reverse auctions, buyer aggregation, rebates and rewards);
2) Experience value (customer choice, personalization, automation, lower latency and any device any time);
3) Platform value (marketplaces, crowdsourcing, peer-to-peer, sharing economy and data monetization).

Thus, companies collect, store and analyze (Big) Data to develop existing businesses, to create actual business value and to develop totally new BMs. Of the earlier contributions in the DBM research stream, Davenport (2006) is among those presenting a number of primarily anecdotal examples of companies drawing a competitive advantage from the use of data and analytics. This is further supported in the empirical analysis by McAfee and Brynjolfsson (2012), who suggest that companies that rely more on data-driven decision-making perform better in terms of productivity and profitability. Another stream of DBM literature focuses on data as a service and analytics as a service as new service types and/or emphasizes DBM partnerships. Otto and Aier (2013) suggest different BMs in the business partner data domain using a case-study approach. Another stream focuses on the analytics ecosystem and, for example, Chen et al. (2011) define the two new types of BMs as relying on data from a structural perspective. However, most of the present DBM/DBMI research focuses on technical or organizational aspects (Delen and Demirkan 2013).

Rong et al. (2015) develop an integrated 6C framework to systemize the understanding of the IoT-based business system, namely Context, Cooperation, Constructive elements, Configuration, Capability and Change. Context is the environmental setting for the ecosystem development. Cooperation incorporates the mechanisms by which the partners interact to reach the strategic objectives. Constructive elements constitute the fundamental structure and supportive infrastructure of the ecosystem. Configuration identifies the external relationships among partners. Capacity implies the key success features of a supply network from the functional view of design, production, in-bound logistics and information management. And finally, each business ecosystem faces the challenge of Change. Through case studies, Rong et al. (2015) reveal that the ecosystem is very open at an early stage in which the focal firm needs more stakeholders to add value to the product platform.

Bucherer et al. (2012) describe some of the key issues when designing IoT BMs, including information between nodes and win–win information exchange for all stakeholders. Moreover, Westerlund et al. (2014) identify three contemporary challenges of IoT: (1) the diversity of objects, which refers to a multitude of different types of connected objects and devices without commonly accepted or emerging standards, (2) the immaturity of innovation, referring to today's quintessential IoT innovations that have not yet matured into products and services, and (3) the unstructured ecosystems, which refer to the lack of defined underlying structures and governance, stakeholder roles and value-creating logics. Despite these challenges, several IoT BM frameworks exist, as will be presented in Section 3. However, there are still some major gaps in IoT that must be properly addressed (Chan 2015).

2.1 Drivers and Challenges of Digital Business Models

The exponential growth and adoption of digital technologies in businesses has resulted in significant improvements in many business processes and plays a significant role in the BM and innovation field (e.g. Yoo et al. 2012; Holmstrom and Partanen 2014; Hylving 2015). As such, companies are moving from stand-alone organizations to multi-firm networks that perform collaborative innovation with partners, suppliers and customers in what is commonly referred to as open or collaborative environments. Digital technologies and IoT play key roles as enablers of communication and in the exchange of quality and timely information, the sharing, storing and protection of knowledge, and provide new platforms for developing existing businesses and totally new DBMs. Hence, established companies are progressively undertaking digital transformations not only to rethink what customers value but also to create operating models that take advantage of what has recently become possible for competitive differentiation (Berman 2012).

However, as value creation in the traditional product mindset shifts from solving existing needs in a reactive manner to addressing real-time and emerging needs in a predictive manner, filling out well-known frameworks and streaming established BMs will not be enough (Hui 2014). Through the exchange and adoption of data, businesses can evolve their operations and value creation using DBMs and IoT across three drivers/layers: manufacturing, supporting and value creation (Mejtoft 2011). The manufacturing layer implies that manufacturers or retailers can provide items such as sensors and terminal devices: the supporting layer collects data that can be utilized in the value creation processes and the value creation layer applies IoT as a cocreative partner, as the network of "things" can think for itself.

Another key driver in adopting and leveraging DBMI opportunities is to apply the SD logic lens (Vargo and Lusch 2004; Spring and Araujo 2009; Maglio and Spohrer 2013), implying that companies focus on client solutions rather than just selling a product. The SD logic view brings together joint consideration of a DBM, IoT, opportunities for customer interaction and the evolution of supporting external service platforms, which helps move the enterprise perspective from a focus on (just) value proposition to a focus on customer value cocreation and value in use as well.

New technologies and innovations are often commercialized through start-up companies (Criscuolo et al. 2012). A new phenomenon emerging in the context of digitalization is digital entrepreneurship, which may be viewed as a socio-economic and technological phenomenon that joins traditional entrepreneurship with an emphasis on leveraging new digital technologies in novel ways (e.g. social, mobile, artificial intelligence, analytics, cloud and cyber-solutions) in order to develop the traditional way of creating and doing business in the digital era. The digital entrepreneurs and digital start-ups are characterized by a high intensity of utilization of new digital technologies (particularly social, mobile, analytics and cloud solutions) to improve business operations, invent new DBMs, sharpen business intelligence and engage with customers and stakeholders through new (digital) channels (Ries 2011).

Some authors foresee a new wave of digital start-ups linked to Industry 4.0 and the Internet of Everything, where digital platforms will be coupled and connected with sophisticated infrastructures of sensors, cyber-physical systems and robots (Case 2016). As stressed by Hartmann et al. (2016), digital start-up companies are not bound by the legacy systems of established firms built over a period of time, and it is therefore easier for newer firms to get the right infrastructure in place to exploit their data. Thus, leveraging the advantage of starting from a blank page instead of being constrained by an existing business, start-ups create a variety of (presumably) "purer" BMs. The potential first-mover advantages, unexplored BMs and growing population size and needs make start-up companies an optimal venue for adopting DBMs.

3 (Digital) Business Model Frameworks

In the exploration of what DBMs contain, numerous BM (innovation) frameworks are presented by various authors. Most of these frameworks describe these BMs in detail as meta-models and/or activity systems. However, the aim of this chapter is not explore all possible BM frameworks or to select one such framework over another, but rather to present some of the variety in how the DBM concept is explained and explored across the different dimensions of BM frameworks. As such, BM frameworks have three distinct advantages, as they offer: (1) a "common language" that fosters dialogue, (2) scaled-down representations and the opportunity to experiment with ideas and (3) representations that boost legitimacy and activate resources (Amit and Zott 2012).

This chapter is not a complete literature review of (D)BMI tools and frameworks; rather, it is based on the UNIFY-IoT report, which identifies a number of important BMI tools that have been used specifically for IoT and relevant digital BMI. A total of six BMI frameworks were identified in the literature, which were considered suitable for this analysis—three traditional BM/BMI frameworks (Business Model Canvas, Business Model Navigator and Value Design Model) and three new/recent IoT/digital-focused DBM/DBMI frameworks (DNA Model, BM Type for IoT Model and IoT Business Model Framework). As the first three BM frameworks are fairly well known, extensive description is unnecessary. However, the latter three models are relatively new and will therefore be explained in greater detail.

One important point to keep in mind in this discussion of frameworks for mapping DBMs is that some of these frameworks/models were invented before digitalization and before DBMs were adopted and became "mainstream" in the business literature. One might therefore question or discuss if the existing BM frameworks can be applied in a digital context and whether these frameworks integrate the necessary dimensions to accommodate for this new commodity of data in business development and in mapping DBMs and DBMI.

3.1 Business Model Canvas

The most famous and widely applied BMI framework is the Business Model Canvas by Osterwalder and Pigneur (2010). Through this graphical explanation of the content of BMs, the Business Model Canvas provides an overview and potentials for comparisons and development. It is an industry standard and celebrated as an easy approach to business model innovation. The canvas consists of nine building blocks that are distributed in a rectangular sheet, and the blocks are studied separately and linearly. Osterwalder and Pigneur (2010) argue that the customer segment is the center of the BM, and the business should therefore be built around the understanding of a specific customer segment's needs. They state that the whole right side of the canvas is about value, where the left side is about efficiency (Fig. 1.2).

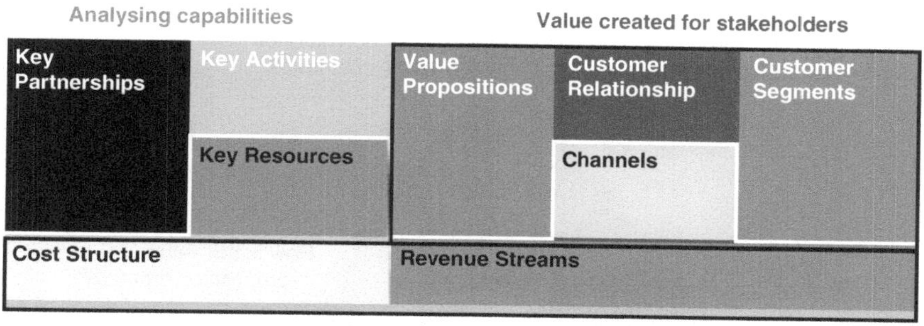

Fig. 1.2 Business model canvas. (Source: Inspired from Osterwalder and Pigneur (2010))

The Benefits and Challenges of Using the Business Model Canvas for DBM

Today, the Business Model Canvas is acknowledged for its high usability and maturity. It is a well-documented model, user friendly and ready for application by the ordinary user. The handbook guide contains some lean start-up elements, for instance how to choose customer channels through prototyping and feedback loops. However, the model does not address the technological aspect of business modeling and does not consider data as a specific value. Furthermore, it builds on the assumption that the customer need is known, which may not be the case for disruptive new DBMs.

3.2 St. Gallen Business Model Navigator: Magic Triangle

The St. Gallen Business Model Navigator Magic Triangle model by Gassmann et al. (2014) (see Fig. 1.3) argues that any BM consists of four main building blocks: "Who?," "What?," "How?" and "Value?" In contrast to the previous two models, this is a distinct approach, defining the minimum requirements of a BM. Gassmann et al. (2014) argue for business modeling as the new competitive advantage. Businesses that do not

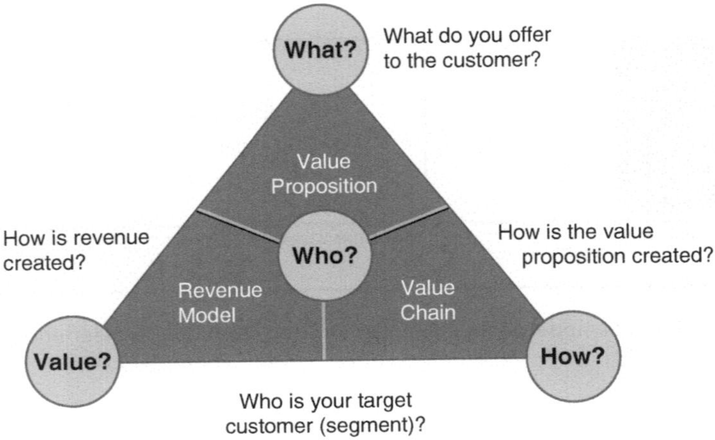

Fig. 1.3 St. Gallen Magic Triangle. (Source: Gassmann et al. (2014))

consider business modeling are generally less successful and tend to disappear faster from the market. The original purpose of the tool is for businesses that are stuck in conventional thinking to think outside the box and create new revenue streams. However, its simplicity has given birth to new BMs by building on the four core dimensions.

The Benefits and Challenges of Using the Business Model Navigator for DBM

The Gassmann et al. Business Model Navigator is commercialized, mature and highly usable. It is simple to use and therefore quick to map the overall elements of a BM. However, its simplicity comes with the drawbacks of not producing a more detailed mapping of a (D)BM. The framework/tool comes with online courses, a software tool and 55 BM patterns stimulating ideation. However, it suffers many of the same issues as the Business Model Canvas in mapping DBM, as it does not address/integrate technology or data explicitly.

3.3 Value Design Model

Westerlund et al. (2014) propose a conceptual framework, the Value Design Model, that takes a holistic approach to mapping participants and their interrelations in value creation through the BM. Value Design consists of four main blocks interacting with one another: Value Drivers, Value Nodes, Value Exchanges and Value Extracts (see Fig. 1.4).

Value Drivers comprise both individual and shared motivations for participants to be part of the ecosystem. Value Nodes are the actors in the ecosystem and refer to the links between them that create value. Value Exchange describes the flow of value between the nodes (the relationship between Value Flow and Value Node). Value Extract functions as a zoom-in/zoom-out tool relative to the Value Flows for companies to explore and identify possibilities to capture value and create new revenue streams. Thus, Value Exchange can explain what fuels the engine, which is at the core of network-centric BMs. The exchanges can be monetary and non-monetary, but the Value Extract is the extraction of the value that can be monetized and therefore is the most relevant to the business. Westerlund et al. (2014) claim that a vendor-centric BM concept is similar to Value Design, the difference being that it is applied at an ecosystem network-centric level.

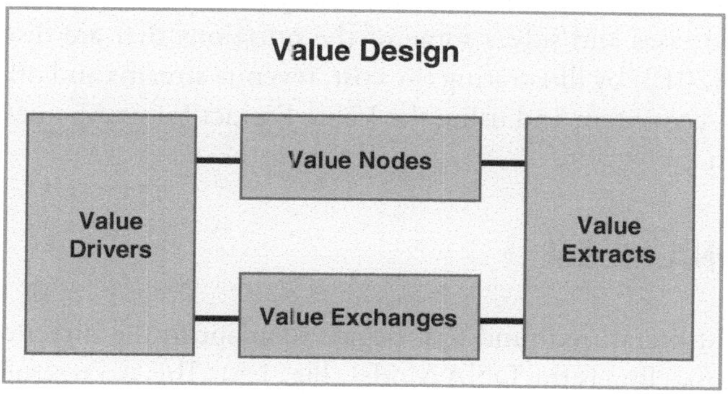

Fig. 1.4 Value Design Model. (Source: Westerlund et al. (2014))

The Benefits and Challenges of Using the Value Design Model for DBM

The Value Design Model discusses an ecosystem perspective in IoT business modeling; that is, thinking of IoT business modeling from a collaborative network-centric view rather than something the business does by itself. Ecosystem theory is derived from systems theory, which builds on the notion that the system is more than the sum of its parts. In enabling IoT services, many participatory skillsets are involved. Similarly, then, a company's BM should not be viewed as vendor-centric so that it can capture all flowing value streams. Together, the four blocks illustrate the concept of Value Design; that is, how value is deliberately created and captured in an IoT ecosystem.

Westerlund et al. (2014) develop a new way of how companies should do IoT business modeling, proposing a shift from a vendor-centric to a network-centric view. This requires companies to make a radical mental shift from the conventional way of thinking. Another difference from the two previous frameworks is that the Value Design Model proposes a holistic view of business modeling building blocks to identify the value flows between the dimensions, whereas Osterwalder and Pigneur (2010) isolate the building blocks. The Value Design Model has primarily been created and discussed on a conceptual level, which means that it is lacking in areas such as usability and maturity. However, the Value Design Model addresses and solves some of the questions that are discussed by Sun et al. (2012) by illustrating the cost, revenue streams and other values in the IoT ecosystem and using the Value Extract for companies to profit from them.

3.4 DNA Model

The earliest literature found that begins to adapt in the direction of IoT business modeling is the DNA Model (Fig. 1.5). This is a restructuring of the Business Model Canvas, as it divides the nine building blocks into three block categories: **D**esign, **N**eeds and **A**spirations (DNA). Sun et al. (2012) propose a linear approach to business modeling that consists of

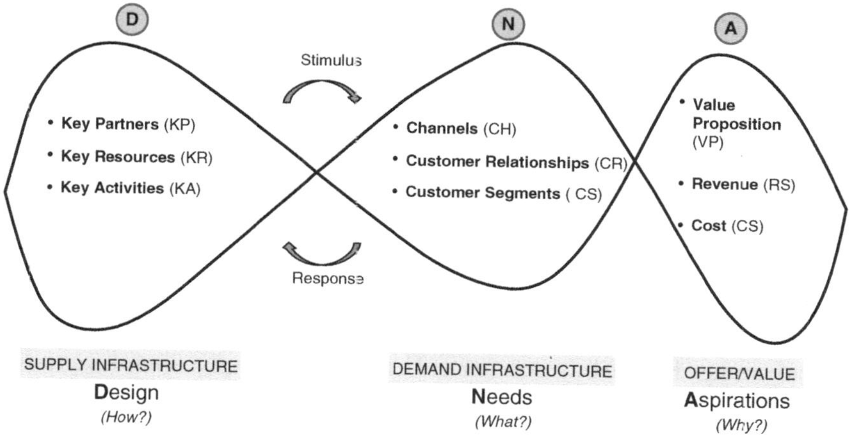

Fig. 1.5 DNA Model. (Source: Sun et al. (2012))

"How?," "What?" and "Why?" Of these, "How?" relates to the supply infrastructure of the design, the key partners, resources and activities, which Sun et al. (2012) call the *design* block. The "What?" (or *needs*) block, equaling the external infrastructure, is the customer channels, relationships and segments, including the business's stakeholders and market presence. Sun et al. (2012) argue that the design and needs blocks are the means to achieving the "end-result," which is the last block called Aspirations—the "Why?" This block contains the value proposition, revenue stream and cost structure.

The Benefits and Challenges of Using the DNA Model for DBM

Sun et al. (2012) describe a three-layered IoT architecture and call for a need for an IoT business modeling approach. They argue that a lot of BMs lack description of the interaction between the layers and how a company is to profit from IoT technologies. However, the DNA Model lacks a reflection of these aspects in the tool and therefore does not solve any of the issues it addresses. Conversely, the model brings forward a conceptual ecosystem perspective by putting together the key partnerships, resources and activity blocks in a single design block.

3.5 BM Type for IoT Model

The BM Type for IoT Model develops a graphical layout for an IoT BM. The model emerges based on the lack of tools able to give a visual presentation of the business's IoT activities, as IoT services sometimes operate on a multi-collaboration dimension. The idea behind the model is to enhance the opportunity for customers or partners to become the cocreators of IoT BMs. The BM type proposes a service-dominant (SD) logic embedded in its tool. An SD logic perceives other participants' successes and surplus in the ecosystem as sustainability for all and a competitive advantage for the business itself. The model's design principles emerge from a kind of mixture of the Magic Triangle's building blocks "Who?," "What?," "How?" and "Value?" and an IoT ecosystem perspective, culminating in a 3D model. The "Who?" undertakes the participants' collaboration in the ecosystem, including that of the suppliers, partners and customers.

Turber et al. (2014) describe how it is important to distinguish between collaborators, as they can function as operant resources to execute parts of the BM. The "What?" refers to each participant's responsibility in offering a digital product. Turber et al. (2014) argue that the value network traces back to the IoT architecture, which makes it a central aspect of the BM. The third dimension is the "Why?," which includes the monetary and non-monetary value drivers that can encourage participants to take part in the ecosystem. By adopting an SD logic, a stable ecosystem can be created. The "How?" is how the collaborating partners are creating value and intersects between the "Who?" and "What?" dimensions (Fig. 1.6).

The Benefits and Challenges of Using the BM Type for IoT Model for DBM

The model brings forth an interesting aspect of what an IoT prototype artifact BM-type visual layout can look like. This model is in an early to mid-stage of development, which is why it lacks in maturity and usability. The authors state that businesses need a better visual tool

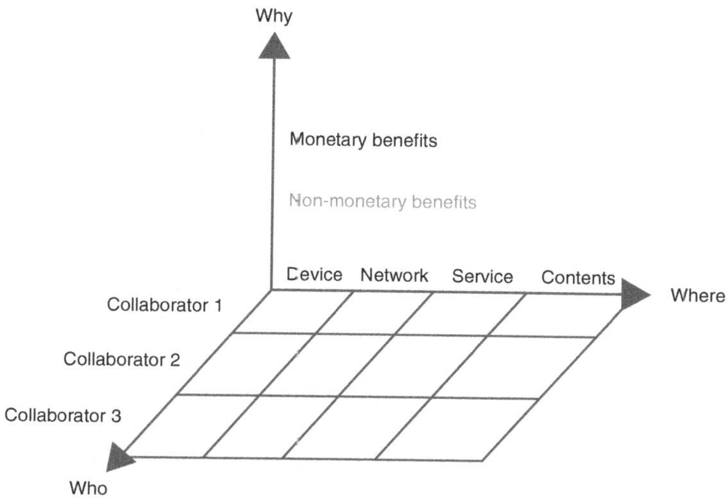

Fig. 1.6 BM type for IoT Model. (Source: Turber et al. (2014, p. 24))

when it comes to IoT business modeling and thus propose a 3D model, assuming this helps. This assumption might be considered a bit weak, as Chan (2015) finds that the model lacks in usability when testing it with study groups.

3.6 IoT Business Model Framework

The IoT Business Model Framework by Chan (2015) is an attempt at improving the BM Type for IoT Model by Turber et al. (2014). Chan (2015) claims transforming the model into a 2D model will increase its usability, arguing that strategic aspects are needed in IoT BM tools to enhance the ability of businesses to assume the first-mover position. Strategy and tactics dimensions are thus added to the BM tool. The author also includes literature from IoT architecture, IoT value chain, the Magic Triangle (Gassmann et al. 2014) and Value Design Model (Westerlund et al. 2014).

The IoT Business Model Framework contains eight dimensions, as illustrated in Fig. 1.7.

Company	Collaborator	Inputs	Network	Service/ processing/ packaging	Content/ Information product	Benefits	Strategy	Tactic
	C1							
ABC	C2							
	C3							

Fig. 1.7 IoT Business Model Framework. (Source: Chan (2015))

Starting on the right is the focal business that initiates the BM, moving to the collaborators, the input, the network, the service, the content, the benefits and finally strategy and tactics. The collaborators comprising the ecosystem are the participants needed to enable/execute the BM, including suppliers and customers. The input is the provided action from the participants, including data from sensors or a GPS location/destination. The network is the communication technology, such as mobile network, Internet or Bluetooth. The service is the offering; it also includes a process or package, which can be anything from a cloud service to data analytics to data collection and/or advertisements. Content/information is the visualization of data, pop-up advertisements and so forth. Benefits are the equivalent of the value captured. A strategy is either "get ahead" or "catch up" in market or technology to indicate the type of BM strategy. Lastly, a tactic is the digital charging approach, such as physical freemium, digital add-on, digital lock-in, product as point of sales, object self-service or remote usage and condition monitoring.

The Benefits and Challenges of Using the IoT Business Model Framework for DBM

The IoT Business Model Framework comprises a vast amount of previous literature on IoT business modeling. It includes aspects of strategy and tactics and increases usability by introducing a 2D format. This framework is an example of the foundational layer of IoT business modeling literature. However, the new add-ons are inconsistent in terms of addressing the issues stated by previous authors. For instance, the revenue streams and cost structures between collaborators remain unclear. Moreover, no tools are provided, making the model lack usability and maturity.

4 Discussion and Concluding Remarks

Until now, the Business Model Canvas (Osterwalder and Pigneur 2010) has been the most popular contribution to business modeling, and businesses also use it for tech-related BMs. However, with the digital transformation and growth in IoT adoption in business, BM frameworks must also be able to capture new types of values and IoT revenue streams as a way of doing business. One of the first shifts toward IoT business modeling was from Sun et al. (2012), who redefine the BM canvas into a new structure implying the ecosystem perspective as a key element in BM and BMI. Further research and new contributions later built on these ideas of considering IoT as a way of doing business. Gassmann et al. (2014) define the four core building blocks any BM should consist of, which creates space for the development of new BM tools. Westerlund et al. (2014), Turber et al. (2014) and Chan (2015) all contribute to how an IoT BM tool can look like, but this is far from mature.

The literature review of the definitions of DBM and IoT reveals a number of commonalities across the BM/IoT and DBM frameworks for IoT business modeling. All of the six frameworks incorporate the overall four-core dimensions also adopted by Gassmann et al. (2014) as the minimum requirements for any BM. These four elements are present in all six tools, which makes it possible to compare them. The other elements are: usability and maturity. Usability is based on the documentation of real-world-use cases of the tools, and maturity shows how well adapted the model is, which is evaluated using the number of citations from Google Scholar. The other part of the comparison considers digitalization and IoT, to show the strengths and weaknesses of the models when they are adopted and applied to designing DBMs and DBMI.

For evaluation, we suggest six characteristics as assumptions about what is important for digital/IoT business modeling and BM frameworks aimed at mapping DBM (Beliatis et al. 2018):

1) *Assisting the "to-be/as-is" transition.* Many DBMs cause a disruptive change in the core business of organizations. Thus, a business modeling process should be able to capture this transitional move from one BM to another.

2) *Mapping the IoT architecture.* It is important for IoT business modeling and DBM frameworks to be able to connect IoT architecture elements to the dimensions of the BM. Even in a simplified matter, the IoT architecture should be able to be mapped, for instance to the ecosystem actors or revenue streams. Other elements that could be relevant are identifying the strengths and weaknesses regarding the coupling of technology choices in different layers, their interoperability and switching costs.

3) *Ecosystem/collaboration approach.* Frameworks for DBM and IoT business modeling have to view the business from an ecosystem perspective going from a business-centric to a network-centric BM approach. Maintaining everyone in the ecosystem in surplus is suggested, which will lead to stability, sustainability and competitive advantage.

4) *The value flow.* DBM frameworks and IoT business modeling must be able to map the value flows in the ecosystem, as value flows from data might include other revenue streams, costs as well as tangible and intangible assets, than those detected in traditional BM frameworks. The BM framework also has to have a built-in ability to identify various value flows that occur across hardware and software collaborators and aid the business in extracting and capturing value flows to generate more revenue streams from data.

5) *Digitalization patterns.* It is important for DBM and IoT business modeling to include concrete DBM patterns. This might include BM patterns such as add-on, freemium, pay per use, hidden revenue, subscriptions and white label.

6) *Think big act small/lean elements.* Finally, it is critical for frameworks for DBM and IoT business modeling to be able to think big but act small. The BM tool must be able to accommodate this principle in terms of allowing for big visions but breaking them down into smaller BMs that facilitate development toward the greater vision. This might include learning in terms of technical competencies, lean start-up ideas (e.g. fail forward) and limited blast radius. Elements of tactical and strategic business decisions must be considered.

The presentation of the six BM frameworks reveals that the first three BM tools are high in usability and maturity. However, they rate low in the suggested six DBM/IoT business modeling characteristics. On the contrary, the new generation of BM tools ranks high in DBM/IoT business modeling aspects and low in usability and maturity. A preliminary conclusion could therefore indicate future research and development in DBM to develop more maturity and usability for the DBM/IoT BM tools.

With the new generation of DBM frameworks, these six extra characteristics are present, and stress the need for the adoption of new BM frameworks capable of capturing the new value and revenue streams of data and the IoT architecture and interconnectivity of ecosystems as central parts of BMs in a digital economy. Thus, in this chapter we have attempted to shed light on some of the new research streams and trends in DBM and IoT business modeling, in which we most likely will see major developments in the coming decades as digitalization transforms business and society. However, numerous researchers stress that without interdisciplinary effort, which involves research performed by scholars belonging to other disciplines (Nambisan et al. 2017) and addressing competing concerns (Svahn et al. 2017), it is unlikely that valuable theoretical advancements will be realized in this field of research.

This chapter has explored the concept, definition, drivers and challenges of DBMs and examines six different (D)BM frameworks and their applicability in mapping DBMs. Numerous BM frameworks and tools exist and others are emerging continuously. However, digitalization provides new venues, opportunities and challenges for established and new businesses in forming DBMs, where this chapter stresses that traditional BM frameworks may not be able to capture and explore DBMs optimally. A number of characteristics or criteria are suggested. In evaluation of this, we suggest that six characteristics are important for digital/IoT business modeling and BM frameworks aimed at mapping DBM. These characteristics are: (1) assisting the "to-be/as-is" transition, (2) the IoT architecture, (3) ecosystem/collaboration approach, (4) the value flow, (5) digitalization patterns and (6) think big act small/lean elements (Beliatis et al. 2018).

In terms of future research, three streams may be envisioned: an operational stream of research exploring how companies organize, manage, collaborate and measure DBMs; a longitudinal stream of studies including performance indicators to shed light on the dynamics, development and evolution of DBMs; and finally, embracing a greater foresight in terms of perspective and research stream as well as exploring the ecosystems and interconnectivity of DBMs, as future DBMs will not be limited by established boundaries and clusters. Thus, much remains uncharted territory in the research and practice of DBMs; international, interdisciplinary, cross-function and cross-sector research is all therefore necessary to uncover the multiple potentials, interconnectivity and challenges (e.g. privacy, security) of DBMs and digital businesses/entities.

References

Afuah, A., and C.L. Tucci. 2001. *Internet Business Models and Strategies*. New York: McGraw-Hill.

Amit, R., and G. Zott. 2001. Value Creation in e-business. *Strategic Management Journal* 22 (6–7): 493–520.

Amit, R., and C. Zott. 2012. Creating Value Through Business Model Innovation. *MIT Sloan Management Review* 53 (3): 41–49.

Arthur, W.B. 2011. The Second Economy. *McKinsey Quarterly* 4 (1): 90–99.

Beliatis J.M., H. Mansour, S. Nagy, A. Aagaard, and M. Presser. 2018. Digital Waste Management Using LoRa Network a Business Case from Lab to Fab. In *IEEE 2018 Global Internet of Things Summit (GIoTS)*.

Berman, S.J. 2012. Digital Transformation: Opportunities to Create New Business Models. *Strategy & Leadership* 40 (2): 16–24.

Bradley, J., J. Loucks, J. Macaulay, A. Noronha, and M. Wade. 2015. Digital Vortex: How Digital Disruption Is Redefining Industries. Global Center for Digital Business Transformation: An IMD and Cisco Initiative. June.

Bucherer, E., U. Eisert, and O. Gassmann. 2012. Towards Systematic Business Model Innovation: Lessons from Product Innovation Management. *Creativity and Innovation Management* 21: 183–198.

Case, S. 2016. *The Third Wave: An entrepreneur's Vision of the Future*. New York: Simon & Schuster. ISBN-10: 1501140752.

Chan, H.C.Y. 2015. Internet of Things Business Models. *Journal of Service Science and Management* 8: 552–568.

Chen, Y., J. Kreulen, M. Campbell, and C. Abrams. 2011. Analytics Ecosystem Transformation: A Force for Business Model Innovation. In *SRII Global Conference* 2011, 11–20.

Chesbrough, H., and R. Rosenbloom. 2002. The Role of the Business Model in Capturing Value from Innovation. *Industrial and Corporate Change* 11 (3): 529–556.

Criscuolo, P., N. Nicolaou, and A. Salter. 2012. The Elixir (or Burden) of Youth? Exploring Differences in Innovation Between Start-Ups and Established Firms. *Research Policy* 41 (2): 319–333.

Davenport, T.H. 2006. Competing on Analytics. *Harvard Business Review* 84 (1): 98–107.

Delen, D., and H. Demirkan. 2013. Data, Information and Analytics as Services. *Decision Support Systems* 55 (1): 359–363.

Dodgson, M., D.M. Gann, and N. Phillips, eds. 2013. *The Oxford Handbook of Innovation Management*. Oxford: Oxford University Press.

El Sawy, O.A., and F. Pereira. 2013. *Digital Business Models: Review and Synthesis, Chapter 2 in Business Modelling in the Dynamic Digital Space: An Ecosystem Approach*, 13–20. New York: Springer.

EU FP7 Project CASAGRAS. 2009. CASAGRAS Final Report: "RFID and the Inclusive Model for the Internet of Things", 43–54.

Gantz, J., and D. Reinsel. 2012. *The Digital Universe in 2020: Big Data, Bigger Digital Shadows and Biggest Growth in the Far East*. Framingham: International Data Corporation.

Gassmann, H., K. Frankenberger, and M. Csik. 2014. *The St. Gallen Business Model Navigator*. Working Paper: University of St. Gallen: ITEM-HSG.

Hartmann, P.M., M. Zaki, N. Feldmann, and A. Neely. 2016. Capturing Value from Big Data: a Taxonomy of Data-driven Business Models Used by Start-Up Firms. *International Journal of Operations & Production Management* 36 (10): 1382–1406.

Holler, J., V. Tsiatsis, C. Mulligan, S. Avesand, S. Karnouskos, and D. Boyle. 2014. *From Machine-to-Machine to the Internet of Things: Introduction to a New Age of Intelligence*. Waltham: Elsevier.

Holmström, J., and J. Partanen. 2014. Digital Manufacturing-driven Transformations of Service Supply Chains for Complex Products. *Supply Chain Management: An International Journal* 19 (4): 421–430.

Hui, G. 2014. How the Internet of Things Changes Business Models. *Harvard Business Review* 92: 1–5.

Hylving, L. 2015. Competing Values in the Era of Digitalization. In System Sciences (HICSS), 2015. *48th Hawaii International Conference,* 4161–4170. IEEE.

Johanson, M., S. Belenki, J. Jalminger, M. Fant, and M. Gjertz. 2014. Big Automotive Data: Leveraging Large Volumes of Data for Knowledge-driven Product Development. In *Big Data IEEE International Conference*, 736–741, October.

Kiel, D., C. Arnold, M. Collisi, and K.I. Voigt. 2016. The Impact of the Industrial Internet of Things on Established Business Models. In *Proceedings of the 25th International Association for Management of Technology (IAMOT) Conference*, Orlando, FL, USA, May 15–19.

Lee, S., M. Choi, and S. Kim. 2017. How and What to Study About IoT: Research Trends and Future Directions from the Perspective of Social Science. *Telecommunications Policy* 41 (10): 1056–1067.

Maglio, P.P., and J. Spohrer. 2013. A Service Science Perspective on Business Model Innovation. *Industrial Marketing Management* 42 (5): 665–670.

Magretta, J. 2002. Why Business Models Matter. *Harvard Business Review* 80 (5): 86–92.

Manyika, J., M. Chui, B. Brown, J. Bughin, R. Dobbs, C. Roxburgh, and A. Hung Byres. 2011. *Big Data: The Next Frontier for Innovation, Competition, and Productivity*. San Francisco: McKinsey Global Institute.

Markides, C. 2013. Business Model Innovation: What Can the Ambidexterity Literature Teach Us? *The Academy of Management Perspectives* 27 (4): 313–323.

Markides, C., and C. Charitou. 2004. Competing with Dual Business Models: A Contingency Approach. *Academy of Management Executive* 18 (3): 22–36.

McAfee, A., and E. Brynjolfsson. 2012. Big Data: The Management Revolution. *Harvard Business Review* 90 (10): 60–68.

Mejtoft, T. 2011. Internet of Things and Co-creation of Value. In *Proceedings of the 2011 International Conference on and 4th International Conference on Cyber, Physical and Social Computing*, Dalian, 672–677, October 19–22.

Nambisan, S., K. Lyytinen, A. Majchrzak, and M. Song. 2017. Digital Innovation Management: Reinventing Innovation Management Research in a Ddigital World. *MIS Quarterly* 41 (1): 223–238.

Osterwalder, A., and Y. Pigneur. 2010. *Business Model Generation: A Handbook for Visionaries, Game Changers, and Challengers*. Hoboken: Wiley.

Otto, B., and S. Aier. 2013. Business Models in the Data Economy: A Case Study from the Business Partner Data Domain. In *Proceedings of the 11th International Conference on Wirtschaftsinformatik (WI 2013)* in Leipzig, vol. 1, 475–489.

Ries, E. 2011. *The Lean Start-up: How Constant Innovation Creates Radically Successful Businesses*. London: Portfolio Penguin. ISBN-10: 0670921602.

Rong, K., G.Y. Hu, Y. Lin, Y.J. Shi, and L. Guo. 2015. Understanding Business Ecosystem Using a 6C Framework in Internet-of-Things-Based Sectors. *International Journal of Production Economics* 159: 41–55. https://doi.org/10.1016/j.ijpe.2014.09.003.

Schroeck, M., R. Shockley, J. Smart, D. Romero-Morales, and P. Tufano. 2012. *Analytics: The Real-World Use of Big Data. How Innovative Enterprises Extract Value from Uncertain Data*. Oxford: IBM Institute for Business Value/Saïd Business School at the University of Oxford.

Spieth, P., D. Schneckenberg, and J.E. Ricart. 2014. Business Model Innovation: State of the Art and Future Challenges for the Field. *R&D Management* 44 (3): 237–247.

Spring, M., and L. Araujo. 2009. Service, Services and Products: Rethinking Operations Strategy. *International Journal of Operations & Production Management* 29 (5): 444–467.

Sun, Y., H. Yan, C. Lu, R. Bie, and P. Thomas. 2012. A Holistic Approach to Visualizing Business Models for the Internet of Things. *Communications in Mobile Computing* 1: 4.

Svahn, F., L. Mathiassen, and R. Lindgren. 2017. Embracing Digital Innovation in Incumbent Firms: How Volvo Cars Managed Competing Concerns. *MIS Quarterly* 41 (1): 239–253.

Taran, Y. 2011. *Re-thinking It All: Overcoming Obstacles to Business Model Innovation*. Center for Industrial Production. Ph.D Thesis, Aalborg University.

Teece, D.J. 2010. Business Models, Business Strategy and Innovation. *Long Range Planning* 43 (2–3): 172–194.

Turber, S., J.V. Brocke, O. Gassmann, and E. Flesich. 2014. Designing Business Models in the Era of Internet of Things. In *Conference Paper. 9th International Conference*, DESRIST 2014, Miami,17–31, May 22–24.

Unify IoT deliverable D02.01 – IoT Business Models Framework. Published 14 July 2016. http://www.unify-iot.

Vargo, S.L., and R.F. Lusch. 2004. Evolving to a New Dominant Logic for Marketing. *Journal of Marketing* 68 (1): 1–17.

Veit, D., E. Clemons, A. Benlian, P. Buxmann, T. Hess, D. Kundisch, J.M. Leimeister, P. Loos, and M. Spann. 2014. Business Models: An Information Systems Research Agenda. *Business & Information Systems Engineering* 1: 45–53.

Westerlund, M., S. Leminen, and M. Rajahonka. 2014. Designing Business Models for the Internet of Things. *Technology Innovation Management Review* 4 (7): 5–14.

Yoo, Y., R.J. Boland Jr., K. Lyytinen, and A. Majchrzak. 2012. Organizing for Innovation in the Digitized World. *Organization Science* 23 (5): 1398–1408.

Zott, C., R. Amit, and L. Massa. 2011. The Business Model: Recent Developments and Future Research. *Journal of Management* 37 (4): 1019–1042.

2

The Internet of Things as Driver for Digital Business Model Innovation

Mirko Presser, Qi Zhang, Anja Bechmann, and Michail J. Beliatis

1 Introduction

Up until the middle of the first decade of the twenty-first century, the principal devices for accessing the Internet were personal computers and laptops controlled and used by people. This changed rapidly in the years that followed. First came smartphones, which changed the way in which people consumed online services and even interacted with the world, leading to a profound impact on business practices and society alike. Other computing devices followed the trend of becoming internet enabled, mainly for consumer electronics but also for significantly different devices in contexts such as manufacturing, transport and farming. It was still a time when the number of devices more or less scaled linearly with the number of users and growth was mainly driven by market penetration and

M. Presser (✉) • M. J. Beliatis
Aarhus University, Aarhus, Denmark
e-mail: mirko.presser@btech.au.dk

Q. Zhang • A. Bechmann
Aarhus University, Aarhus, Denmark

A. Aagaard (ed.), *Digital Business Models*,
https://doi.org/10.1007/978-3-319-96902-2_2

the accessing of new geographical markets. It was easy to tell what was connected to the Internet and what was not.

After first decade of the twenty-first century, something dramatic happened. Connections to the Internet started picking up beyond the linear scale with respect to people: connections became decoupled from people and machines and things started to take over, communicating with each other in addition to people. By 2017, 30 billion devices were linked to the Internet. This is what is called the emergence of the Internet of Things (IoT).

1.1 What Is the Internet of Things?

The IoT is a term that has been much discussed in the literature and is considered a growth engine in both vertical and horizontal industries. It has brought about a major industrial and societal paradigm shift, equivalent to technologies such as steam driving the industrial revolution in the eighteenth century or electricity a century later. The definition of IoT depends on the target audience and it describes the different usages of the IoT. Four main categories of definitions can be determined in the literature according to Lee et al. (2017):

1. Intelligent objects. For example, Gubbi et al. (2013) define the interconnection of sensing and actuating devices, thereby providing the ability to share information across platforms through a unified framework, developing a common operating picture that enables innovative applications.
2. An extension of the internet. For example, Rose et al. (2015) define the extension of network connectivity and computing capability to objects, devices, sensors and items not ordinarily considered to be computers.
3. A global network infrastructure. For example, CASAGRAS (2011) define a global network infrastructure that links physical and virtual objects through the exploitation of data capture and communication capabilities.
4. An interaction of information. For example, techniques or environments that attach sensors to objects and exchange necessary information in real time.

Throughout this chapter, the IoT is defined as a global ecosystem based on an infrastructure linking physical and virtual objects through the exploitation of data capture and communication, according to CASAGRAS (2011). This clarifies that IoT is more than a set of technologies that when "glued" together make up the IoT, but also involves the entire ecosystem in which the IoT is present—which can be described both through technologies as well as business constructs. For a wider set of definitions Minerva et al. (2015) have, via the Institute of Electrical and Electronics Engineers (IEEE) IoT Initiative, released a document that tries to work towards a definition of the IoT.

2 IoT Technologies

As described by CASAGRAS (2011), IoT systems seamlessly connect the physical world with the digital world, which enables real-time monitoring and interaction with physical objects, as well as information and knowledge extraction from massive sensor data generated by heterogeneous IoT devices, enabled by an IoT technology stack. An end-to-end IoT solution is basically built on an IoT technology stack that is composed of multiple layers including hardware, embedded software, communication and connectivity, a cloud-based platform, a suite of security tools, a gateway towards external data sources and other elements. Figure 2.1 illustrates the key components of the IoT technology stack. We will present IoT devices, IoT connectivity and cloud-based platforms in the following subsections.

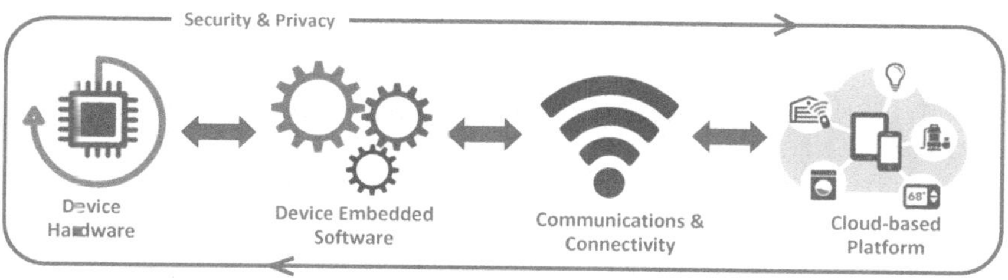

Fig. 2.1 Key components of the IoT technology stack

2.1 IoT Devices

There is a wide range of IoT devices, from tiny implantable devices to diverse wearables and gadgets, smart meters, robots, vehicles and even aircraft. They are often also referred to as "things" embedded with hardware and software. The basic hardware of an IoT device consists of sensors/actuators, a controlling processor, a communication transceiver and a power supply (Fig. 2.2). There are many commercial off-the-shelf embedded systems available that are open for developers to develop novel IoT applications; examples of a few popular systems are ESP8266, Ardurio Yun, Raspberry Pi, CloudBit, LoPy, FiPy and Samsung Artik.

With advances in sensor technologies, a plethora of sensors is available. These are able to continuously or periodically measure a variety of real-time parameters, for example physical (e.g. vibration, pressure and humidity), chemical (e.g. CO_2 and PH value), optical (e.g. radiation and ultraviolet), energy (power, voltage, current) and biometric (e.g. ECG, EEG and PPG). Similarly, various actuators are able to convert the electric input into physical actions to interact with the physical world. The communication interface connects the IoT devices with the IoT network infrastructure. It can be wired or wireless; however, wireless communication interfaces are preferred. A number of wireless communication technologies with different communication capabilities are available. According to the needs of IoT applications, an appropriate communication technology can be selected considering the transmission range, data rate, energy consumption, reliability, mobility and others. The primary power supply in IoT devices relies on battery power. In the past decade,

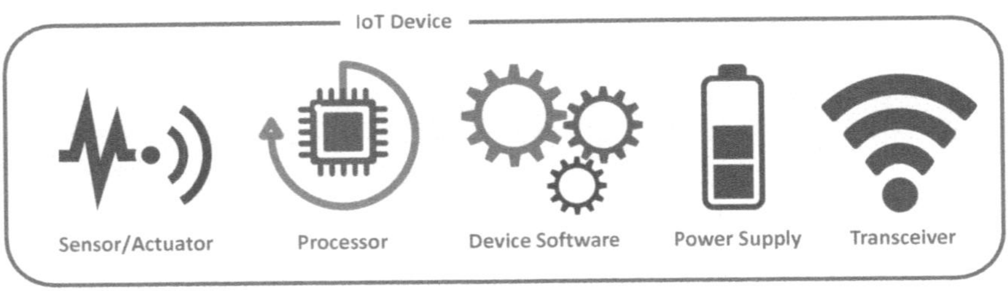

Fig. 2.2 Typical IoT device components

the battery capacity development has not followed Moore's law Schlachter (2013), and remains one of the major critical challenges in IoT to support long-term and self-sustaining operation. Therefore, a large number of energy-efficient communication protocols and computation algorithms, as well as low-power radio transceivers, have been developed for wireless sensor networks and the IoT. Additionally, it is promised that battery lifetimes can be prolonged by energy harvesting technology; see Adila et al. (2018). For instance, energy can be harvested from various sources in the environment, such as thermal, solar and vibration. In particular, wireless radio frequency is a new energy source that is widely available in the form of transmitted energy, and it has the advantages of low cost and small form factor implementation (Kamalinejad et al. 2015).

IoT devices cannot work without software. This includes embedded operating systems, onboard software applications and communication protocols. Onboard software applications take care of many tasks, such as data acquisition, data pre-processing (e.g. aggregation in time domain, outline detection), scheduling of duty cycle, time synchronization and localization.

2.2 IoT Connectivity

IoT connectivity is the fundamental technology that enables geographically distributed and heterogeneous IoT devices to transmit acquired sensor data to the cloud for further data analytics, visualization, knowledge extraction and value creation. It is an important part of the IoT infrastructure, which can be implemented by diverse underpinning communication technologies and the upper layer communication protocols in the communication protocol stack.

IoT connectivity, de facto, includes the connections between IoT devices, and the connection between IoT devices and gateways, cloud platforms and service providers. The possible underlying paradigm of machine-to-machine communication (M2M) for IoT has a wide span in terms of transmission range, data rate, energy consumption, reliability, mobility support, deployment cost and many other areas. Based on the transmission range, IoT communication technologies can be classified as proximity communication (e.g. RFID), short-range wireless personal area network (e.g. BLE, Zigbee (IEEE 802.15.4), WirelessHart), wireless local area networks (e.g. WiFi IEEE 802.11 a/b/g/n/ac and low-power WiFi 802.11 ah), low-power wide area network (LPWAN) (e.g. NB-IoT, LoRa, SigFox), cellular networks (GPRS, 3G and 4G) and even satellite communications. They not only compete with each other but also complement each other, as individual communication technologies have their own strengths and weaknesses. For example, BLE and Zigbee can only support a communication range of 10–100 m, which is suitable for IoT applications with static IoT devices within relatively small areas, such as home automation and e-health. For applications requiring large coverage areas such as smart parking and smart waste management, if using short-range technologies, the IoT devices have to rely on a multi-hop mesh network to connect to repeaters, and repeaters are connected to gateways (Andreev et al. 2015; Beliatis et al. 2018), allowing for interconnected larger networks. Such a network topology set-up leads to higher total energy consumption of the system, longer delay and higher outage probability owing to multihop and high wireless channel dynamics (Andreev et al. 2015). For such use cases, LPWAN technologies or low-power WiFi (802.11 ah) are better choices. LPWAN has a transmission range of 30+ km, which can simplify the network topology and network deployment using fewer base stations, thereby reducing latency and outage probability, as well as minimizing the infrastructure and operation cost. Low-power WiFi (802.11 ah), a new communication technology in the WiFi family, has extended coverage of up to 1 km and can support 8000 IoT devices from one access point.

It is worth mentioning that to select an appropriate communication technology not only depends on technical requirements but also on the ecosystem in which the technology operates. Although BLE and Zigbee are both personal area networks, developed based on the IEEE 802.15 family, they have different features and aim at different applications. For instance, for e-health applications BLE is one of the best candidates, as it has relative to ZigBee a shorter communication range and lower power consumption; furthermore, most smartphones and tablets are equipped with BLE interfaces and naturally become the data hub to forward sensor data from the IoT devices to the cloud. In the above-mentioned cases, it can be seen that the selection of communication technologies is crucial to fulfil the requirements of IoT applications and services.

From an IoT communication protocol stack point of view, the above-mentioned communication technologies mainly correspond to the lower two layers, the physical layer and medium access control layer of the Open Systems Interconnection model. The networking layer, particularly IPv6, is regarded as the dominant protocol allowing communication between all IP-based devices over the Internet, whatever the underlying communication technologies. Since IPv6 was not originally designed for resource-constrained devices in IoT, an adaption layer 6LoWPAN has been developed to enable IPv6 communication over IEEE 802.15.4, using header compression, fragmentation and link layer forwarding techniques.

The application layer of IoT, instead of using HTTP, adopts several lightweight protocols, for example MQTT and CoAP, which have been developed in the application layer to enable communication between resource-constrained IoT devices and the Internet. They are different in terms of their communication models and the underlying protocol. They have their own strengths and weaknesses, and are suitable for different types of IoT applications. For example, Message Queuing Telemetry Transport (MQTT) a messaging protocol, uses a publish/subscribe model and requires a central MQTT broker which effectively decouples the communication in space and time, allowing duty cycle implementation to save IoT devices' energy. In other words, the nodes can publish the sensor data regardless of the other nodes' state (e.g. sleep or active). The other nodes receiving the data can retrieve it from the central broker when they become active. MQTT can be regarded as many-to-many communication. Additionally, MQTT uses Transmission Control Protocol (TCP) as a transport protocol and therefore features its reliability. Constrained Application Protocol (CoAP) is a client/server protocol based on a one-to-one request/report interaction model. CoAP is designed to work with HTTP or RESTful web through light proxies, which make it compatible with the Internet. CoAP runs on UDP transport protocol, which facilitates fast communication with low overheads; however, CoAP lacks the reliability and service guarantee of TCP-based MQTT.

2.3 IoT Platforms

In order to create value from connected IoT devices, it is indispensable to have an intelligent entity to facilitate and orchestrate key interactions between different components in the IoT technology stack as well as other information technology systems and services used in businesses. IoT platforms play this pivotal role, which is a crucial component in the IoT technology stack. The main objective of IoT platforms is to make it easier for developers, service providers, managers and users to work on IoT solutions. IoT applications often share large parts of their core functionality with each other. For instance, no matter if the application is working with smart metering, smart agriculture or logistic tracking, regardless if the aim is to offer predictive maintenance or business process optimization, they need common functions such as rules for thresholds and alerts, communication through multiple networks, over-the-air firmware downloads and update, remote diagnosis and reconfiguration and many others. IoT platforms allow IoT developers to reuse common functionalities by providing a suite of software tools, which enables the developer to focus on the unique features of the applications. IoT platforms can significantly reduce entry barriers for businesses to implement and deploy IoT applications in terms of investment, expertise and overall risks (Lucero 2016).

IoT platforms have many functions or subplatforms running in the back end, such as cloud/edge computing, application enablement, data management, connectivity management, device management, providing tools for data analytics and visualization, and security (Fig. 2.3).

Cloud/Edge Computing This offers computing and data storage resources to IoT platforms through Infrastructure as a Service (IaaS), Platform as a Service (PaaS) or Software as a Service (SaaS). For example, IBM Watson IoT platform is hosted on IBM Bluemix PaaS. With the fast growth of sensor data volume, it causes significant stress to the core network to transport all of the sensor data from devices to the cloud. Furthermore, more and more emerging IoT applications require ultra-low latency, such as industry 4.0 and driverless cars. The conventional

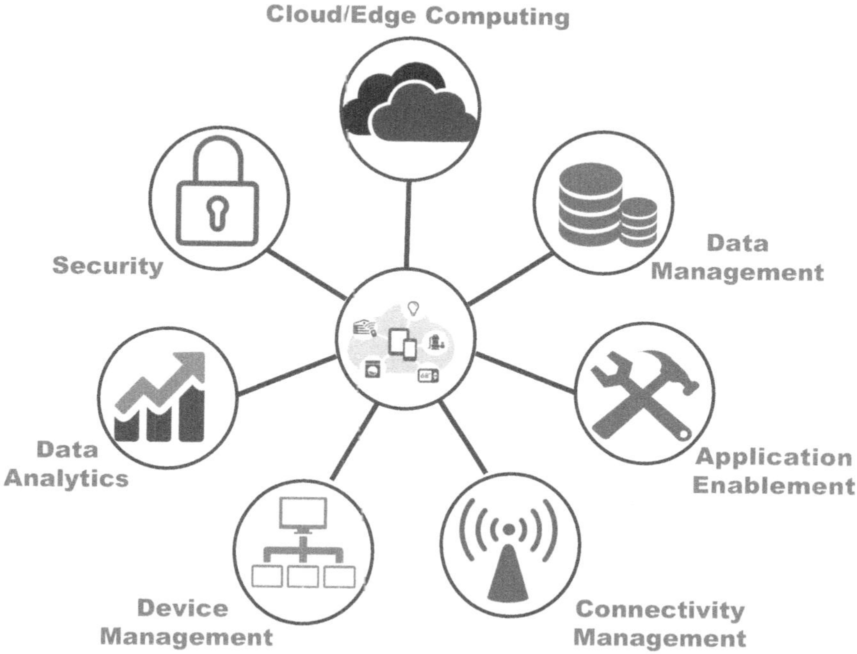

Fig. 2.3 Overview of IoT platform functionalities

cloud architectures fall short of the Quality of Service (QoS) requirements of these IoT applications; therefore, the cloud architecture is evolving and the cloud is moving towards the edge of the network. Edge computing and fog computing are promising technologies to complement the traditional cloud computing paradigm (Bonomoi et al. 2012). In edge and fog computing, the IoT devices send the data to the nearby edge servers that can process and store part of the data. In this way, the system is able to provide extra flexibility, reduce response latency, support mobility and create novel location-based IoT services.

Application Enablement This abstracts many common features from the logic of specific applications and provides application programming interfaces (APIs), which make it feasible to develop diverse IoT applications without knowing the intricate underlying hardware and software layers.

In this way, it enables application developers to streamline the programming and reduce the cost of developing and maintaining applications. For instance, a good IoT platform should be hardware-agnostic and is able to integrate any IoT devices into the solution. Some IoT platforms have pre-integrated a list of devices, for example Arduino, Microchip, ST, NXP, TI and Renesas prototype boards. Additionally, IoT platforms also provide various development kits for fast development of IoT solutions. It is worth mentioning that a third-party vendor can offer a standalone application enablement platform as a part of a larger IoT platform.

Data Management Aimed not only at orchestrating the data flows from geographically distributed and different types of sensors, this also allows businesses to integrate massive data from machines and sensors with the existing data from, for example, enterprise resource planning systems, open government databases and social media feeds, crossing multiple technologies and protocols.

Connectivity Management This provides connectivity support to all primary IoT communication networks, covering a wide span of communication ranges and capacities, and thereby offering greater flexibility, reliability and scalability in designing IoT solutions. As mentioned above, there are many different underlying communication networks for connecting the IoT devices. An IoT solution might need to connect different IoT devices that are deployed under different propagation conditions, for example in tunnels and in rural areas. In such cases, the IoT solution will need a multi-network connectivity using multiple communication technologies.

Device Management This monitors devices' running status and ensures they are all working properly. It contains operations such as location updates, firmware downloads and updates, remote diagnosis, search and discovery of devices and operational status, reboots, factory resets, collecting error codes and log messages.

Data Analytics Extracting insights and knowledge from big data (structured or unstructured data) from sensors and machines, and external data sources, data analytics creates value for business and society. Analytics and machine learning algorithms can process and visualize the historical data to study the long-term underlying data pattern so that the root causes in health, harmful or otherwise unwanted social behavior, climate, agriculture, city planning and so on can be diagnosed, or future events can be predicted based on the data pattern in order to do predictive maintenance. Furthermore, analytics can also do online real-time analytics to discover anomalies in sensor data, thereby detecting operation errors and system defects, and sending alarms and alerts. Analytics is realized by a set of tools equipped in the IoT platform or the analytics software offered by third-party vendors via APIs.

The current IoT platform market is immature and there are many IoT platforms. They are developed with different capabilities, all of which have specific tradeoffs. IoT platform functionality is not standardized in the market (Lucero 2016). Until now, there has been no converged IoT platform that comprehensively contains all the envisioned capabilities and can fit all applications. For example, InfoBright is particularly strong in data analytics as it provides Knowledge Grid architecture (an IoT-based analytical database platform) that allows storage and analysis of and actions on the sensor data, as well as setting up communication with several leading business intelligence platforms (e.g. Micro-Strategy, Pentaho, Jaspersoft) to enable interconnected business ecosystems. The Arrayent IoT platform enables major heterogeneous brands, such as Maytag, Whirlpool, OSRAM and SALUS to connect their products to smart handsets and web applications (Ray 2016). Hence, in practice, full platform functionality is often realized by assembling different key components from multiple partners in the ecosystems.

2.4 Challenges in IoT Technologies

One of the critical challenges when it comes to encouraging more businesses to adopt IoT applications is the fragmentation of IoT and the lack of interoperability in IoT ecosystems. State-of-the-art IoT platforms lack standardization and offer heterogeneous ways to access IoT devices and acquire sensor data, Bröring et al. (2017). This leads to interoperability issues, in particular when developers attempt to create cross-platform and cross-domain applications. This becomes a serious barrier for small and medium-sized businesses that are attempting to provide their solution across multiple platforms.

Furthermore, various existing IoT systems are developed and deployed for different verticals, which have unique characteristics and requirements and connect with different ecosystems. For example, a smart home focuses on connected appliances and manages indoor climate, e-health systems continuously record personal physiological data and monitor body condition, and smart city systems generate data about traffic, air quality, pollution, noise and so on. There is, however, vast potential in interconnecting verticals: for example, e-health systems can leverage data from smart home and smart city systems to diagnose the causes of diseases. Furthermore, the separate deployment of each vertical is not cost effective. To enable data sharing and interworking, a horizontal platform approach is needed to integrate or interwork these vertical systems (Kim et al. 2016).

3 IoT Application Examples

There is a wide variety of IoT applications already deployed in the real world. These can be categorized into several types of applications in terms of their scale (i.e. number of IoT devices) and utilization of the network effect (i.e. how much they use each other to create a gain in value, such as information based on the number of nodes in the network).

Intelligent objects as described by Gubbi et al. (2013) offer value through their basic functionality often as individual devices, with limited scale and limited network effect. If we add many intelligent objects into a system that collects data from each of the devices into the cloud, the application is able to compute new knowledge based on vast amounts of sensor data and make decisions for optimization in the future—often referred to as business intelligence or big data analytics. Once these devices start collaborating, exchanging information and making autonomous decisions, the network effect is leveraged and additional value is unlocked: only then can we tap into the real value of IoT.

3.1 Industry 4.0: Predictive Maintenance

A typical cloud-based application, collecting vast amounts of data from various sensors over a prolonged period of time, is called predictive maintenance. This is based on condition-monitoring techniques that involve machine-learning algorithms, and it replaces the business practice of either scheduled maintenance or reactive maintenance. It often allows for a vast amount of uptime improvement of physical assets, such as trucks, windmills and manufacturing equipment (Yan et al. 2017).

3.2 Smart Logistics: Supply Chain Optimization

Nagy et al. (2018) describe a system of sensors that tracks goods while they are being shipped from a factory to a customer location. The system tracks different sensor parameters such as location and condition, and the application presents this data to different stakeholders offering various service logics, for example allowing the ordering of replacement goods if damage occurs in transit, or accounting for unforeseen delays owing to traffic conditions. This generally provides a better relationship with the customer and allows for the optimization of supply chain and logistics.

3.3 Smart City: Citizen Services

In Hernández-Muñoz et al. (2011) and Vestergaard et al. (2015) the smart city is described as a system of systems that allows a vast amount of IoT data to be collected in complex networks. The aim in most industries is to build vertical solutions for specialized applications, whereas in smart cities the vision is to create a single horizontal platform that integrates all IoT devices and offers many applications and services on top. This allows for a more efficient use of resources as well as the ability to leverage data from many different systems in novel applications and services.

In contrast to the notion of optimization of resources stands the idea of leveraging technology in cities in order to improve citizenship, equality and fairness. This often stands in contrast to the more engineering-focused optimization problems mentioned in the previous paragraph, discussed for example by Kitchin (2015).

3.4 Smart Energy: Grid

With the era of renewable energy sources installation, excess power generation during low power demand times can lead to instabilities in the grid. Therefore, the involvement of smart energy meters, smart loads, smart energy storage systems, smart building, accurate predictive weather diagnosis and load distribution over different time zones around the globe is required to maintain a balance of energy requirements in terms of generation and dissipation. Such grids and energy sources, which require substantial IoT infrastructure for their operation, are known as smart energy/grid.

3.5 Smart Appliances, Welfare and Agriculture

Home appliances, which can connect through the Internet to remote servers either for receiving data on the fly, such as kitchen recipes, or energy tariffs to allow effective regulation of consumption and cost at individual house level or in communal buildings level, are known as smart appliances—which scale up into smart buildings. Their impact at society level is known as smart welfare. In a similar manner, wirelessly remote sensors which can monitor the location and health of animals enabling precision farming and smart food processing by delivering data-driven decisions and automating the process of food growing and animal welfare, are known as smart agriculture.

4 IoT Business Model Innovation

IoT is a complex area from a technology perspective, creating new classes of applications such as the examples above. There are many business opportunities for technology companies, new application and service providers, and businesses that are developing new business models.

Business models seek to make sense of how businesses operate. In essence, they provide a hypothesis that needs to be implemented and proven. They are presented at different levels of abstraction in the literature. Magaretta (2002) discusses business models as narratives that describe the customer, customer value, revenue collection and delivery of value. Another level of abstraction is made by Gassmann et al. (2013), who describe the business model as an archetype of 55 different business model building blocks that can be combined in various ways to accommodate how the business operates.

The most frequently adopted breakthrough on another level of abstraction is the graphical framework. The most-cited of these is the Business Model Canvas by Osterwalder and Pigneur (2010), and this subsection focuses on analyzing frameworks at this level of abstraction.

4.1 IoT and Business Model Innovation

When it comes to innovation, IoT is a disruptive force, and traditional business model canvases are relatively weak in offering descriptive features to allow for IoT characteristics to be properly reflected (Mansour et al. 2018). The following characteristics are important for IoT-based business model innovation (BMI) and need to be able to be reflected.

BMI Transition

Many business models in the IoT cause a disruptive change in the core business of organizations. A business modeling process should be able to capture this transitional move from the as/is model to the to/be model. As an example, the idea of predictive maintenance as mentioned above transforms the business model drastically. Whereas the as/is situation offers an opportunity for selling a product and then selling services to repair a product, the new business model encourages the use of pay-per-use or subscription-based models, including performance-based contracts to maintain products over a given period of time. This transition is not easily captured in BMI.

IoT Ecosystem, Technology Stack and Value Flow

IoT business modeling needs to be able to connect the IoT technology stack to the dimensions of the business model. Even in a simplified form the IoT technology stack should be able to be mapped, for instance to the ecosystem actors, technology providers and service providers. Other elements that could be relevant are identifying the strengths and weaknesses regarding the coupling of technology choices in different layers, their interoperability and their switching costs. Taking the example of predictive maintenance, a service is typically enabled by a set of sensors measuring the state of a device, a communication network collecting data, a cloud platform storing and analyzing data, and the service itself. Businesses can of course make the investment to build an end-to-end system, but the trend is for more and more businesses to tend towards ecosystems when they are developing complex technology stacks, in other words by mixing and matching the different layers and components that are best suited for the application/service.

In this respect it is important to think of a network-based business modeling approach rather than a value chain or business-centric approach. This points towards the idea of value flows and value networks, which describe how value can be shared by involved ecosystem members. Value flows might include revenue streams and costs as well as tangible and intangible assets.

Think Big Act Small/Lean Elements

It is also important for IoT business modeling to be able to think big but act small. The business model tool needs to be able to accommodate this principle in that it allows for drafting big visions, but breaks them down into smaller business models that facilitate development towards the greater vision. This might include learning in terms of technical competencies and lean start-up ideas, such as fail forward and limited blast radius. It looks at elements of tactical and strategic business decisions.

4.2 IoT Business Model Innovation Canvases

Mansour et al. (2018) analyzes different business model canvases with respect to the previously mentioned characteristics.

- The business model canvas of Osterwalder and Pigneur (2010) is an industry standard, and offers an easy approach to BMI. The business model canvas has elements that allow for the mapping of technologies in terms of key resources and also of the ecosystem in terms of key partners, but lacks a mapping of the technology stack and network-based elements that is needed in developing IoT applications.
- The DNA model by Sun et al. (2012) builds on Osterwalder and Pigneur (2010), and brings forward a conceptual ecosystem perspective by putting together the key partnerships, resources and activity blocks in one design block.
- The original purpose of the St. Gallen Business Model Navigator tool (Gassmann et al. 2013) is to allow businesses that are stuck in conventional thinking to think outside the box and create new revenue streams; it brings business modeling back to its basics, and with that it also remains technology agnostic.
- The Value Design Model of Westerlund et al. (2014) was created and discussed mainly on a conceptual level, which means it is lacking in areas such as usability and maturity. However, Value Design takes a step in the right direction, and will stimulate future research and development in IoT business modeling. It addresses and solves questions that were discussed by Sun et al. by illustrating the cost, revenue streams and other values in the IoT ecosystem, using Value Extract so that companies can profit from these values.
- The BM Type for IoT Model (Turber et al. 2014) brings forth an interesting aspect of how an IoT prototype artifact business model type visual layout can look. This model is in an early to mid-stage of development, which is why it lacks maturity and usability. The authors state that businesses need a better visual tool when it comes to IoT business modeling and thus propose a 3D model, assuming this helps.

- The 3DCM model (Chan 2015) includes aspects of strategy and tactics and increases usability by introducing a 2D-format. The 3DCM is an example of the foundational layer of IoT business modeling literature. However, the new add-ons are inconsistent in addressing the issues stated by previous authors. For instance, revenue streams and cost structures between collaborators remains unclear. Moreover, no tools are provided, meaning the model lacks usability and maturity.

Osterwalder and Pigneur (2010) has until now been one of the most popular contributions to business modeling. Businesses use the business model canvas for technology-related business models as well. But to gain a full visual representation that is able to capture new values and revenue streams, the preference is for the model to acknowledge IoT as one way of doing business.

The first signs of a shift to IoT business modeling came from Sun et al. (2012) who started to redefine the business model canvas into a new structure that implies the ecosystem perspective. More research was built upon the ideas about considering IoT as a way of doing business. Gassmann et al. (2013) defined the four core building blocks for any business model, thereby creating space for new business model tools to arise. Westerlund et al. (2014), Turber et al. (2014) and Chan (2015) are all contributions to how an IoT business model tool can look.

4.3 Challenges in IoT Business Model Innovation

There are still no good tools available to capture the complexity of IoT business models. Mature but technology agnostic tools such as Osterwalder and Pigneur (2010) are used widely, and have brought about limitations to how IoT business models are developed (Vermesan et al. 2016). This is a mimicry of the technology challenges previously discussed, specifically on the topics of interoperability and standardization.

It is only through standards for and the development of interoperability that we will be able to build more network-based business models. If we cannot imagine and communicate network-based business model because of a lack of tools, there will also be a lack of interest in focusing on standards and interoperability, continuing with common practices for building silo applications, proprietary technology stacks and creating technology lock-ins. This also encourages the creation of data lakes and the aggregation of vast amounts of data, with the consequent ethical issues that are discussed in the following section.

5 IoT and Ethics

Instances especially of personal data theft and device take-overs in connection with IoT have proven that security and ethics are central issues, both when it comes to IoT in general and especially concerning digital BMI. This chapter defines ethics in close relation to Floridi & Taddeo's understanding of data ethics:

> problems related to data (including generation, recording, curation, processing, dissemination, sharing and use), algorithms (including artificial intelligence, artificial agents, machine learning and robots) and corresponding practices (including responsible innovation, programming, hacking and professional codes), in order to formulate and support morally good solutions (e.g. right conducts or right values). (Floridi and Taddeo 2016)

Yet in a particular IoT context it is important to underline that the violation of such data ethics not only includes broken expectations, hacking and breaches on the data level, but also hacking on the device level that results in potential device take-over. In the following section we will show what we mean by data expectations and device take-over by providing examples of fear scenarios and instances of potential violation of expectations.

5.1 Cases of Data Sharing, Breaches and Device Take-Over

Issues of data theft, data leakage or device take-overs that have violated user privacy or security have been a strong weapon against business innovation related to IoT. A range of famous consumer device cases have shown the vulnerability of IoT technologies, and have generated fear about how IoT will delimit control by or even physically injure the end user.

Application and Device Take-Over

The short history of IoT contains many cases of instability and thereby potential take-over. The case of the Mirai botnet attack on IoT devices (Woolf 2016) in particular showed how service take-over is possible owing to the many access points in IoT, which we initially outlined as one of the defining characteristics of IoT, that were not updated. Health cases also raise concerns, as the cyborg fallacy is created and the fear grows of not being in control of one's own body in line with general robotics and automation resistance (Calo 2017). An example is the case of the St. Jude Medical implantable cardiac devices, which were able to be hacked and thereby potentially kill people (Larson 2017). The same goes for potentially deadly hacks of self-driving cars such as Jeep (Greenberg 2015) and Tesla (Solon 2016), which could be taken over by hostile actors. Another genre of take-overs is the use of cameras in various devices and contexts, such as toys or cities, where the camera takes over—such as in the Trendnet case (Adhikari 2013).

Data Sharing for Other Purposes

Yet, another fear or "creep" scenario (Shklovski et al. 2014) that plays on factors such as lack of control and mistrust is the case in which users share data with a company, and the company agrees to use it for other purposes than those the user would normally expect. One of the issues here is that the average user seldom reads the informed consent contracts in which such terms of services are stated (Bechmann 2013). Here, IoT adds significant complexities to this equation as interfaces become even more integrated in the everyday context. Warnings are therefore potentially difficult to establish and guidelines for making sure people read End User License Agreements (EULAs) primarily use laptops and smartphones when showing best practices. This falls short when the interface is, for instance, sound or movement based in IoT.

Some of the most famous recent cases of data expectations and the fear of expectations being violated involve home devices. One such relates to the robotic vacuum cleaner company iRoomba, which possesses highly valuable data about people's homes (Reilly 2017). Furthermore, media stories about the Amazon loudspeaker Echo, with an Alexa social bot interface that it was presumed could listen to conversations in the room even when it was not being operated (Field 2018), served as a case of fearing surveillance (Lyon 2007) and broke expectations about how a home device should act ethically bought by users and allowed to be part of their intimate and private spaces.

The interoperability or more precise the intraoperability (Bechmann 2013) of IoT not only connects to services that are tied to particular spaces such as home devices, but also and especially to data services that transgress physical places and collect a massive amount of data. Just a few players (Facebook, Alphabet, Apple, Microsoft, Amazon) have control over this ecosystem, and this in some ways makes the manipulation of data easier because users and services are interconnected. This is a defining characteristic of the present IoT infrastructure, and especially when it comes to social media as an application, infrastructure and data service that connects to various IoT solutions and access devices. One of the most recent cases, involving Cambridge Analytica, showed that people do not read informed consent contracts. Users taking quizzes allowed Facebook data from 87 million friends and friends of friends to be collected by third parties (which was a standard procedure in the API set-up until 2015), presumably helping to manipulate elections (Chaykowski 2018).

5.2 Ethics as Corporate Social Responsibility in IoT

All these cases potentially have a chilling effect on innovation, business models and value creation in connection with IoT. Ethics as corporate social responsibility, along with regulation such as the General Data Protection Regulation in the European Union (EU), therefore becomes a way in which to make sure that companies address issues of data theft, leakage or device take-over in the wake of security breaches that are due to unstable technological solutions or data management. Ethics is here understood as a way to protect organizations against intellectual property theft or blackmail and the individual against violation of privacy, as well as to secure solutions and services against hostile take-over in order to protect the individual from harm and serve the common good in society. However, doing this is not without obstacles.

5.3 Individual Rights and the 'Common Good'

The balance between individual rights such as privacy and the common good (or public good) is a well-known ethical dilemma that moral philosophy in connection with IoT needs to and continuously has addressed (Vayena and Gasser 2016; Wigan and Clarke 2013; Floridi 1999). How do we make sure that we can protect user privacy and at the same time use data and infrastructure to optimize knowledge about users for product and service innovation and serve the common good at the same time? To address this question, at least five associated aspects can be identified in the research on information ethics and critical algorithmic studies: governance, transparency, accountability, privacy and trust.

5.4 Governance

Some of the defining characteristics of IoT such as increased openness, inter(or intra)operability, mobility and accessibility at the same time make the infrastructure vulnerable to attacks (Bechmann and Lomborg 2014), and the scale of damage done increases with the extension of network connectivity and global network infrastructure, as we have identified in the defining characteristics of IoT. This calls for stronger attempts to govern IoT in a way that makes sure data collection, processing, management and sharing live up to general regulatory issues such as anti-trust, anti-discrimination, protected classes, privacy, freedom of speech and right to information, to name just a few.

Many issues of IoT governance have been raised, and here two will be emphasized. In a global society should we have shared standards and code of conducts that we need to govern for, and if not then how are we making sure that international IoT companies live up to standards on a national level? And how are we making sure that they follow existing regulation and values in a given market at all?

5.5 Transparency

Here, transparency has been a hot topic within existing data, machine learning and IoT policy research. Transparency is often used as a concept to comply with privacy regulations (e.g. the General Data Privacy Regulation in the EU) and to provide an understanding of where data is being used, for what purposes, by whom and for how long. This is often considered a part of privacy-by-design compliance, but the issue of transparency paradox may prevent transparency from being the solution of such complex network accounts, simply because users will not be able to understand the complexity, will not read it because of the complexity and continue to use the service without consulting further (Nissenbaum 2011). These issues are not decreasing with IoT, and in fact the opposite is the case as interfaces become more tangible and integrated. Some researchers find that transparency of the algorithms and the code itself can make sure that companies follow general regulations on human rights and specific regulation within the different markets (Sandvig et al. 2014). However, other scholars have suggested that transparency of the algorithm will not solve the problem of governance, since algorithms are intertwined and often to some degree work autonomously, meaning that it is when the algorithm meets the data that the outcome on values can be measured (Bechmann and Bowker 2017; Kroll et al. 2016; Ananny and Crawford 2016).

5.6 Accountability

Accountability to some extent combines the goals of transparency and governance, not by claiming direct transparency for the code in the algorithms but by focusing more on how to make sure that companies and organizations can document and account for how they meet criteria relating to, for instance, anti-discrimination, and showing what has been manipulated, for whom and how (e.g. content in political campaigns) without violating intellectual property rights. Supplementary accountability also highlights how actors such as companies and organizations comply with the general regulation and values of a given market, culture and society (Kroll et al. 2016; Bechmann and Bowker 2017). However, accountability is also not without obstacles.

The intelligent processing of data in IoT using machine learning and artificial intelligence such as deep neural networks makes it difficult to account for why predictions end up as they do. However, accounting for these processes cannot only be done just by having access to the algorithms (Ananny and Crawford 2016), but needs, according to existing studies, to be done by storing data processing outcomes on a continuous basis and making that information available for independent audits, for instance (Kroll et al. 2016; Bechmann and Bowker 2017). Yet one of the largest obstacles in such audits is the issue of time: once an audit is finished the algorithm might have changed or picked up new patterns in the closed machine learning cycle that makes the prediction different, and potentially violating some of the values tested for.

5.7 Privacy

Two overarching themes in ethics are transparency on one side and privacy on the other. To some degree these two issues may be mutually exclusive and not necessarily work in tandem. An example of this conflict is the spread of disinformation and the combating thereof. In order to prevent disinformation, data scientists and regulators need to understand the circulation at scale, but in providing access to information exposure, regulators will violate the privacy of the networks that have shared that information (EU Commission 2018). Yet, in the light of potential data expectations, privacy has with the introduction of the General Data Protection Regulation (GDPR) a high priority in governance supported by EU. However, privacy is not only a way in which to comply with regulation; it also serves as a way to communicate corporate social responsibility to the user that will potentially increase the trust relationship between company and user that IoT increasingly relies on, in order to attract and keep users despite the creep factor and fear scenarios, as exemplified in the sections above.

5.8 The Currency of Trust: A Challenge and Potential for IoT

Trust is a concept that shows an uneven power relationship between two or more actors, in this case the company and the user(s) where one actor holds more knowledge than the other (Giddens 2013). Trust therefore becomes the essential currency in IoT and needs to be integrated into future innovative IoT solutions to secure a sustainable and trustworthy relationship with users. How are companies going to prevent attacks on trust building, as we have seen with the fear scenarios and attacks through carefully constructed disinformation campaigns? More research needs to be done in order to answer this important question in depth and on different levels, not only relating to interface design, but also to infrastructure and protocols.

6 Conclusion

This chapter offers an insight into three intertwined disciplines related to the development of IoT. It is clear that we are only at an early stage of offering tools and understanding in terms of technology, business and ethics for developing IoT applications and services, and in turn driving novel business models. Technology can be seen as driving the innovation, with the business and ethics conversations lagging behind.

The technology challenge is looking at how to collaborate with business and ethical challenges to foster solutions that are interoperable, secure and efficient at the same time, as well as offering the right level of privacy mechanisms for ethical IoT use. The business challenge provides another side, modeling the businesses' operations in a digital world with tools that are agnostic to novel technologies and fail to capture the full potential of IoT. A mismatch between understanding and drivers is starting to emerge, and we are seeing attempts to bridge the gap, as shown by Vermesan et al. (2016) and Mansour et al. (2018). The final side of the triangle, IoT and ethics, offers an insight into the exploitation of technology that reflects this immaturity.

References

Adhikari, Richard. 2013.Webcam Maker Takes FTC's Heat for Internet-of-Things Security Failure. *TechNewsWorld*.

Adila, Afghan Syeda, Almusawi Husam, and Géza Husi. 2018. Towards the Self-Powered Internet of Things (IoT) by Energy Harvesting: Trends and Technologies for Green IoT. In *Small-scale Intelligent Manufacturing Systems (SIMS), 2018 2nd International Symposium on*, 1–5. IEEE.

Ananny, Mike, and Kate Crawford. 2016. Seeing Without Knowing: Limitations of the Transparency Ideal and Its Application to Algorithmic Accountability. *New Media & Society*: 1461444816676645.

Andreev, Sergey, Olga Galinina, Alexander Pyattaev, Mikhail Gerasimenko, Tuomas Tirronen, Johan Torsner, Joachim Sachs, Mischa Dohler, and Yevgeni Koucheryavy. 2015. Understanding the IoT Connectivity Landscape: A Contemporary M2M Radio Technology Roadmap. *IEEE Communications Magazine* 53 (9): 32–40.

Bechmann, Anja. 2013. Internet Profiling: The Economy of Data Intraoperability on Facebook and Google. *MedieKultur: Journal of Media and Communication Research* 29 (55): 19.

Bechmann, Anja, and Geoffrey C. Bowker. 2017. AI, Discrimination and Inequality in a 'Post' Classification Era. In *ICA* 2017.

Bechmann, Anja, and Stine Lomborg, eds. 2014. *The Ubiquitous Internet: User and Industry Perspectives*. Vol. 25. New York: Routledge.

Beliatis, Michail J., Hussam Mansour, Nagy Szabolcs, Aagaard Annabeth, and Presser Mirko. 2018. Digital Waste Management Using LoRa Network a Business Case from Lab to Fab. To be published in IEEE 2018 Global Internet of Things Summit (GIoTS). IEEE.

Bonomi, Flavio, Rodolfo Milito, Jiang Zhu, and Sateesh Addepalli. 2012. Fog Computing and Its Role in the Internet of Things. In *Proceedings of the First Edition of the MCC Workshop on Mobile Cloud Computing*, 13–16. ACM.

Bröring, Arne, Stefan Schmid, Corina-Kim Schindhelm, Abdelmajid Khelil, Sebastian Käbisch, Denis Kramer, Danh Le Phuoc, Jelena Mitic, Darko Anicic, and Ernest Teniente. 2017. Enabling IoT Ecosystems Through Platform Interoperability. *IEEE Software* 34 (1): 54–61.

Calo, Ryan. 2017. Artificial Intelligence Policy: A Primer and Roadmap. *UCDL Rev* 51: 399.

Casagras, R.F.I.D. 2011. The Inclusive Model for the Internet of Things Report. *EU Project* 216803: 16–23.

Chan, Hubert C.Y. 2015. Internet of Things Business Models. *Journal of Service Science and Management* 8 (04): 552.

Chaykowski, Kathleen. 2018. Facebook Says Data On 87 Million People May Have Been Shared in Cambridge Analytica Leak. *Forbes*. https://www.forbes.com/sites/kathleenchaykowski/2018/04/04/facebook-says-data-on-87-million-people-may-have-been-shared-in-cambridge-analytica-leak/#4a5ff8173e8b. Accessed 1 June 2018.

EU Commission. 2018. *HLEG on Fake News Report: A Multi-Dimensional Approach to Disinformation*. Brussels: EU Commission.

Field, Matthew. 2018. Amazon Fixes Alexa Bug that Let Echo Keep Listening. *The Telegraph*. https://www.telegraph.co.uk/technology/2018/04/27/amazon-alexa-bug-let-hackers-turn-echo-speakers-covert-listening/. Accessed 1 June 2018.

Floridi, Luciano. 1999. Information Ethics: On the Philosophical Foundation of Computer Ethics. *Ethics and Information Technology* 1 (1): 33–52.

Floridi, Luciano, and Mariarosaria Taddeo. 2016. *What Is Data Ethics?* 20160360.

Gassmann, Oliver, Karolin Frankenberger, and Michaela Csik. 2013. *The St. Gallen Business Model Navigator*. University of St.Gallen.

Giddens, Anthony. 2013. *The Consequences of Modernity*. Hoboken: John Wiley & Sons.

Greenberg, Andy. 2015. Hackers Remotely Kill a Jeep on the Highway—With Me in It. *Wired* 7: 21.

Gubbi, Jayavardhana, Rajkumar Buyya, Slaven Marusic, and Marimuthu Palaniswami. 2013. Internet of Things (IoT): A Vision, Architectural Elements, and Future Directions. *Future Generation Computer Systems* 29 (7): 1645–1660.

Hernández-Muñoz, José M., Jesús Bernat Vercher, Luis Muñoz, José A. Galache, Mirko Presser, Luis A. Hernández Gómez, and Jan Pettersson. 2011. Smart Cities at the Forefront of the Future Internet. In *The Future Internet Assembly*, 447–462. Berlin: Springer.

Kamalinejad, Pouya, Chinmaya Mahapatra, Zhengguo Sheng, Shahriar Mirabbasi, Victor C.M. Leung, and Yong Liang Guan. 2015. Wireless Energy Harvesting for the Internet of Things. *IEEE Communications Magazine* 53 (6): 102–108.

Kim, Jaeho, Jaeseok Yun, Sung-Chan Choi, Dale N. Seed, Lu Guang, Martin Bauer, Adel Al-Hezmi, Konrad Campowsky, and Jaeseung Song. 2016. Standard-based IoT Platforms Interworking: Implementation, Experiences, and Lessons Learned. *IEEE Communications Magazine* 54 (7): 48–54.

Kitchin, Rob. 2015. Making Sense of Smart Cities: Addressing Present Shortcomings. *Cambridge Journal of Regions, Economy and Society* 8 (1): 131–136.

Kroll, Joshua A., Solon Barocas, Edward W. Felten, Joel R. Reidenberg, David G. Robinson, and Harlan Yu. 2016. Accountable Algorithms. *University of Pennsylvania Law Review* 165: 633.

Larson, Selena. 2017. FDA Confirms That St. Jude's Cardiac Devices Can Be Hacked. *CNN*. http://money.cnn.com/2017/01/09/technology/fda-st-jude-cardiac-hack/. Accessed 1 June 2018.

Lee, So-Eun, Mideum Choi, and Seongcheol Kim. 2017. How and What to Study About IoT: Research Trends and Future Directions from the Perspective of Social Science. *Telecommunications Policy* 41 (10): 1056–1067.

Lucero, Sam. 2016. IoT Platforms: Enabling the Internet of Things. *IHS Technology White Paper*.

Lyon, David. 2007. *Surveillance Studies: An Overview*. Cambridge: Polity.

Mansour, Hussam, Mirko Presser, and Torben Bjerrum. 2018. Comparison of Seven Business Model Innovation Tools for IoT Ecosystems. In *Internet of Things (WF-IoT), 2018 IEEE 4th World Forum on*, 68–73. IEEE.

Magretta, Joan. 2002. Why Business Models Matter. *Harvard Business Review*: 86–92.

Minerva, Roberto, Abyi Biru, and Domenico Rotondi. 2015. Towards a Definition of the Internet of Things (IoT). *IEEE Internet Initiative* 1.

Nissenbaum, Helen. 2011. A Contextual Approach to Privacy Online. *Daedalus* 140 (4): 32–48.

Nagy, Szabolcs, Hussam Mansour, and Mirko Presser. 2018. Case Study of IoT as a Driver for Business Model Innovation in the Wind Industry. In *Internet of Things (WF-IoT), 2018 IEEE 4th World Forum on*, 74–79. IEEE.

Osterwalder, Alexander, and Yves Pigneur. 2010. *Business Model Generation: A Handbook for Visionaries, Game Changers, and Challengers*. Hoboken: John Wiley & Sons.

Ray, Partha Pratim. 2016. A Survey of IoT Cloud Platforms. *Future Computing and Informatics Journal* 1 (1–2): 35–46.

Reilly, Michael. 2017. Roomba, the Cute Little Robovac, Has Got a Side Hustle. *MIT Technology Review* https://www.technologyreview.com/s/608344/your-roomba-is-also-gathering-data-about-the-layout-of-your-home/. Accessed 1 June 2018.

Rose, Karen, Scott Eldridge, and Lyman Chapin. 2015. The Internet of Things: An Overview. *The Internet Society (ISOC)*: 1–50.

Sandvig, Christian, Kevin Hamilton, Karrie Karahalios, and Cedric Langbort. 2014. Auditing Algorithms: Research Methods for Detecting Discrimination on Internet Platforms. *Data and Discrimination: Converting Critical Concerns into Productive Inquiry*, 1–23.

Schlachter, Fred. 2013. No Moore's Law for Batteries. *Proceedings of the National Academy of Sciences* 110 (14): 5273–5273.

Shklovski, Irina, Scott D. Mainwaring, Halla Hrund Skúladóttir, and Höskuldur Borgthorsson. 2014. Leakiness and Creepiness in App Space: Perceptions of Privacy and Mobile App Use. In *Proceedings of the SIGCHI Conference on Human Factors in Computing Systems*, 2347–2356. ACM.

Solon, Olivia. 2016. Team of Hackers Take Remote Control of Tesla Model S from 12 Miles Away. *The Guardian*, September.

Sun, Yunchuan, Hongli Yan, Cheng Lu, Rongfang Bie, and Peter Thomas. 2012. A Holistic Approach to Visualizing Business Models for the Internet of Things. *Communications in Mobile Computing* 1 (1): 4.

Turber, Stefanie, Jan Vom Brocke, Oliver Gassmann, and Elgar Fleisch. 2014. Designing Business Models in the Era of Internet of Things. In *International Conference on Design Science Research in Information Systems*, 17–31. Cham: Springer.

Vayena, Effy, and Urs Gasser. 2016. Between Openness and Privacy in Genomics. *PLoS Medicine* 13 (1): e1001937.

Vermesan, Ovidiu, Bahr, Roy, Gluhak Alexander, Boesenberg Frank, Hoeer, Anne, and Osella Michele, 2016. IoT Business Models Framework. H2020: UNIFY-IoT Project. http://www.internet-of-things-research.eu/pdf/D02_01_WP02_H2020_UNIFY-IoT_Final.pdf. Accessed 1 June 2018.

Vestergaard, Lasse Steenbock, João Fernandes, and Mirko Alexander Presser. 2015. Towards Smart City Democracy. *Geoforum Perspektiv* 14 (25): 38–43.

Westerlund, Mika, Seppo Leminen, and Mervi Rajahonka. 2014. Designing Business Models for the Internet of Things. *Technology Innovation Management Review* 4 (7): 5.

Wigan, Marcus R., and Roger Clarke. 2013. Big Data's Big Unintended Consequences. *Computer* 46 (6): 46–53.

Woolf, Nicky. 2016. DDoS Attack that Disrupted Internet Was Largest of Its Kind in History, Experts Say. *The Guardian,* 26.

Yan, Jihong, Yue Meng, Lei Lu, and Lin Li. 2017. Industrial Big Data in an Industry 4.0 Environment: Challenges, Schemes, and Applications for Predictive Maintenance. *IEEE Access* 5: 23484–23491.

3

Value Creation for Intelligent Connected Vehicles: An Industry Value-Chain Perspective

Xiangxuan Xu

Great technological achievements commonly fail commercially because little attention has been given to designing a business model to take them to market properly. This can and should be remedied.
David J. Teece (*2010*: 192)

1 Introduction

Digital transformation is at the top of the list for automakers (Dremel et al. 2017; Hanelt et al. 2015; Svahn et al. 2017). Tech companies and original equipment manufacturers (OEMs), once separated by the digital/physical dichotomy, are now reconfiguring their positions and strategies in this fast-changing competitive landscape. As witnessed in the mobile phone industry a decade ago, for today's OEMs embracing digital innovation is not just an add-on feature, but rather an action to remain

X. Xu (✉)
Department of Business Administration, School of Business, Economics and Law, University of Gothenburg, Gothenburg, Sweden
e-mail: emily.xu@handels.gu.se

A. Aagaard (ed.), *Digital Business Models*,
https://doi.org/10.1007/978-3-319-96902-2_3

relevant. Owing to digital disruption, together with the imperative for sustainable mobility and the rise of the sharing economy, the global automotive industry has witnessed a paradigm shift.

Incumbents that cannot adapt to this new reality are risking the loss of competitive advantages to new entrants and business models that disrupt markets. Thus, OEMs and suppliers, ride-hailing firms, and tech companies are facing a battle for digital supremacy regarding future mobility (The Economist 2018). Despite growing expectations, such radical change has so far not been researched in depth by business and innovation scholars (Ferràs-Hernández et al. 2017). One explanation is that the market has just recently begun to emerge. For example, Uber still had a net income loss of $1.1 billion during the fourth quarter in 2018 (Hook 2018). The hype-pivoting disruptive technologies such as autonomous driving and blockchain have not reached mass adoption yet. However, it is not impossible to draw insights from pioneering investments and initiatives in this new business arena. An industry value-chain perspective can help to envision the potential business models, because the changes to value-added distribution provide a catalyst for value creation (Teece 2010). Value creation is an essential part of any successful business model (Teece and Linden 2017; Wirtz et al. 2015). This chapter focuses on the value creation and strategy for intelligent connected vehicles (ICVs).

The empirical cases presented are mainly from West Sweden. The automotive industry has been Sweden's largest export industry, with a share of around 14% of the national merchandise exports in 2016 (Pohl 2017:7). The West Sweden region has always been the center of the automotive industry in the country. It is the home of many leading OEMs and specialized subcontractors and suppliers as well as a growing number of tech start-ups. The region has the most significant share of the research and development (R&D) investment in the country's vehicle development and over a third of its national automotive labor force. The digital transformation has boosted the region's automotive sector in recent years in the area of connected vehicles, autonomous driving, and electric mobility. Therefore, the region offers a dynamic context for this timely topic.

The advent of digital technologies impacts the value added and creates space to capture new value points. By applying an industry value-chain perspective, this chapter aims to shed light on the emerging business model development that varies in terms of the different parts of the automotive industry value chain; that is, the upstream and downstream value added. The implications can help automakers rethink their digital innovation strategies based on a full spectrum of value points, from the supply side to the demand side of aftersales services and new usage modes.

The study aims to contribute to the research on the business model innovation of smart, connected vehicles by using an industry value-chain perspective. An analytical framework of new value creation logic and strategies for the different value-added points of ICVs is proposed. Empirical cases from one of the world's innovation hubs within the auto sector add timely observations and reflections regarding this ongoing paradigm shift. The study provides pertinent analytical insights for academic researchers and industry practitioners at this uncertain phase of industry transformation.

The chapter is divided into five parts. After the introduction, the second part introduces the current studies on industry value-chain change that is driven by digital transformation in the automotive industry. Based on the changes in value-added distribution, the third section further elaborates the implications for ICV business value creation on the demand and supply sides. In this section, an analytical framework is proposed to facilitate the discussions about the empirical cases. After the method and data collection section, the fifth part discusses the empirical findings. The chapter ends with a conclusion and implication section.

2 How Does Digital Conversion Change the Industry Value Chain for ICVs?

Tomorrow's vehicles are intelligent, connected, and ultimately driverless (Kellerman 2018; Pohl 2017). For ICVs, digital technologies are embedded in the products and services offerings, as well as the processes that underpin them. The path towards such transition is built upon codevelopment of technological advancements and business innovation in the industry value chain (Habeck et al. 2014). Studies show that the digital domain will dominate the core value added.

2.1 Core Value-Added Shift to the Digital Domain

Porter and Heppelmann (2014:4) reviewed the new technology stack driven by the Internet of Things and concluded that smart, connected products alter the industry structure and introduce a new set of strategic choices related to how value is created and captured, hence exposing companies to new, competitive opportunities and threats. This paradigm shift is happening within the automotive industry now. New entrants are shaping the ecosystem of vehicle development, disrupting the "old fortress" that was dominated by the traditional OEMs and tier-one suppliers. They can include new OEMs such as Google and Tesla, tech-savvy start-ups, digital fleet platforms, venture capitalists, and research institutes. Ferràs-Hernández et al. (2017) investigated 156 start-ups and concluded that the competitive battle is in the digital arena to control critical technologies and the user interfaces of the future, and the disruption seems to be led by outsiders from the digital domain.

Recent trends of merger and acquisition deals in the auto industry indicate that trends have shifted from consolidation to expansion into new technologies, new services, and new business models (Zaleski et al. 2017). The traditional OEMs are incompatible in the offline world when it comes to making vehicles. This marks a truly global industry. The big OEMs have an elaborate global production and knowledge network as well as a top R&D budget to guard their market supremacy (Castelli et al. 2011). However, they are latecomers in the digital world, particularly regarding data processing and analytics, system integration and security, and digital platforms and services, in which the tech companies are the masters. Meanwhile, the tech companies lack the domain knowledge of producing the hardware—vehicles. Consequently, automakers add technology to their core capabilities through acquisition, investment, and the creation of strategic partnerships (Dawson 2016).

2.2 A Deeper and Extended "Smile Curve"

The digital conversion of ICV value creation will impact the value-added distribution. Kuang et al. (2018) illustrated this changing shape as a deeper and extended "Smile Curve" (Fig. 3.1). The new value added is most dramatic at the two ends of the value chain.

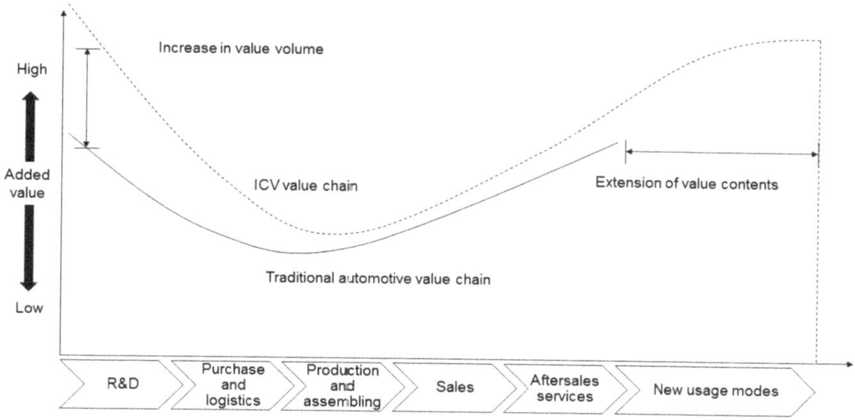

Fig. 3.1 Changes in industrial value distribution of ICV. (Source: Kuang et al. (2018:13))

On the supply side, the R&D of cutting-edge technologies such as autonomous driving, infotainment, and intelligent human/machine interface is likely to provide the competitive advantages for future auto leaders. At the same time, services such as vehicle management and device management are also active areas of the innovation race. Table 3.1 lists the major acquisition, investment, and partnership in the auto industry. It shows that traditional OEMs mostly invest in autonomous driving and enable connected device services. The tier-one suppliers focus on technologies for autonomous driving, infotainment, and human/machine interface, while new entrants participate in all fields, especially autonomous driving and connectivity and cloud-connected vehicle services.

On the demand side, the diversification of new service modes is expected to create high value-added potential for aftersales and new usage market. Examples can be found in maintenance, safety, insurance, vehicle rental, parking, second-hand transactions and recycling, assisting/autonomous driving, shared mobility, vehicle management, entertainment, navigation, and so on.

A few consulting estimations studied the different scenarios for growth trends in the auto industry by 2030 (Baker et al. 2016; Mckinsey & Company 2016). The numbers support the above assumption. The total

Table 3.1 Deals, investments, partnerships, and new entrants at the supply side

	Technology				Enabling services	
	Adaptive driver assistance systems	Technologies Infotainment	Human–machine interface	Communications, computing, and cloud	Connected vehicle services	Connected device services
OEMs (major automakers) Acquisition	**Acquisition** Audi/Daimler/BMW: Here (2015) GM: Cruise Automation (2016) **Investment** Volvo: Peloton (2015) **Partnership** Audi & Nvidia (since 2005) Bosch & TomTom (2015) GM & Mobileye (2015) VW & Mobileye (2015) BMW & Intel & Mobileye (2016) Hyundai & Cisco (2016)	**Investment** Ford: Livio (2013) **Partnership** Audi & Nvidia (since 2005)		**Partnership** Daimler & Qualcomm (2015) Hyundai & Cisco (2016) Toyota & KDDI (2016)	**Partnership** Ford & State Farm (2012) BMW & Pivotal (2015) Ford & Microsoft Azure (2015) Volvo & Microsoft (2015) Nissan & Microsoft Azure (2016)	**Acquisition** Daimler: Mytaxi (2014) GM: Sidecar (2016) **Investment** BMW: RideCell (2014) BMW: Zendrive (2014) GM: Telogis (2014) BAIC: Didi Chuxing (2015) Ford: Pivotal (2016) GM: Lyft (2016) Toyota: Uber (2016) VW: Gett (2016) **Partnership** BMW & Baidu (2015) BMW & Microsoft Azure (2016) Seat & Samsung & SAP (2016) Toyota & Microsoft Azure (2016)

Traditional suppliers	**Acquisition** Continental: Elektrobit (2015) Delphi: Ottomatika (2015) ZF: TRW (2015) Continental: ASC (2016) **Investment** Delphi: Quanergy (2015) Bosch: AdasWorks (2016) **Partnership** Valeo & Mobileye (2015)	**Acquisition** Harman: Aha (2010) Harman: S1nn (2014) Continental: Elektrobit (2015) Harman: Symphony Teleca (2015) **Partnership** Ha rman & Luxoft (2011) Harman & Microsoft (2016)	**Acquisition** Continental: Elektrobit (2015) **Partnership** Valeo & Safran (2013)	**Acquisition** Bosch: ProSyst (2015) Valeo: Pelker (2015	**Acquisition** Harman: Redbend SW (2015) Harman: TowerSec (2016) **Partnership** Valeo & Capgemini (2015)	**Acquisition** Harman: Aditi (2015)
New entrants from outside automotive	**Acquisition** Panasonic: Ficosa (2014) Google: FCA (2016) Nvidia: AdasWorks (2016) **New entrants:** Apple, Baidu, Google	**New entrants** AdasWorks, Baselabs, Vector, Velodyne, Wind River	**Investment** Intel: Omek (2013) **New entrants** Atmel, Fujitsu, Kyocera, LG, Toshiba	**Acquisition** Cisco/NXP: Cohda Wireless (2013) **New entrants** Cohda Wireless, Kymeta, Veniam	**Investment** Verizon: Hughes (2012) **Partnership** Airbiquity & Arynga (2016) **New entrants** Airbiquity, Allstate, Fleetmatics, Pivotal, Progressive, SiriusXM, Trimble, Verisk	**Partnership** Daimler Moovel & IBM (2014) Airbiquity & Arynga (2016) **New entrants** Airbiquity, Apple, Contigo, Dash, Google, iTrack, Lyft, MyCarTracks, Uber

Source: Baker et al. (2016:35–36)

revenue streams from new value points can vary from $1.5 trillion (30% of the total revenue pool) to $3.5 trillion (45% of the total revenue pool). Despite the difference in math, it is clear that value creation is moving from traditional one-time vehicle sales and aftermarket value to a diverse range of recurring revenues from new usage modes.

3 Implications for ICV Business Value Creation

3.1 Demand-Side Value Creation Logic Shifting to the Network Effect, Long-Tail Effect, and Multi-Sided Platforms

Network Effect

On the downstream side, the convergence of digital forces into the physical auto industry value chain has just begun. This conversion leads to the coupling of the physical value chain and virtual value chain (Rayport and Sviokla 1995). The virtual value chain often mirrors the structure of the physical one, but with different value creation logic—the network effect (Shapiro and Varian 1999; Xu 2012, 2017). The network effect indicates that the value of a product and service increases according to the number of others using it. It amplifies the scaling effect of the user networks. As fast scaling requires the accumulation of positive feedback loops, it thereby emphasizes first-mover advantages.

Long-Tail Effect

The second mindset change for value creation is the long-tail effect (Brynjolfsson et al. 2014). Traditionally, many consumer markets are dominated by a few bestsellers, which reflects the Pareto principle (e.g. the classic 80/20 divide). Owing to the increase in product selection and lower search costs on the Internet, such sales concentration has been reduced to a more extended distribution of sales of niche products. The long-tail effect is user-centric. Traditional automotive value chains are producer-driven (Dijk and Yarime 2010). The big auto brands lead the product innovation and strategies. For ICVs, this is no longer the case. The long-tail effect extends the range of personalized on-demand services based on user preferences and data analytics. Therefore, it is user-centric and data-driven.

The third game changer is the platform mindset. When vehicles become the platform of on-demand real-time personalized services, they are no longer just physical products, but also the platform upon which to connect with digital resources. This took place in the mobile phone industry a decade ago. It might even be the case that the future auto leaders will dominate the vehicle platform, as with today's Android/iOS oligopoly on the mobile device platform.

Multi-Sided Platforms

The platform mindset alters the value creation logic for producers. According to economic theories, traditionally producers are one of three types: vertically integrated firms, resellers, or input suppliers. The economy of platform introduces the multi-sided platform (MSP) business model (Hagiu and Wright 2015). MSP enables direct interactions between two or more distinct sides that are affiliated with the platform. Therefore, MSP changes the nature of the transaction and then redefines the interorganizational boundaries. Hagiu and Wright (2015) suggest that MSP can best achieve motivating unobservable efforts by a variety of actors because they can adapt their own decisions to their private information (Fig. 3.2).

MSPs generate recurring value creation such as e-hailing, car sharing, and data-connectivity services including apps, remote services, and software upgrades (Mckinsey & Company 2016). Therefore, automakers are shifting their role from product developers to system and service integrators. For instance, Shelly (2015) suggested that developing cutting-edge software and integrating the car with the Smartphone ecosystem would provide strategic differentiation factors for automotive leaders.

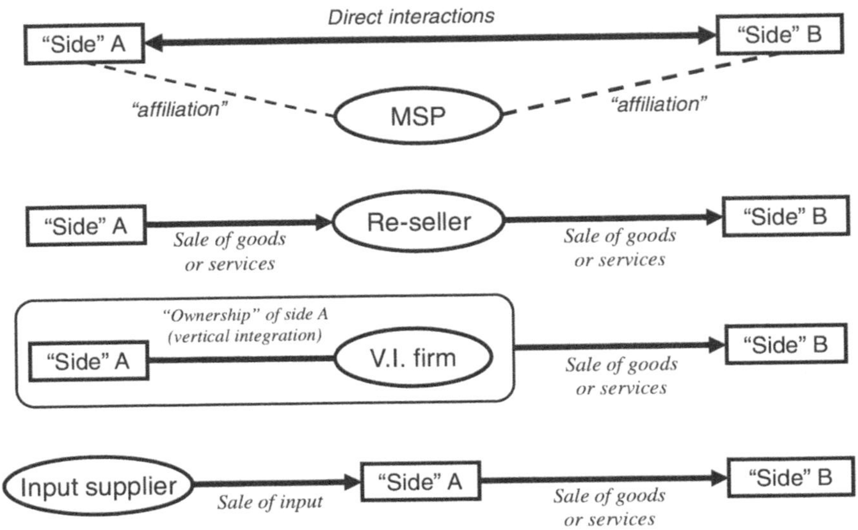

Fig. 3.2 MSPs versus alternative business models. (Source: Hagiu and Wright (2015:165))

3.2 Supply-Side Value Creation Logic Adding Horizontal Integration

The R&D activities in the traditional automotive industry represent a textbook example of vertical integration (Castelli et al. 2011; Williamson 1971). Vertical integration in the business model design tends to bring R&D units together under common ownership. One example is Geely auto's acquisition of Volvo from Ford in 2010. A joint venture R&D center China Europe Vehicle Technology (CEVT) was created afterwards, which was considered to be a strategic asset creation for innovation upgrading (Yakob et al. 2018)

The core capability shift to the digital domain requires automakers to adapt to a more open development environment for technology innovation, which pushes horizontal integration in R&D activities. OEMs cannot possess all knowledge, competencies, and know-how only to develop technologies, but also to collaborate with resources within or outside the traditional industry boundaries for example with the specialized service providers, data analytics, system integrators, and network service providers. Strategic partnerships can be formed between traditional OEMs, between traditional OEMs and new OEMs, or with tech companies. They codevelop cutting-edge smart vehicle operating systems, driverless technologies, and in-car infotainment systems. Examples include Google's first partnership with a major automaker to test self-driving technology with 100 Chrysler minivans; Audi, BMW, and Daimler's $3 billion purchase of Here's digital mapping services; and the joint venture between Intel and BMW to develop self-driving systems (Dawson 2016).

Open Innovation

The value creation of horizontal integration relies on open innovation (Chesbrough 2006) and innovation ecosystem building. Open innovation is a digital era mindset that promotes the use of external ideas as well as internal ideas and internal and external paths to market. It counters the traditional closed-door research units that run as silos. The open innovation practices can vary from transactional to collaborative (Brunswicker and Chesbrough 2018). Narsalay et al. (2016) suggested four modes of open innovation strategies:

1) Traditional IP contract: a market transaction typically used when a single owner controls a specific needed technology.
2) Open-innovation partnership: a bilateral relationship used when projects are ill-structured and complex but relate to well-known technological solution areas (e.g. Huawei, IoT, and HP/DreamWorks).
3) Open innovation platform/contest: a competition used when a problem requires access to the long-tail effect of solution knowledge (e.g. Bosch technology contest and Samsung ARTIK contest).
4) Open innovation community: a collaboration among different parties used when joint problem-solving is required to tackle truly perplexing problems (e.g. Ford OpenXC).

Innovation Ecosystems

Open innovation focuses on firms' R&D activities, while innovation ecosystem building is a company strategy that alters the governance structure of the production network. According to the global value-chain theory (Gereffi et al. 2005), there are five types of the governance structure of production networks (from tight to loose): (1) hierarchy, (2) captive, (3) relational, (4) modular, and (5) market.

Hierarchy and captive are somewhat typical structures in the traditional automotive industry supply chain management. The MSP business model is expected to embrace the relational, modular, or even market governance structures. Since MSPs enable direct interactions among different sides, they enhance the ability to codify complex transactions and motivate adaptations among sides. Therefore, MSPs increase the ability to codify complex transactions and enhance the capabilities of the supply base. According to Gereffi et al. (2005:86), relational forms occur when product specifications cannot be codified, transactions are complex, and supplier capabilities are high. Modular forms arise when the ability to codify specifications extends to complex products and technical standards simplify interactions by reducing component variation and by unifying component, product, and process specifications. Market forms can be expected when transactions are easily codified, product specifications are simple, and suppliers are fully capable.

The future leader ought to be a cross-boundary orchestrator in relational (e.g. science park, innovation district), modular (sub-contractor outsourcing), or distributed (market) innovation ecosystems. This governance structure can overlap with the MSP platform at different sides of integration.

Table 3.2 summarizes the different value creation logic and strategies for the demand side and supply side of the ICV value chain.

Table 3.2 A framework of new value creation logic and strategy for the supply and demand side of ICV value added

Value-added side	New value creation logic	Value creation strategies
Demand-side (e.g. aftersales and new usage modes)	Network effect	Fast scaling, First-mover advantages
	Long-tail effect	User centric, Data centric
	Multi-Sided Platforms	Recurring revenue streams, system and service integrator
Supply-side (e.g. R&D activities)	Horizontal integration	Orchestrating innovation ecosystem (relational, modular, or distributed), Open innovation (contract IP, innovation contest, innovation community, innovation partnership)

Source: Author

4 Method and Data Collection

This research performs a qualitative case study of the digital transformation in the automotive industry in the West Sweden region.

The West Sweden region is the capital of Sweden's automotive industry. According to Business Region Göteborg,[1] the region is one of the world's most knowledge-intensive regions per capita for vehicle development. With more than 25,000 direct employees in the automotive sector, the region contributes to over 60% of the country's total automotive R&D investments. It is the home base to the world's leading OEMs and specialist subcontractors and suppliers, such as Volvo cars, the Volvo Group, CEVT, National Electric Vehicle Sweden (NEVS), SKF, Autoliv, Zenuity, Semcon, Ericsson, and HCL. In recent years, the booming automotive sector has attracted foreign direct investment, especially from the China Geely Group. A new 70,000 sq. meter Geely Innovation Centre is

[1] Source: https://www.businessregiongoteborg.se/en/focus-areas/automotive-and-transport (Retrieved March 17, 2018).

under construction. The digital transformation also opens up new opportunities for new entrant start-ups. Today, the region claims itself as a world-class leader in areas such as electrification, autonomous driving, and connected cars. The West Sweden region has almost the entire vehicle development ecosystem. Therefore, it is an exciting place to explore the latest business models that are emerging for future mobility.

The case study method offers rich and in-depth data on complex social events, and people's perceptions are therefore mostly used to conduct explorative studies (Bryman and Bell 2015; Patton 2014). Multiple data collection methods are typical for qualitative case research (Eisenhardt 1989). Interviews and archived materials such as reports, website information, and news releases were applied for this study. Between November 2017 to March 2018 fifteen interviews were collected, the interviewees being business owners, innovation managers, and business developers from the leading OEMs, new OEMs, tech companies, tech spin-out firms, and start-ups in the region. The interviewers were not from the industry. People from public agencies and innovation arenas related to the regional automotive innovation system also provided their opinions. Therefore, the selection of interviewers provides a broader picture of the current development in the automotive sector.

5 Discussion

5.1 Value-Added Distribution

In the West Sweden region, the automotive industry transforms in its core, owing to the disruptive technology shifts and fast-changing consumer behaviors and needs. The expectations are high, and the pace of technology innovation is faster than ever. Traditional OEMs are entering the uncharted waters of fierce competitions with the new entrants. The race heats up in new usage modes, such as shared mobility, connected services, and autonomous driving. Even though uncertainty is high, they must bet and move quickly. Therefore, both supply-side pull and demand-side push affect the value-added distribution.

One observation from the region is that many of these new entrants are spin-outs from the old OEMs and tier-one suppliers. They can be joint ventures between the OEM and tier one. For instance, Zenuity, specializing in developing new advanced driver assist systems and autonomous driving technologies, is a joint venture between Volvo cars and Autoliv that began in April 2017. Zenuity identifies itself as an automotive new entrant. The rationale for this initiative is to share risk in developing cutting-edge technologies and to move quickly. A business development manager from a new entrant said, "In the old days, the development cycle at OEM was around seven years, and now they can reduce it to three years, but it is still too slow for us... we are talking about months." Zenuity aims to launch the unsupervised highway pilot in 2021 and the unsupervised urban pilot in 2023.

City Trollhättan, where Saab auto was established, has witnessed a wave of new venture creation in the automotive sector since Saab went bankrupt. A majority of these new establishments were funded by former Saab engineers. For instance, the powertrain team created T-Engineering (acquired by Chinese Dongfeng Motor in 2014), while the infotainment team initiated Swedspot. They are both fast-growing auto new entrants in the region. T-Engineering develops in-vehicle control systems, and Swedspot develops embedded user interfaces and on-board diagnostics (OBD) sockets for connected car services. The most prominent new entrant is NEVS (acquired the Saab assets in 2012), which focuses on producing pure electric vehicles and providing mobility services. Most of the new entrants are driven by the new usage modes.

The increasing links between China and investment in the region will have a profound impact on the value-added distribution for the automotive sector. The major foreign direct investment to the automotive sector for West Sweden region is from China. The most prominent investors are Geely auto, Dongfeng motors, and the owners of NEVS—Hong Kong-based National Modern Energy Holdings and the Tianjin Binhai Hi-tech Industry Development Area. For example, the creation of a new "born digital" car brand Lynk & Co was a joint venture between Geely auto and Volvo cars. The first generation of Lynk & Co targeted young urban Chinese consumers. NEVS formed a partnership with China's ride-hailing giant Didi Chuxing for its electric car-sharing platform, which is expected to operate more than 1 million electric vehicles by 2020.

5.2 Demand-Side Value Creation

Digital lifestyles are redefining the relationship between customers and their cars, as well as what a car should be. Today, people use their smartphones for almost everything but making a call. So why should cars still be only for driving? Some emerging trends can be found in areas such as car buying and learning how to own and use a car.

First, *sales go online.* This trend reflects the network effect logic. The most well-known example is Tesla, which does not have any dealerships. Most cars today are still sold at the dealers' network, but sales online are rising. Geely and Volvo's Lynk & Co tested the online format in 2017 for its premier launch on the Chinese market. According to the official news release, the company encountered huge success, receiving 6000 orders in just 137 seconds. Volvo cars' website also offers a personalized online booking option.

Second, companies *go subscribing*. Instead of buying a car, customers can subscribe by paying a monthly fee for different vehicle use and service packages. Subscription is a typical MPS value creation logic to generate recurring revenue streams. Private leasing is a way to create recurring revenues too, but it does not represent a platform mindset. Through private leasing, consumers are buying cars with a package of services. Therefore, it is still a form of one-time vehicle purchase. Subscription shifts the mindset of buying a car to getting access to a variety of vehicle services. For example, Volvo has launched its Care by Volvo subscription services. The plan is based on a 24-month subscription. After two years, subscribers hand the car back, or they can switch to a different Volvo after 12 months. The service package includes insurance, maintenance, repairs, tire changing, and connected car services. In this way, ownership is not what customers buy, but they subscribe to a platform of various vehicle services.

Similar to smartphone subscriptions, a vehicle version of *app stores* is often provided. Since connected car services on a vehicle app store can be quickly updated and added, it uses the extended long-tail effect logic for value creation. Today, most leading car brands provide apps.

Third, companies *go sharing*. Compared with subscribing, shared mobility goes a step further to disrupt car ownership. It can be realized in a peer-to-peer sharing platform, or fleet platform, or ultimately by driverless cars. When reaching that point, most of the population won't need to own a car anymore. The shared mobility enables the long-tail effect logic that is data driven and user centric. The more advanced the platform is, the more data driven it becomes. NEVS, as a new entrant OEM for sustainable mobility, claims to measure the success of how many vehicles are sold by how many trips are generated. They design business models by differentiating between ownership service and non-ownership service. Value creation for non-ownership vehicle usage involves much more than sharing. When the vehicle space turns from private to semi-public or public, it opens new opportunities for a variety of value points, such as advertising, insurance, safety, retailing, and entertainment, and even requires a different design for cleaning. This introduces unlimited possibilities.

No matter whether a company goes online, offers sharing, or provides subscriptions, the demand-side value creation sets the prerequisite for future auto leaders to be system and service integrators. From the history of the smartphone industry and other digital platforms, we know that the winners are few and first-mover advantage is crucial. Most digital platforms such as Google, Facebook, and Uber reached fast market dominance before developing mature business models. This "scaling first then profit" mindset could impact the auto sector now.

5.3 Supply-Side Value Creation

In recent years, the horizontal integration in R&D development has gained increasing visibility. Different from the demand-side value-creation logic that is driven by understanding consumer needs and data analytics, the supply-side logic goes beyond what the consumer wants. The R&D of cutting-edge technologies for tomorrow's mobility must be ahead of the consumer's needs. As the pace of technological change speeds up and the disruptors are outsiders, the level of uncertainty is high. The traditional OEMs are forced to open up, and the West Sweden region is no exception.

Currently, *open innovation partnership* and *open innovation community* offer the most common paths for horizontal integration in R&D activities. For instance, Volvo cars and Google formed a partnership to bring Android into infotainment and user experience development. HiQ is also helping Volvo with autonomous driving technology development. Furthermore, Volvo's collaboration with Ericsson on connected car services can be traced back to 2012. A recently acquired partner for the company is the Swedish Nobel Media for research in enduring innovation. As mentioned earlier in the chapter, NEVS formed a partnership with China's Didi for electric shared mobility.

An open innovation community often overlaps with relational innovation ecosystems. The physical community can be based on geographical proximity such as innovation arenas at a science park. A virtual community can take the form of an industry alliance that is based on business networks. MobilityXlab, founded by Volvo Cars, Ericsson, Volvo Group, Veoneer, Zenuity, and CEVT, is a recent establishment to bring pioneering start-ups closer to the founders. It is physically hosted by the Lindholmen Science Park, where the founding partners all have a physical presence. In March 2018, Geely auto, which owns Volvo cars and CEVT, revealed its smart ecosystem network for the first time at the Sanya Geely global ecopartner conference. Geely's smart ecosystem covers a broad spectrum of industries, new media, and tech entrants, including the big tech Tencent, e-commerce giant JD, telecom ZTE, insurance CPIC, global industry leader Bosch, HP, Autoliv, and BASF. According to the news release, the conference has attracted over 4000 participants from all over the world, including suppliers, distributors, finance, and internet companies.[2] Geely is building a 70,000 sq. meter global innovation center at Gothenburg to bring its ecosystem partners together.

However, the reality looks more complicated than the open/closed dichotomy. Going open does not equal horizontal, and vice versa. There can be many grey areas. For example, Zenuity is created as a joint venture by Volvo cars and tier-one Autoliv to focus on R&D for autonomous driving. Since Autoliv is the tier-one supplier for Volvo cars, from

[2] Source: http://global.geely.com/2018/03/16/geely-auto-launches-2018-bo-yue-suv-with-leading-gkui-interface/ (Retrieved March 31, 2018).

a supply chain perspective it is vertical integration. But from an organizational perspective, this joint venture can be categorized as interorganizational horizontal integration. Another example is CEVT, which was created in 2013 as Geely group's first overseas R&D center to supply Compact Modular Architecture (CMA) modular technologies for both Geely and Volvo cars. As a subsidiary of Geely, it is a clear vertical integration case. However, owing to the post-acquisition strategy that "Volvo is Volvo, Geely is Geely," CEVT thereby also represents a horizontal integration regarding actual organizational boundaries.

Opening up innovation processes is a delicate task. The combination of horizontal and vertical integration is a consequence of the changing competitive pace and landscape. Opening such processes provides the means to get access to ideas, resources, and Intellectual Properties (IPs) outside the organizational boundary so that the OEMs can maintain a softer leadership style in the battle for the best and fastest technology innovation.

6 Conclusion

This chapter discusses the ongoing digital transformation for value creation in the automotive industry. The innovation of this contribution is the use of an industry value-chain perspective to construct an analytical framework for ICV value creation. Owing to the disruptive technology innovation and changing customer expectations and needs, the growth of ICV value added is most dramatic on the demand side of the aftersales and new usage modes and on the supply side of R&D activities. The Smile Curve of ICVs then gets deeper and bigger.

Value creation on the demand side is shifting from one-time vehicle sales to recurring revenue streams. The study suggests that such a shift requires new value creation logic; that is, the network effect, the long-tail effect, and platform mindset (MSP). The cases in the West Sweden region show the trends of *selling online*, *go subscribing*, and *go sharing*. Automakers are developing app stores and transforming their role from vehicle producers to system and service integrators.

Horizontal integration on the supply side is increasing, since automakers have realized that they cannot have all the competence and know-how alone. R&D embraces open innovation. The old OEMs and new entrants in the West Sweden region form open innovation partnerships and open innovation communities to develop cutting-edge technologies for the future mobility. In reality, such an openness movement is supported by a mix of horizontal and vertical integrations, for example through the creation of new R&D centers by OEMs and tier-one suppliers through the establishment of global innovation centers to support interorganizational R&D collaboration within the same group. The open mindset is extended to overall company strategies. Leading OEMs are entering the race of building innovation ecosystems. Innovation arenas are founded to bring pioneering start-ups closer to the big players. The global ecopartner network is constructed to support cross-boundary collaborations. The role of the automaker is thereby transformed into an ecosystem orchestrator.

Speed is crucial. Strategies such as "scaling first then profits" are commonly used in the digital platform economy. When vehicles become the next digital platform, automakers can play this card too. The automotive industry is traditionally a very cost-controlled industry. To play the platform card, it requires an entirely different mindset as well as risk evaluation methods, operational processes, and organizational culture. All changes cannot happen at once, and this will impose significant challenges to the traditional OEMs.

7 Funding

This work was supported by the Adlerbert Research Foundation 2017–2018.

References

Baker, Edward H., David Crusius, Marco Fischer, Walter Gerling, Kaushik Gnanaserakan, Henning Kerstan, Felix Kuhnert, Julia Kusber, Joachim Mohs, Manuel Schule, Jonas Seyfferth, Juliane Stephan, and Trent Warnke. 2016. *Connected Car Report 2016: Opportunities, Risk, and Turmoil on the Road to Autonomous Vehicles*. Strategy&. PwC.

Brunswicker, Sabine, and Henry Chesbrough. 2018. The Adoption of Open Innovation in Large Firms. *Research-Technology Management* 61 (1): 35–45.

Bryman, Alan, and Emma Bell. 2015. *Business Research Methods*. New York: Oxford University Press.

Brynjolfsson, Erik, Yu (Jeffrey) Hu, and Duncan Simester. 2014. Goodbye Pareto Principle, Hello Long Tail: The Effect of Search Costs on the Concentration of Product Sales. *Management Science* 57 (8): 1373–86.

Castelli, Cristina, Massimo Florio, and Anna Giunta. 2011. How to Cope with the Global Value Chain: Lessons from Italian Automotive Suppliers. *International Journal of Automotive Technology and Management* 11: 236.

Chesbrough, Henry William. 2006. *Open Innovation: The New Imperative for Creating and Profiting from Technology*. Boston: Harvard Business School Press.

Dawson, Chester. 2016. Big Tech Reshaping Auto Supply Chain With Latest Deals. *The Wall Street Journal*, March 14.

Dijk, Marc, and Masaru Yarime. 2010. The Emergence of Hybrid-Electric Cars: Innovation Path Creation Through Co-Evolution of Supply and Demand. *Technological Forecasting and Social Change* 77: 1371–1390.

Dremel, Christian, Jochen Wulf, Matthias M. Herterich, Jean-Claude Waizmann, and Walter Brenner. 2017. How AUDI AG Established Big Data Analytics in Its Digital Transformation. *MIS Quarterly Executive* 16: 81–100.

Eisenhardt, Kathleen. M. 1989. Building Theories from Case Research. *The Academy of Management Review* 14: 532–550.

Ferràs-Hernández, Xavier, Elisenda Tarrats-Pons, and Núria Arimany-Serrat. 2017. Disruption in the Automotive Industry: A Cambrian Moment. *Business Horizons* 60: 855–863.

Gereffi, Gary, John Humphrey, and Timothy Sturgeon. 2005. The Governance of Global Value Chains. *Review of International Political Economy* 12: 78–104.

Habeck, Andreas, John Newman, Michele Bertoncello, Matthias Kässer, Florian Weig, Martin Hehensteiger, Julian Hölz, Ralf Plattfaut, Chad Wegner, Michal Guminski, and Zexiong Yan. 2014. *Connected Car, Automotive Value Chain Unbound*, 1–50. McKinsey & Company.

Hagiu, Andrei, and Julian Wright. 2015. Multi-Sided Platforms. *International Journal of Industrial Organization* 43: 162–174.

Hanelt, Andre, Everlin Piccinini, Robert W. Gregory, Björn Hildebrandt, and M. Lutz. 2015. Digital Transformation of Primarily Physical Industries – Exploring the Impact of Digital Trends on Business Models of Automobile Manufacturers. *12th International Conference on Wirtschaftsinformatik* 10: 1313–1327.

Hook, Leslie. 2018. Uber Pares Quarterly Losses and Lifts Revenues. *Financial Times*, February 14.
Kellerman, Aharon. 2018. *Automated and Autonomous Spatial Mobilities*. Cheltenham/Northampton: Edward Elgar Publishing.
Kuang, Xu, Fuquan Zhao, Han Hao, and Zongwei Liu. 2018. Intelligent Connected Vehicles: The Industrial Practices and Impacts on Automotive Value-Chains in China. *Asia Pacific Business Review* 24: 1–21.
Mckinsey & Company. 2016. Automotive Revolution – Perspective Towards 2030. *Advanced Industries*, January.
Narsalay, Raghav, Sabine Brunswicker, and Mehdi Bagherzadeh. 2016. The Smart Way to Open Your Innovation Process. Accenture Outlook.
Patton, Michael Quinn. 2014. *Qualitative Research & Evaluation Methods: Integrating Theory and Practice*. Thousand Oaks: SAGE Publications.
Pohl, Hans. 2017. *The Automotive Industry in Sweden*. Vinnova.
Porter, Michael E., and James E. Heppelmann. 2014. How Smart, Connected Products Are Transforming Competition. *Harvard Business Review*.
Rayport, Jeffrey F., and John J. Sviokla. 1995. Exploiting the Virtual Value Chain. *Harvard Business Review* 73: 75–85.
Shapiro, Carl, and Hal R. Varian. 1999. The Information Economy. In *Information Rules: A Strategic Guide to the Network Economy*, vol. 21, 1–18. Boston: Harvard Business School Press.
Shelly, Patrick. 2015. Addressing Challenges in Automotive Connectivity: Mobile Devices, Technologies, and the Connected Car. *SAE International Journal of Passenger Cars – Electronic and Electrical Systems* 8: 161–169.
Svahn, Fredrik, Lars Mathiassen, and Rikard Lindgren. 2017. Embracing Digital Innovation in Incumbent Firms: How Volvo Cars Managed Competing Concerns. *MIS Quarterly* 41: 239–254.
Teece, David J. 2010. Business Models, Business Strategy and Innovation. *Long Range Planning* 43 (2–3): 172–194.
Teece, David J., and Greg Linden. 2017. Business Models, Value Capture, and the Digital Enterprise. *Journal of Organization Design* 6 (1): 8.
The Economist. 2018. *Autonomous Vehicles*, Special Report. March 3.
Williamson, Oliver E. 1971. The Vertical Integration of Production: Market Failure Considerations. *American Economic Review* 61 (2): 112–123.
Wirtz, Bernd W., Adriano Pistoia, Sebastian Ullrich, and Vincent Göttel. 2015. Business Models: Origin, Development and Future Research Perspectives. *Long Range Planning* 49 (1): 36–54.

Xu, Xiangxuan. 2012. Internet of Things in Service Innovation. *The Amfiteatru Economic Journal* 14 (6): 698–720.

———. 2017. *The Internet of Things: Projects – Places – Policies*. Doctoral Thesis. Gothenburg: Gothenburg University.

Yakob, Ramsin, H. Richard Nakamura, and Patrik Ström. 2018. Chinese Foreign Acquisitions Aimed for Strategic Asset-Creation and Innovation Upgrading: The Case of Geely and Volvo Cars. *Technovation* 70: 59–72.

Zaleski, Jeff, Gonzalo Nespolo, and Christopher Sutton. 2017. *Global Automotive M&A Deals Insights Year-End 2016*, 1–7. PwC.

4

Digitization of Value Chains and Ecosystems

Srdjan Krčo, Rob van Kranenburg, Miloš Lončar, Xenia Ziouvelou, and Frank McGroarty

1 In the (Very) Near Future, Internet of Things Will Be Everywhere

Internet of Things (IoT) technology is reinforcing two emerging trends in the business world:

1. The necessity to operate within ecosystems,
2. The necessity to transform into a software company, regardless of the industry vertical in which an organization originates.

S. Krčo (✉)
DunavNET, Novi Sad, Serbia

DunavNET, Dublin, Ireland
e-mail: srdjan.krco@dunavnet.eu

R. van Kranenburg
Resonance Design BV, Tilburg, The Netherlands

M. Lončar
Microsoft Austria, Wien, Austria

A. Aagaard (ed.), *Digital Business Models*,
https://doi.org/10.1007/978-3-319-96902-2_4

Not only will it impact and drive changes in society and life; it will become an integral part of them, even in more conservative industries that still believe the wave of changes will not affect them. What these incumbent industries are forgetting is that no matter how their industry might be protected from technology disruptions, their customers are not. Buyers and users will drive the change because they will expect the same experience they get in other areas of life that run on IoT systems. The IoT has the potential to significantly change business as we know it, while its added value goes beyond operational cost savings from smart devices that report failures before they occur. Many see the biggest value of the IoT technology in a very singular form, where it helps one company with insights gained through the collected and analyzed disparate data, in real time and across time, to drive innovation or at least product improvement. However, when you look at the big picture, IoT is driving much greater value. Deloitte's "The Internet of Things Ecosystem" white paper finds that: "These developments will play out within and across enterprises, offering opportunities for sustained value creation and even disruption for those who can imagine possibilities beyond the incremental."[1] IoT can completely reshape the business landscape with its natural drive to create digital business ecosystems, where:

- everyone is a partner and a competitor at the same time;
- companies exist *because of* codependency;
- value is cocreated;
- every organization offers software solutions based on an open source technology approach.

X. Ziouvelou • F. McGroarty
University of Southampton, Southampton, UK

---

[1] https://www2.deloitte.com/us/en/pages/technology-media-and-telecommunications/articles/internet-of-things-iot-enterprise-value-report.html.

2 Emerging Value Models and Business Models

Until recently, rules of engagement in the business world relied on firm boundaries and closed systems. You had a company and a product or a service, and you were competing with others in a marketplace. The company owned its data, which was highly protected, and collaboration was ongoing only inside the organization. Everyone from the outside was seen as a potential threat.

However, today those boundaries are collapsing. As Kevin Kelly (2016) argues in his book *The Inevitable*,[2] the organization of work has evolved: from a single company to a broader marketplace provided by that company, which further grew into a platform—a foundation started by one organization that lets other companies build their products or services upon it. As they all rest upon the same platform, those products are often highly interdependent, developing from each other or upgrading one another. Over time, the platform creates an ecosystem, which is a type of biological codependence, a mixture of competition and cooperation. Take a natural ecosystem, such as a forest, and you will see the same phenomenon: everything is interconnected in a food chain and the success of one species depends on others. Although analogies of these biological ecosystems with the business (Moore 1993) and the economic (Rothschild 1990) fields have been made for quite a few years, we see that nowadays they are more relevant than ever before. Business ecosystems, like biological ecosystems, are characterized by high complexity, interdependence, cooperation, competition and coevolution (Moore 1996; Lehto et al. 2013; Jansson et al. 2014), and "conscious choice" differentiates the two (Moore 1996) among others.[3] All technology and business giants of today, Apple, Microsoft, Google, Facebook, are multi-sided platforms that:

[2] https://www.amazon.com/Inevitable-Understanding-Technological-Forces-Future/dp/0143110373.

[3] See Ziouvelou and McGroarty (2017) for a detailed overview of ecosystems.

- employ third-party vendors to increase the value of their platforms;
- encourage others to play with application platform interfaces (APIs), which is a set of subroutine definitions, protocols and tools for building application software;
- enable robust ecosystems of derivative yet interdependent products and services.

Digital transformation in the era of hyperconnectivity acts thus as a key driver for change both in the business and the social environments. In the business context, this change has started to become evident, as new opportunities for value creation and value capture have emerged. Value flows have been extended to include new value creating actors, technologies, and novel cocreation and coinnovation processes across interconnected and constantly evolving value-driven ecosystems empowered by the cutting edge technology. The report by MacArthur and Waughray (2016) titled: *Intelligent Assets: Unlocking the circular economy potential*, finds that "pairing circular economy principles with the information generated by intelligent devices creates a fertile ground for innovation that could enable this decoupling, and lead to broad social benefits." (p.30). With up to 50 billion connected devices by 2020, pervasive digital transformation will reshape the economy. Will this "fourth industrial revolution" lead to an "acceleration of the extractive, 'linear' economy of today, or will it enable the transition towards a society in which value creation is increasingly decoupled from finite resource consumption?"

Products will communicate with users, collectors and remanufacturers to ensure they are returned and reused after their first lifecycle. Additionally, condition monitoring of sensitive goods during transport, storage and use will expand product lifetime, says Frank Appel, CEO of Deutsche Post DHL.[4] Intelligent Assets establishes an interplay between the 'value drivers' of a circular model, and the potential benefits offered by a network of connected devices and information. "The internet of things, with its smart sensors and connected technologies, can play a key

[4] Circular economy meets the IoT, February 11, 2016 in Innovation http://brand-e.biz/economy-goes-circular-as-products-become-smart-and-connected-to-internet-of-things_37126.html.

role in providing valuable data about things like energy use, under-utilized assets, and material flows to help make businesses more efficient. Their role in building a future with a more circular economy is critical and we are excited about the role of technology will play in realizing this vision."

The European Commission published *EU Circular Economy Package* in December 2015,[5] with an action plan addressing the "full circle" from production and consumption to waste management and the market for secondary raw materials, to create a circular flow of materials necessary for a regenerative economic system. There are also sector-specific measures on plastics, food waste, critical raw materials, construction and bio-based products. The proposed actions will contribute to "closing the loop" of product lifecycles through greater recycling and reuse and will bring benefits for both the environment and the economy.[6]

2.1 From Linear to Circular, Participatory Value Models

Digital transformation signifies a broad structural shift in the way value is created, captured and distributed in today's networked society, from stand-alone companies to open, integrated ecosystems. The changing firm boundaries, the emerging value cocreation practices and technological advancements have enabled companies to "unlock" distributed value in an increasingly more complex environment. As such the linear, centralized value creation process (company-centric value creation and capture processes, where the buyer captures value by consuming the product/service), have evolved into distributed, decentralized value mechanisms, embedded within the whole ecosystem, making value creation and capture a collaborative effort (Le and Tafardar 2009; Lehto et al. 2013; Iivari

[5] Communication:

http://eur-lex.europa.eu/resource.html?uri=cellar:8a8ef5e8-99a0-11e5-b3b7-01aa75ed71a1.0012.02/DOC_1&format=PDF.

List of actions:

http://eur-lex.europa.eu/resource.html?uri=cellar:8a8ef5e8-99a0-11e5-b3b7-01aa75ed71a1.0012.02/DOC_2&format=PDF.

[6] http://ec.europa.eu/environment/circular-economy/index_en.htm.

et al. 2016; Letaifa 2014). Thus, value is not only cocreated (Allee 2003; Prahalad and Ramaswamy 2004) and cocaptured, but also codistributed among network participants and collaborating parties, as an open "value sharing" process, acting as an ongoing circular and participatory value model (Ziouvelou et al. 2016). To seize the full potential of this emerging value model, it is critical that each value domain operates efficiently, since a weakness in any domain will undermine the performance of the whole value-driven ecosystem.

The challenge is to look beyond solutions for any single sector (manufacturers, retailers or recyclers) and to think about the entire value chain. For instance, in the study *Growth Within: A Circular Economy Vision for a Competitive Europe*,[7] one key recommendation for Europe is to develop a "material backbone"—a system to optimize the circulation of materials,[8] and minimize the need for virgin resources—to strengthen its competitiveness.

2.2 From Closed, Static, Firm-Centric to Open, Dynamic, Crowd-Driven Ecosystem-Centric Business Models

This change in value logic aligns with the change in the logic of business models. More specifically, the emergence of technology advanced value-driven ecosystems has redefined corporate and industrial boundaries and operations, while fundamentally changing the essence of business mod-

[7] http://www.ellenmacarthurfoundation.org/news/circular-economy-would-increase-european-competitiveness-and-deliver-better-societal-outcomes-new-study-reveals.

[8] See also the Flanders Materials Program:

- A long term vision: Plan C is the circular economy hub in Flanders, created by OVAM to encourage a change in mind-set from waste to resources and to accelerate the move towards a circular economy.
- Policy-relevant scientific research: SuMMa (Policy Research Centre for Sustainable Materials Management) brings together a broad spectrum of researchers and investigates which economic, policy and social conditions need to be fulfilled in order to realize the transition towards a circular economy.
- Actions and projects in the field: Agenda 2020 is a list of 45 concrete projects with active partners and a clear time schedule.

http://www.ellenmacarthurfoundation.org/case-studies/belgium-flanders-materials-programme.

els. The notion of business models has advanced from a corporate blueprint-linking strategy and business processes to a constantly evolving network architecture, which describes embedded interconnected value processes that represent a new dimension of innovation, which is highly critical in today's hyperconnected network economy (Ziouvelou and McGroarty 2018). Business models are no longer firm-centric, static and closed structures of the industrial era (Magretta 2002; Osterwalder et al. 2005; Casadesus-Masanell and Ricart 2010), but rather open and dynamic ecosystems-centric (Westerlund et al. 2014; Rong et al. 2015; Schladofsky et al. 2016), as well as crowd-driven ecosystemic structures (Ziouvelou and McGroarty 2017, 2018) of a hypernetworked economy. The latter type represents the third phase of ecosystems (see Fig. 4.1, upper right quadrants: crowd-driven ecosystems and crowd-driven IoT ecosystems), adopting an evolutionary perspective that classifies them based on their value model and their innovation system (Ziouvelou and McGroarty 2018).[9]

To seize the full potential of this structural shift, companies need to align with the new value-driven business logic while at the same time effectively managing complexity. Product, process and organizational innovation alone are no longer sufficient for companies to stay competitive (Zott et al. 2011; Massa and Tucci 2014). Business models represent a key innovation component that complement existing ones (Zott et al. 2011) facilitating success in contemporary complex business ecosystems. The new inclusive and distributed value mechanisms assimilate interdependencies and side effects that need to be considered in order not to ripple through the entire ecosystemic structure. As a consequence, business models need to be open, dynamic, ecosystem-centric constructs that take into account the needs and specifications of today's environment while making business model reinvention a continual and inclusive process (Derfus et al. 2008).

[9] Following Ziouvelou and McGroarty (2018), this taxonomy is based on two differentiating aspects of ecosystems, namely the (a) *value model*: denoting the orientation of the ecosystem in relation to value creation, capture and distribution practices, and the (b) *innovation system*: specifying the innovation orientation of the ecosystem in relation to the innovation process and architecture (knowledge production and knowledge application (innovation); Carayannis and Campbell 2010).

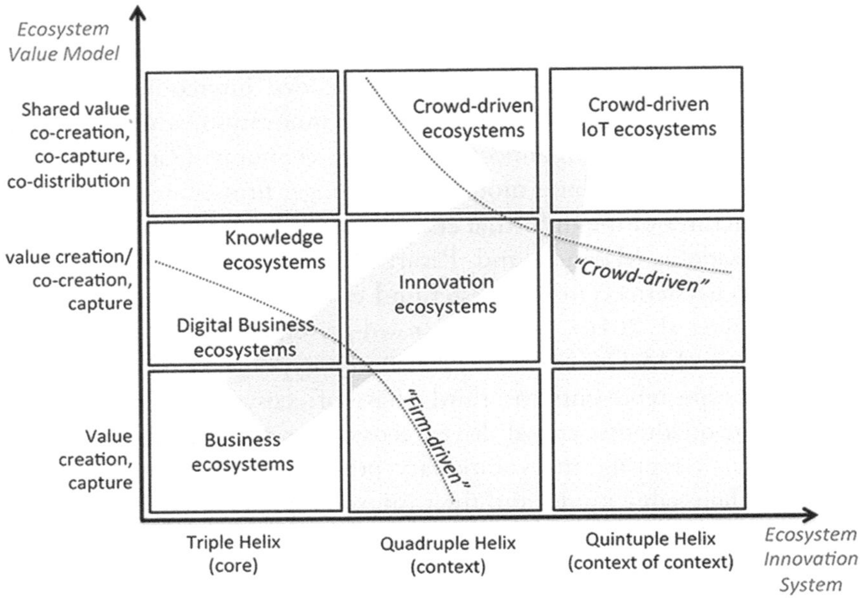

Fig. 4.1 Ecosystems taxonomy. (Source: Ziouvelou and McGroarty (2018))

2.3 New Business Models and New Regulatory Models Need to be Co-Created with Different Actors

Lee Vinsel and Andrew Russel claim in *Hail the Maintainers* that innovation is the dominant ideology of our era, embraced in America by Silicon Valley, Wall Street and the Washington DC political elite. This pursuit of innovation has inspired technologists and capitalists; it has also provoked critics. What happens after innovation, they argue, is more important: "Maintenance and repair, the building of infrastructures, the mundane labor that goes into sustaining functioning and efficient infrastructures, simply has more impact on people's daily lives than the vast majority of technological innovations." They emphasize a shift from means to ends, including the many kinds of social beneficence and improvement that technology can offer.

The roles of individuals, companies, city, government and the European Union (EU) are becoming more fluid. It becomes clear that private over the top players cannot regulate the negative effects of their success for the local living ecosystem. It is also clear that individuals will not go back on their connected powers. Agency must be shared. Cities and the EU need more control over the data from their citizens, machines, and processes, to facilitate sharing services. Individuals need control over the data from their wearables, homes, cars and civic identities. Companies need to have assurances that their investments are safe while providing scalability, guaranteed up time, and sustainability.

New business models and new regulatory models therefore need to be co-created with the different actors: the EU, non-governmental organizations (NGOs), City, small and medium-sized enterprises (SMEs), individuals and large service providers. An important philosophical building block in a larger policy framework and potential inspiration for scenarios is to move the decision-making capabilities into a more relevant balance between actions taken from IoT scenarios and current party politics.[10] In accelerationist thinking, "quantification is not an evil to be eliminated, but a tool to be used in the most effective manner possible. Economic modelling is—simply put—a necessity for making intelligible a complex world. The tools to be found in social network analysis, agent-based modelling, big data analytics, and non-equilibrium economic models, are necessary cognitive mediators for understanding complex systems like the modern economy."

Creating a productive and vital scope with a variety of stakeholders in an open and dynamic ecosystem requires taking a discussion beyond the immediate deliverables and the concrete outcomes, enablers, applications and services in order to accommodate new developments and trends. These developments are tuned to new situations. These situations do not

[10] #ACCELERATE MANIFESTO FOR AN ACCELERATIONIST POLITICS: https://syntheticedifice.files.wordpress.com/2013/06/accelerate.pdf. "Any transformation of society must involve economic and social experimentation. The Chilean Project Cybersyn is emblematic of this experimental attitude – fusing advanced cybernetic technologies, with sophisticated economic modelling, and a democratic platform instantiated in the technological infrastructure itself."

look back, but look ahead to new and immediate recognition. It is important for a vital ecosystem that these new developments can be accommodated in the current set-up.

3 Open, Dynamic, Ecosystem-Centric Constructs

One could say that no ecosystem means no success in IoT. A well-developed ecosystem with a diverse set of partners bringing in a set of complementary skills, services and geographical coverage is essential for the successful delivery of IoT solutions.

Why is this so?

IoT solutions are applicable to many business domains, and this fact alone means that expertise is required in a diverse set of domains, not only to understand business requirements, but also to be able to process captured data and generate reports in the most meaningful manner for the business needs. This is not easy for a single company, not even a large one. Further to this, the development, provision and maintenance of IoT solutions is complex and requires knowledge of several technical areas. First, edge devices (sensors, actuators, gateways) must be selected based on the use case requirements and environment conditions (availability of network connectivity, planned maintenance, etc.). The number of communication networks which can be used is growing every day (WiFi, GPRS, 3G, Bluetooth, LoRa, NB-IoT, LTE-CAT1, Weightless, etc.), thus requiring a very good knowledge of the intrinsic details of each communication interface/protocol and how they impact the performance of the planned IoT solution. Security is one of the major concerns across all industries, requiring a detailed knowledge of the potential threats and how to minimize associated risks. Similarly, growing concerns over data privacy and upcoming introduction of General Data Protection Regulation (GDPR: https://www.eugdpr.org/) require extensive experience of this domain, including options for integrating adequate tools in commercial IoT solutions. Finally, the deployment of IoT solutions requires physical presence at the client site, thus presenting demands for geographical coverage. While it might look to be everyday business for an information technology system integrator, in many cases it is not. Often, installation of sensors requires substantial domain knowledge and has to be done carefully to ensure that captured information/measurements are of adequate quality for the solution.

Let us look at this using the example of a smart home. If an organization wants to sell smart homes, it needs to partner up with several different companies because machines and objects in the house come from various manufacturers. All of them need to talk to each other: the lights need to talk to the fridge, which needs to talk to the furniture, and so on, and they all "report" to the central control system. Moreover, when certain parts of that system require upgrades or add-ins, a new manufacturer that is already in the business of producing such products and has the right skills may join this ecosystem. With the velocity of changes in today's world, nobody has the time to develop an innovative product or service from the ground up and spend six months or a full year on development. The solution is to partner up with someone who already does it successfully and then leverage each other's competencies into a novelty in the market. That is the biggest power of a digital ecosystem: **creating added value through partnerships**.

The benefits of a well-developed IoT ecosystem are numerous. First and foremost, it allows easy access to domain specialists' know-how and expertise at reasonable costs, an essential factor in the success of IoT projects. Then it accelerates the time to market thanks to the reuse of multiple components and a more distributed workload. The result of this is improved return on investment for each stakeholder and enhanced customer experience as visible results are achievable in a very short timeframe. Last but not least, an IoT solution built inside a well-developed ecosystem provides assurance to customers that their investment will have continued support and innovation across the entire value chain. This is particularly important bearing in mind that many, if not all, IoT solutions are being deployed with long-term exploitation plans.

3.1 Open Platforms

Platforms have upgraded and changed over time. Kelly explains it well in "The Inevitable," stating that one of the first platforms was Microsoft's OS operating system, and that anyone with the ambition could build and sell a program that ran on an OS that Microsoft owned. Apple's iTunes was an example of the second generation of platforms, which also became a marketplace for mobile apps. Apple owns the platform, sets rules and protocols, tracks financial exchanges and so on. The marketplace itself (iTunes) is, therefore, one of Apple's products. The tech giant continued to improve the iPhone device, while different contributors to its platform continued to innovate the software that runs on those devices. The third generation of platforms is also a combination of a market and a company, but has more complex market attributes. Unlike the traditional two-sided market, this platform ecosystem became a multi-sided market. Initially, Facebook, for example, created a set of rules and protocols that formed a marketplace where independent sellers produced their profiles, which were matched up in a marketplace with their friends. But then it went further: the attention of the users was sold to advertisers, game companies sold to users, third-party apps sold to other third-party apps and so on. This ecosystem with multiple matches is based on interdependent products, and it will expand as long as Facebook is managing the rules and grows as a company.[11] In the more business to business segment of successful platforms are popular cloud platforms from leading providers, including Microsoft Azure, Amazon Web Services and Google Cloud. While platforms collect partners that are focused around one service or product (such as Apple's iOS), ecosystems are much broader than that.

Just like the entire suite of technologies currently in existence, IoT is a true ecosystem where many different, interconnected and codependent parts (devices, IoT software, data platform, analytic tool, virtual desktop, etc.) are orchestrated to generate useful information; in a

[11] https://www.amazon.com/Inevitable-Understanding-Technological-Forces-Future/dp/0143110373.

similar way, IoT replicates that same environment for businesses that use it. James F. Moore provided one of the most accurate definitions of the business ecosystem back in 1993 in his article titled "Predators and Prey: A New Ecology of Competition," for which he won the McKinsey Award for the article of the year:[12] "In a business ecosystem, companies co-evolve capabilities around a new innovation: they work cooperatively and competitively to support new products, satisfy customer needs, and eventually incorporate the next round of innovations." Moore adds: "The economic community produces goods and services of value to customers, who are themselves members of the ecosystem. The member organisms also include suppliers, lead producers, competitors, and other stakeholders. Over time, they co-evolve their capabilities and roles, and tend to align themselves with the directions set by one or more central companies. Those companies holding leadership roles may change over time but the function of ecosystem leader is valued by the community because it enables members to move toward shared visions to align their investments, and to find mutually supportive roles."

Writing about the importance of an open digital ecosystem in Industrial IoT for the "IoT for All" web portal, Michael Reimer elaborates on digital ecosystems as an interdependent group of actors—such as: enterprises, competitors, customers, regulators, individuals, IoT devices, and other stakeholders—that share standardized digital platforms to achieve mutual benefit.[13] For a digital ecosystem to succeed, it needs a platform with an open technology approach. This is the key because platforms and ecosystems cannot thrive on closed systems and protected data; instead of data ownership, they nurture data access.

Enrique Andaluz, Microsoft Director of Strategic Business Development said "It's important to note that it is not just about technology, but it's about how you do business across your operations, employees, partners, and customers. It's about becoming ready to take a bolder

[12] http://blogs.harvard.edu/jim/files/2010/04/Predators-and-Prey.pdf.

[13] https://www.iotforall.com/open-digital-ecosystem-iiot/.

approach at reengineering old operational processes. It's about seizing the opportunity to redefine the customer journey and change the products and services that you offer."[14]

3.2 Ecosystem Roles

Overall, ecosystem stakeholders can take one of three roles:

- ***Horizontal***: providing scalable, interoperable and cost-effective technologies, reusable and future-proof functionality, not specific to any particular business domain or user scenario. Examples are cloud infrastructure, security solutions, device management and networking.
- ***Vertical:*** addressing market-specific challenges and use cases, providing functionalities specific to a specific business domain and enabling full integration of IoT products into existing systems and lines of business. These stakeholders have to understand business operational and technical environments and their unique requirements, to have relationships with the business lines, operational technology or building technology teams.
- ***Geographic:*** responsible for local solution deployment, compliance with user's work processes and national legislation, first-line customer support.

Taking another, more detailed, perspective, ecosystem roles can be divided into two broad categories: technical and business with examples of different positions inside both categories given in Table 4.1.

The important aspect of working in an ecosystem and delivering a solution in collaboration with multiple partners is teamwork. In other words, it is important to have well-defined roles and a business value flow among the partners, not only to set expectations, but also to enable efficient execution in a cooperative environment. A typical business value flow when provisioning a IoT solution is presented in Fig. 4.2.

[14] https://enterprise.microsoft.com/en-us/articles/industries/discrete-manufacturing/building-the-industrial-iot-ecosystem-that-is-right-for-your-business/.

Table 4.1 Ecosystem roles

	Technology				Enabling services	
	Adaptive driver assistance systems	Technologies Infotainment	Human–machine interface	Communications, computing, and cloud	Connected vehicle services	Connected device services
OEMs (major automakers) Acquisition	**Acquisition** Audi/Daimler/BMW: Here (2015) GM: Cruise Automation (2016) **Investment** Volvo: Peloton (2015) **Partnership** Audi & Nvidia (since 2005) Bosch & TomTom (2015) GM & Mobileye (2015) VW & Mobileye (2015) BMW & Intel & Mobileye (2016) Hyundai & Cisco (2016)	**Investment** Ford: Livio (2013) **Partnership** Audi & Nvidia (since 2005)		**Partnership** Daimler & Qualcomm (2015) Hyundai & Cisco (2016) Toyota & KDDI (2016)	**Partnership** Ford & State Farm (2012) BMW & Pivotal (2015) Ford & Microsoft Azure (2015) Volvo & Microsoft (2015) Nissan & Microsoft Azure (2016)	**Acquisition** Daimler: Mytaxi (2014) GM: Sidecar (2016) **Investment** BMW: RideCell (2014) BMW: Zendrive (2014) GM: Telogis (2014) BAIC: Didi Chuxing (2015) Ford: Pivotal (2016) GM: Lyft (2016) Toyota: Uber (2016) VW: Gett (2016) **Partnership** BMW & Baidu (2015) BMW & Microsoft Azure (2016) Seat & Samsung & SAP (2016) Toyota & Microsoft Azure (2016)

(*continued*)

Table 4.1 (continued)

	Technology				Enabling services	
	Adaptive driver assistance systems	Technologies Infotainment	Human–machine interface	Communications, computing, and cloud	Connected vehicle services	Connected device services
Traditional suppliers	**Acquisition** Continental: Elektrobit (2015) Delphi: Ottomatika (2015) ZF: TRW (2015) Continental: ASC (2016) **Investment** Delphi: Quanergy (2015) Bosch: AdasWorks (2016) **Partnership** Valeo & Mobileye (2015)	**Acquisition** Harman: Aha (2010) Harman: S1nn (2014) Continental: Elektrobit (2015) Harman: Symphony Teleca (2015) **Partnership** Harman & Luxoft (2011) Harman & Microsoft (2016)	**Acquisition** Continental: Elektrobit (2015) **Partnership** Valeo & Safran (2013)	**Acquisition** Bosch: ProSyst (2015) Valeo: Pelker (2015	**Acquisition** Harman: Redbend SW (2015) Harman: TowerSec (2016) **Partnership** Valeo & Capgemini (2015)	**Acquisition** Harman: Aditi (2015)
New entrants from outside automotive	**Acquisition** Panasonic: Ficosa (2014) Google: FCA (2016) Nvidia: AdasWorks (2016) **New entrants:** Apple, Baidu, Google	**New entrants** AdasWorks, Baselabs, Vector, Velodyne, Wind River	**Investment** Intel: Omek (2013) **New entrants** Atmel, Fujitsu, Kyocera, LG, Toshiba	**Acquisition** Cisco/NXP: Cohda Wireless (2013) **New entrants** Cohda Wireless, Kymeta, Veniam	**Investment** Verizon: Hughes (2012) **Partnership** Airbiquity & Arynga (2016) **New entrants** Airbiquity, Allstate, Fleetmatics, Pivotal, Progressive, SiriusXM, Trimble, Verisk	**Partnership** Daimler Moovel & IBM (2014) Airbiquity & Arynga (2016) **New entrants** Airbiquity, Apple, Contigo, Dash, Google, iTrack, Lyft, MyCarTracks, Uber

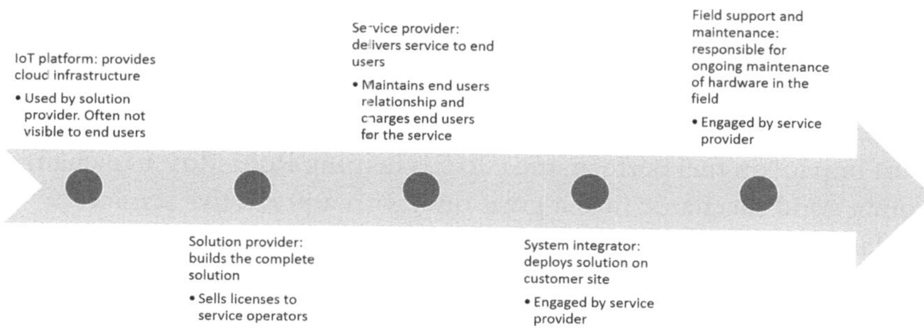

Fig. 4.2 Typical business flow in an IoT ecosystem

4 Supply Chain Use Cases

All leading disruptive companies have one thing in common: they adopt new business models and technologies much faster than others. Their secret sauce is their ability to share information across the value chain partners and cocreate that value in partnerships. This trend is freeing up trapped business value, enhancing innovation and driving the evolution of product offerings into service offerings.

With more than 13,000 engines for commercial aircraft in service around the world, for the past 20 years Rolls-Royce has offered customers comprehensive engine maintenance services.[15] However, data coming from many different types of aircraft equipment was increasing too rapidly, which hindered the company's ability to analyze and gain quality insights. They deployed a new IoT solution and the Microsoft Azure platform to transform their customer experience, but something else happened as well. By examining these growing data analysis challenges, Rolls-Royce came up with a new plan to address the changing market with a more compelling set of services by providing meaningful insights across more of the airlines' operations. One of them relates to

[15] https://customers.microsoft.com/en-us/story/rollsroycestory.

fuel efficiency. By analyzing new data against existing forecasts, reference tables and historical trends, Rolls-Royce is now able to help airlines understand exactly which factors—including flight plans, equipment maintenance, weather and discretionary fuel—have the most impact on fuel performance. IoT is helping Rolls-Royce to change from a good mechanic into a great one, with a predictive service.

Many manufacturers have already taken the first steps towards the digital transformation of their facilities by creating "smart factories," where the quick wins are seen mostly through the increase in productivity. By developing complex ecosystems of self-regulating machines and sites, the output is customized and resources are optimally allocated, while a seamless interface between the physical and virtual segments of construction, assembly, and production is created. In this ecosystem we usually have manufacturers as factory owners, producers of different machines as their suppliers, logistic companies connected to their production process, their customers that want to get insights in production process real time, raw materials suppliers, IoT platform providers, solution providers (Independent Software Vendors) and system integrators. The main challenge is to connect machines produced more than 20 years ago that were never meant to be connected, as well as to stay open for new players that will become part of the value chain and ecosystem. Because of all that has been mentioned above, it is mandatory to have structured data governance and openness to all members of the ecosystem. All big cloud providers (Microsoft, AWS, Google) as well as solution providers for the manufacturing industry (Siemens, ABB, General Electric) realized that IoT is ecosystem play, and they alone are not capable of satisfying the needs of the new digital world. One good example of how companies are changing their strategy is given by Microsoft, which now provides many pre-configured solutions (e.g. Connected Factory, see Fig. 4.3) as open source solutions as well as community efforts, such as the open source OPC foundation (https://opcfoundation.org/), aiming to overcome the challenge of multiple protocols used in manufacturing.

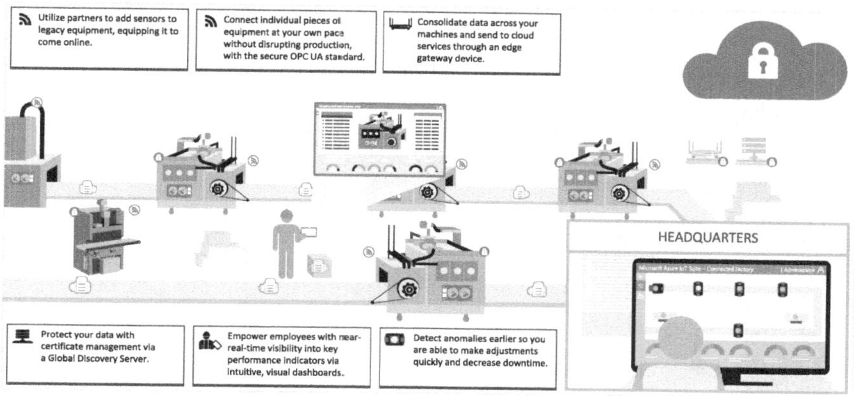

Fig. 4.3 Connected factory, a Microsoft Azure IoT pre-configured solution

4.1 From Manufacturing to Recycling

When talking about IoT and connecting devices, we usually have in mind devices such as those mentioned above: jet engines, factory machines and so on. What is still out of reach owing to technological limitations and the cost of deployment are connected mass-market products: a carton of milk, a package of steak, a basket of apples, a book, a CD. Today, these products are identified by printed tags (barcodes, QR codes). These codes relate to the product they tag, not to the unique unit/object that holds the tag. Once attached to an object, tags are usually static and the information they provide does not change, regardless of the state or events happening in the immediate environment of that product.

Leveraging the features of functional codes (QR codes printed using functional inks) to change according to the context changes of each tagged product, together with the wide availability of smartphones that can capture/record/transmit these codes (Fig. 4.4), we can create context sensors for mass-market products and convert mass-market products into connected mass-market products with a unique identity that can report on their environment. This opens up possibilities for a whole new range of services to be created for and consumed by the user.

In order to address this opportunity, TagItSmart! project (www.tagitsmart.eu) is creating a set of tools and enabling technologies that are integrated into a platform with open interfaces, enabling users across the value chain to

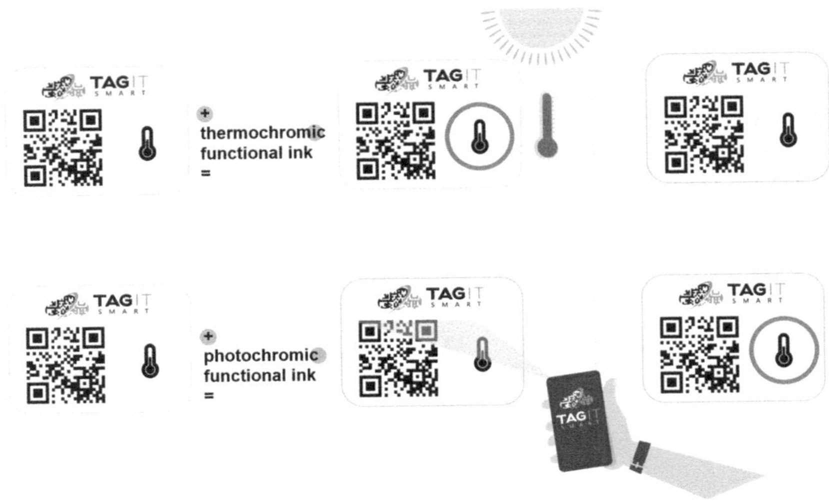

Fig. 4.4 Temperature and light sensitive smart tags

fully exploit the power of condition-dependent smart tags to connect mass-market products with the digital world across multiple application sectors.

Overall, TagItSmart! targets the creation of digital fast-moving consumer goods (FMCG) enhanced with supporting cloud functionality for provision of added value services suitable for a given context. Manufacturers can control products that leave their factories throughout their lifecycle, for example where and how the products are transported and in what conditions, when they have been delivered to the retail stores and when sold to the consumers (Fig. 4.5). It also creates a new channel for manufacturers to communicate with the consumer, so that they can enable easy access to related information on product and item level, which is not only static but depends on the lifecycle and historical data of the item.

Lifecycle Management/Recycling

The lifecycle management/recycling use case (Fig. 4.6) is built around the concept of consumers buying products in the supermarket and engaging with them in different ways, focusing on the recyclability of the product. This creates an ecosystem where consumers are provided with information about

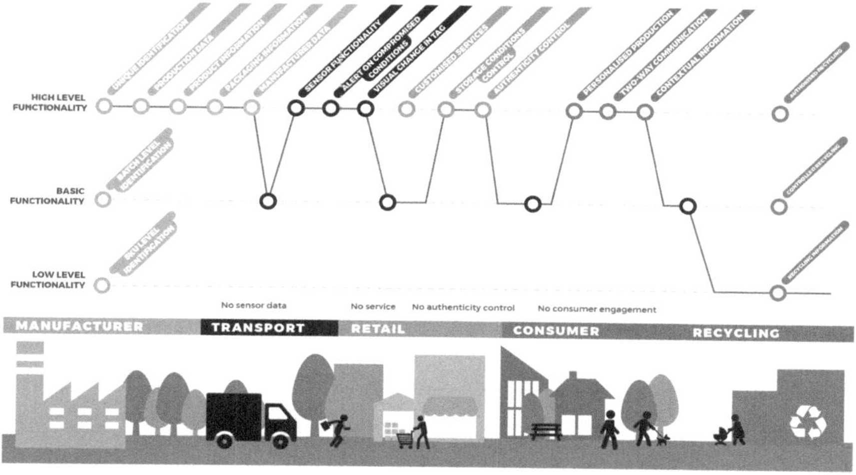

Fig. 4.5 Digital FMCG product lifetime

Fig. 4.6 Lifecycle management/recycling use case

how to recycle a product based on contextual information (location, local regulations) and product recyclability (materials), information that is linked to the SmartTags on the products. SmartTags in this use case enable the creation of consumer-oriented services that are based on information that has been generated at different stages of the lifecycle of a product, involving different stakeholders, from the brands, to the retailers as well as the ultimate focus, the consumers and the authorities that regulate the recycling policies.

Business model canvas for the lifecycle management/recycling use case is presented in Fig. 4.7

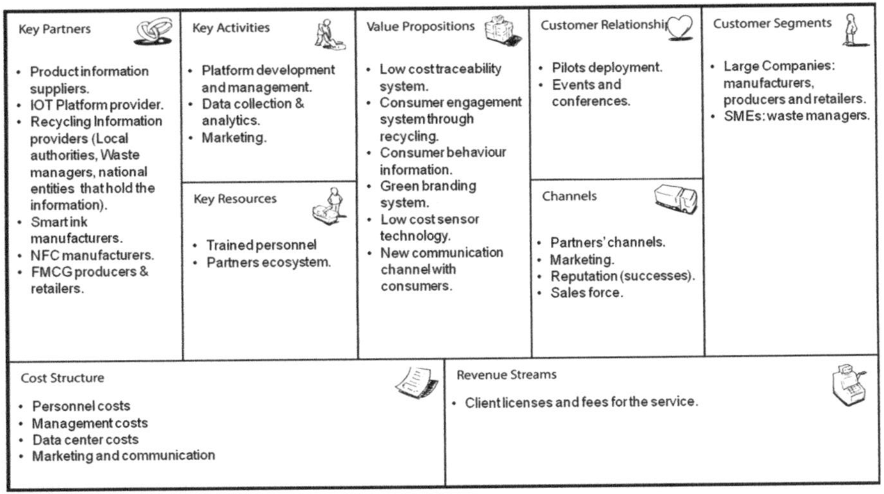

Fig. 4.7 Lifecycle management/recycling use case business model canvas

Brand Protection

The brand protection use case (Fig. 4.8) aims at providing brands and consumers with a mechanism to test the authenticity of their products and reduce counterfeiting. SmartTags and their capabilities to change based on environmental conditions (such as light and temperature) are used to first uniquely identify the item at hand and second to provide means to avoid fake or misplaced products by enabling contextual scanning. Business model canvas for the brand protection use case is given on (Fig. 4.9).

Dynamic Pricing Use Case

Manufacturing first provides general information about the products (ingredients, recycling information, best before, consumable before, etc.) as well as reference thresholds for the type of product. Then the SmartTag (the ID) is encoded and is printed and attached to the prod-

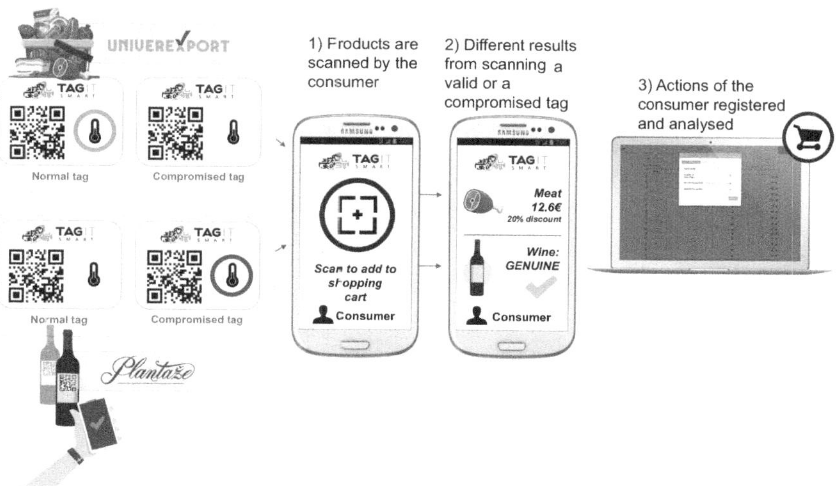

Fig. 4.8 Dynamic pricing and brand protection use cases

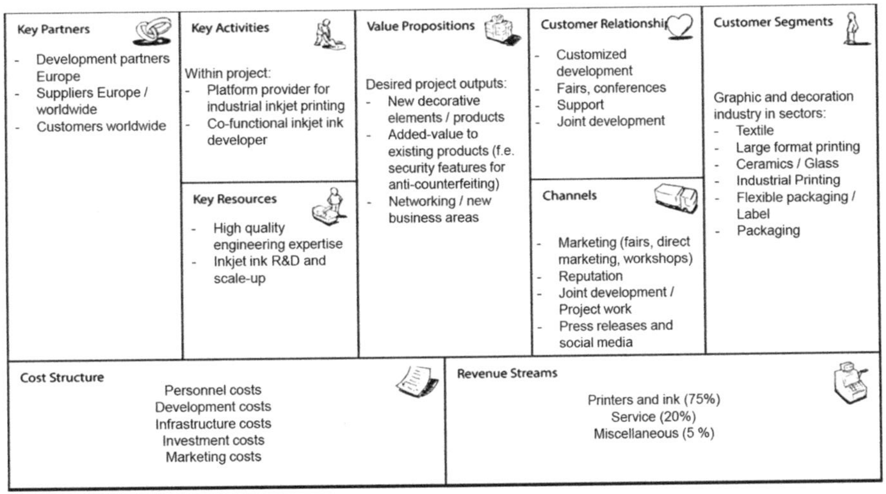

Fig. 4.9 Brand protection use case business model canvas

uct package. As a part of internal process control, the manufacturer scans the SmartTag while the product is still in the factory (e.g. meat processing plant). Then the product is ready for transport to the retailer. Afterwards, the transport provider scans SmartTag as a part of the process control. In retail, the retailer provides additional information about the products to support consumers (recipes, how to use, etc.). Availability of information is defined: general or when scanned at selected locations only (in their shops). Then the retailer scans SmartTag as a part of the supply chain control process. Scanning results (pack ID and result) are forwarded to the platform and the dynamic price calculation process is invoked. The consumer scans SmartTags using a smartphone application and obtains information about the product (best before, price, recycling, recipes and other information approved by retailers). The retrieved information depends on the location and time of scanning. Business model canvas for this use case is described in (Fig. 4.10).

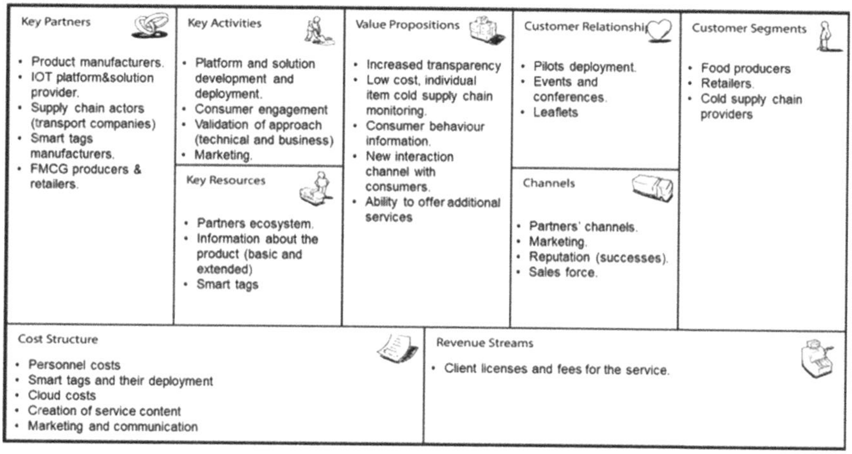

Fig. 4.10 Dynamic pricing use case business model canvas

5 Building an Ecosystem

If we analyze the above use cases, the following ecosystem constellation can be identified:

As can be seen in the canvas above, the envisioned ecosystem includes multiple stakeholders:

- Product information suppliers: organization providing information about the product lines, manufacturing description, usage instructions and so on. This type of service facilitates faster deployment of new services, in particular when a large number of product lines is to be included in the solution. Provided information is usually consumed via APIs.
- IoT platform provider: this operator provides access to data, creation of unique identities, permanent storage, data analytics algorithms, integration with external information systems and interaction with third-party services.
- Solution providers: organizations providing appropriate web and smartphone applications for consumers, enabling them to scan and validate products as well as for retailers to register products and provide required services to consumers.
- Domain specific information providers: organizations providing domain-specific information about products of interest, usually as a service. In the case of recycling, information about the correct recycling procedure of different parts of the products is provided, taking into account local/regional recycling legislation. In other cases, information can be included about how to consume or store a product.
- Smart ink manufacturers: organizations providing functional ink required to create smart tags on product packaging.
- Near-Field Communication (NFC) manufacturers: organizations providing adequate NFC labels to create smart tags on product packaging and to identify bins.
- Smart tag design and printing: organizations providing design of smart tags based on the use case requirements and their printing.
- Transport/logistics service providers: organizations providing transport and storage of products on the way from the manufacturing point to shops.

- FMCG producers and retailers: organizations manufacturing products and offering them to the consumers, leveraging services to provide added value to consumers and increase the efficiency of their processes.

As can be seen, ecosystems can become rather complex, involving organizations with different business focus, expertise and, consequently, roles in the value chain. Building such an ecosystem requires substantial effort and interaction with multiple actors. This is particularly challenging in a new domain where no established players are present and where the value flow and roles of different stakeholders have to be defined and later validated. To address these challenges, one of the key activities throughout the TagItSmart! project was the establishment and expansion of an ecosystem. Having in mind that establishing a new ecosystem from scratch is a complex task, TagItSmart! decided to leverage the existing ecosystems and communities as much as possible by practically embedding smart tags and TagItSmart! enablers into other ecosystems by providing adequate technology hooks. In essence, the project was creating an overlay ecosystem capable of efficiently using TagItSmart! outputs for the creation of sustainable business and services for a range of entities.

The main facilitator was the pilots undertaken in real business environments, with the involvement of interested parties—business stakeholders. To achieve this, TagItSmart! needed to involve: third-party businesses (the smart tags provider, ink manufacturers, technology vendors involved in cloud infrastructure and solutions, service providers as well as consumers) to confirm/comment upon findings and implementations from the business benefits point of view. One of the key challenges was "co-opetition" as the delivery of TagItSmart! solutions required the participation of multiple suppliers of complimentary industries, which in some cases provided the same or similar services.[16]

In the rest of this chapter, we describe the activities undertaken by the project first to establish an ecosystem and then to extend it.

The main tool used was open calls. These enabled the project to involve new stakeholders in selected domains (use cases) interested in using selected TagItSmart! features to create a new business solution. This

[16] http://www.sciencedirect.com/science/article/pii/S0048733311000187.

approach not only helped the project in extending the number of served domains, but also facilitated promotion of the project at both EU and global level. The open calls helped to build bridges between the research and business units, between the enablers and SMEs, and between the services created and the end users, with the overall ambition to create and expand TagItSmart!'s ecosystem. The assumption here is that because of its scope, size and speed, digital transition is creating a new space where the actual practices in research and innovation actions and the business sales and production patterns are becoming intermixed and intertwined. This space is just opening up, and the tools enabling utilization of the benefits provided by such an environment are therefore interesting for both sides.

5.1 Open Calls

The TagItSmart! project (www.tagitsmart.eu) is a H2020 project and is financed by the European Commission in the context of the IoT European Platform Initiative (IoT-EPI: www.iot-epi.eu). The project started in January 2016 and will run for 36 months. The overall goal of the initiative is to address interoperability in the IoT domain and to create sustainable ecosystems, which will take forward and further develop outcomes of all financed projects. In addition to TagItSmart!, six more research and innovation as well as two supporting projects are active. With the sustainability of the results as one of the main drivers, unlike the traditional project structure where everything was fixed at the beginning of the project and not subject to changes, in this initiative the concept of open calls is being used. The primary goal of this concept is to enable projects to expand and tune the overall project's scope based on the progress made and on general global technology developments. In practice, this means the following: addressing new use cases by adding new partners with adequate technical and business skills into a consortium, and extending the functionality of the projects by adding features identified as missing during project execution, based on the initial validation and trials. Leveraging these measures, the projects are not only able to improve project outcomes, but at the same time extend the ecosystem to various domains and generate a "buzz" that leads to further expansion of the ecosystem as interested parties get in contact and establish collaboration outside the open calls.

In total, the IoT-EPI initiative has a budget of approx. 5 million Euros for the open calls, of which TagItSmart! contributes 1.2 million Euros. Having such an ecosystem in place significantly helps execution of the open calls for each individual project. The collective power of the ecosystem in terms of both online and offline presence and reach is of immense help when it comes to reaching out to stakeholders coming from different domains and different geographic regions. Joint online presence combined with organization of joint events, meetups and presence at exhibitions facilitates the promotion and engagement of a large number of potential ecosystem members, much larger than each individual project would be able to do on its own. Further to that, being part of an ecosystem also contributes to a more convincing story when it comes to sustainability of project outcomes beyond project lifetimes.

However, ecosystem establishment does not stop at promotion and meetup presentation. Despite the financial attractiveness of the open calls, in particular for the individual entrepreneurs and SMEs, reaching out to a large number of potential ecosystem members requires much more than just putting money on the table. First, one must have an interesting offering, one to which potential ecosystem members can relate to, understanding the long-term potential as well as their potential role and benefits to them. Once this "big picture" understanding and interest are established, engagement on a more detailed level has to be undertaken, in order to understand the new ideas, to put them into the context of the ecosystem offering and to assess the feasibility of implementation given the available tools. Finally, a substantial amount of work has to be invested in explaining formal procedures and requirements that apply to the open calls. This is especially important if new organizations, previously not active in such programs, are to be involved, which is key if ecosystem expansion is the goal. Further to this and beyond the open calls as a formal tool, interaction with all applicants who are not selected for funding is another important activity that leads to the expansion and strengthening of an ecosystem. Interacting with the open call winners requires skillsets that are not always present in technical projects populated with engineers and researchers. The role of the coordinator as a "welcoming host" and the ecosystem manager as a bridge between the partners in the project, following up the individual projects and their outreach is important. In TagItSmart! the kickoff of the new projects was aligned with a general assembly for all project partners. This worked very well in creating a common vocabulary and realistic expectations for the TagItSmart! enablers.

TagItSmart! had three rounds of open calls, enabling the project to fine tune the strategy in an agile manner and to target specific domains and activities which were deemed most suitable for successful expansion of the ecosystem and sustainability of the project outcomes.

Information Moments

Information moments are not formal "clinics" with more than one partner involved, but more like meetings with the local community where the host, a project partner, explains the overall goal of the project, the main features, the existing scenario and so on. Potential applicants are put in touch directly with the most suitable project partner for further explanation and the more detailed technical discussions that are required for successful preparation of an open call proposal. These activities lead to strong local links, which can result in a deep relationship leading to greater IoT and digital transition, as all drivers are local and global at the same time. A typical example of an open call informal moment interaction follows:

> This morning I had a very good call with Peter who was referred by VTT to have a talk with me on Open Calls. He was very enthusiastic and will for sure go for Call 2, but also try Call 1 although it is close. After explaining the project, he immediately was thinking of a case that a client had put to him recently. A producer of … realized he will need a direct relationship with his customer and asked Peter if a tag/app would be appropriate, so that a buyer can give direct feedback and so to establish a channel of communication. This case touches on the heart of TagItSmart!—how can monitoring the full lifecycle lead to better recycling and reuse and extreme personalization?

These moments are not about quantity, but quality. In the Information Moment Barcelona there was only one participant, but that interaction led to the submission of a successful proposal. In the Ghent Meetup one participant was already considering a proposal, but more interestingly a group of five very dedicated participants who met for the first time there joined forces to write a joint proposal. This kind of light and informal interaction with the companies and the enablers not only contributed to the large number of received proposals in the open call, but also to general awareness of the broader objectives.

Policy Meetings as Drivers of Ecosystem Expansion

An important feature of ecosystem building is the introduction of a higher level of abstraction that is not disputed or competed on by all stakeholders. By focusing on one level of abstraction above the immediate project problem at hand, identity management at the level of the product and the lack of sharing data, TagItSmart! initiated an ongoing discussion in the form of joint policy meetings with the European Environmental Bureau (EEB) in Brussels, inviting DG Connect, DG Grow and DG Environment together with business and recycling stakeholders, as well as a debate via mail, social media and LinkedIn with individual participants. This high-level debate was created to position not only the TagItSmart! project but also its partners and the partners of partners, and to explore the growing interest in blockchain (which was not initially in the project) to link up different contexts around a single item-level product. Because a high-level open policy discussion was created, Open Call 3 could be created in such a way that several proposals addressed the product passport in a very innovative way.[15] This is a proposition that is currently not on the radar in European legislation, but is a key building block in consumer IoT.

In *Data sharing and analytics drive success with IoT. Creating Business Value with the Internet of Things*, Stephanie Jernigan, Sam Ransbotham and David Kiron find that obtaining business value using IoT depends on companies' willingness to share data with other organizations. One of the TagItSmart!bottlenecks involves the quantity, quality and granularity of data shared among all stakeholders, public, private and personal. The EEB in its text *Circular Economy Package 2.0: Some ideas to complete the circle* (March 2015) states that inadequate information passed on from one business to another concerning the resources a product contains and how it can be repaired or recycled is hindering efforts to improve resource efficiency, and the use of a product passport is explored. In 2013 the European Resource Efficiency Platform issued recommendations that product passports would improve resource efficiency, encourage innovation and generate jobs across Europe. Working on shared data propositions throughout a value chain along the lines of a product passport might be a strong enabler for helping companies to explore and adopt new business models.

Steering something as varied and diverse as "goods" has always required thorough domain expertise and scope of focus (on market share, sustainability, brands, competition). The current digitization allows feedback and agency at item level. This is a game changer. IoT is a horizontal process that individuates each object (or good) and adds reading capabilities in a subset, especially via smartphones. For the first time these capabilities are cheap and ubiquitous, with the potential to identify goods uniquely (via various cheap technologies such as barcodes, QR codes, RFID, NFC and smart tags) being ambient and affordable. Most important, we have the ability to store numerous data points virtually for nothing in different clouds.

The key to having a fresh eye on this space is a mentality change for all parties. Currently digital and circular are disconnected. The meetings have indicated that all stakeholders need to rethink their assumptions and position. NGOs still see large companies as unfriendly parties unwilling to share data. Companies still hang on to their individual brands but begin to see that they should harness their own identities across a value chain or a value model. Economic models that do not take into account the disruption of supply chains by top players and their new payment and funding models fueled by this new item level paradigm, will not be able to make productive predictions. Technology is still seen by interested parties as the problem, whereas it is currently more of a solution—bringing transparency across value chains, tracing fakes, allowing receptivity on the right scale and introducing pricing schemes. Legal frameworks such as the EU's General Data Protection Regulation can hamper recycling and reuse schemes as the value models (including companies) need a granular insight into citizens and traceability across various contexts.

The arbitrary divisions in the supply chain and value model of industry as well as in the policy realm that are creating a situation in which the full challenge is being broken up into actionable pieces within its own fields of thought and action (connectivity, economic growth, sustainability, circular) before the new big picture can be observed. The new tools should be able to deal with the dynamic status of goods. Facilitating linear models is no longer tuned to economic realities; it will be seen as unwelcome and irrelevant interference. As we go from product to service in business models and from service to over the top service, the quest for the digital twin is no longer relevant solely in industrial IoT, as we are talking about consumer digital twins: cardboard milk boxes, packets of tofu, Perrier bottles. Digital beer is such a digital twin, allowing stakeholders in the ecosystem around a single bottle to read information and give feedback. This combination of extreme transparency (the temperature of brewing and other production data) throughout the lifecycle (including transport and retail), extreme personalization (consumers can order exactly the same process that led to their one unique bottle) and extreme recycling (whether the bottle is returned or not, with actions and incentives being taken on both) is within five to ten years of production. This example uses smart tags, but we envisage combinations of barcodes, QR codes, RFID, NFC and smart tags as the glue that will enable this linking up of different contexts around a single item level product.

By reintroducing the product passport in policy meetings, TagItSmart! created a debate that led to internal use in Open Call 3 and external discussion in various policy and business environments. Its timing in relation to the recent work in blockchain and distributed ledger technology (DLT) led to a range of innovative proposals that centered around providing relevant information to food professionals and final consumers through ensuring multi-party and transparent information. A novel information sharing model tuned to DLT, integrating product data from the biggest brands and the biggest distributors, tackling real-time data consulting from multiple platforms as well as the lifecycle management, will deliver a product passport concept, maybe even a European product passport, as one of the key ingredients facilitating the processes driving the circular economy.

6 Conclusions

We have described three tools for ecosystem building in TagItSmart!, addressing the three roles, horizontal, technical, geographic (described above in Fig. 4.1) as well as identifying the weak parts in the technical ecosystem model. TagItSmart! is offering a scalable technical printing solution, a horizontal enabler. Vertically it is addressing specific use cases that are extendable, as the functionaries are not tied to any particular domain. Geographically it deals with very local requirements and implementations relating to legislation on recycling. The information moments help to build the opportunities to connect locally.

In the technical model, it is building relationships with all parties (vendors, platforms, domain experts and solution providers) regarding viable business cases and potential revenue streams. As the enablers are generic, it is the last step (to the end user) that is most problematic in terms of visibility for the TagItSmart! ecosystem. This is addressed through the open calls. The open call winners become part of the ecosystem and expose their service to the end user with a visible acknowledgement of TagItSmart!. In this way, the face of the service becomes part of the ecosystem.

References

Allee, V. 2003. *The Future of Knowledge. Increasing Prosperity Though Value Networks*. Burlington: Elsevier.

Carayannis, E.G., and D.F.J. Campbell. 2010. Triple Helix, Quadruple Helix and Quintuple Helix and How Do Knowledge, Innovation and the Environment Relate to Each Other? A Proposed Framework for a Trans-Disciplinary Analysis of Sustainable Development and Social Ecology. *International Journal of Social Ecology and Sustainable Development* 1 (1): 41–69.

Casadesus-Masanell, R., and J.E. Ricart. 2010. From Strategy to Business Models and Onto Tactics. *Long Range Planning* 43 (2–3): 195–215.

Dame Ellen MacArthur, Founder, Ellen MacArthur Foundation; Intelligent Assets: Unlocking the Circular Economy Potential, February 2016, Online Publication. https://www.ellenmacarthurfoundation.org/publications/intelligent-assets.

Derfus, P.J., P.G. Maggitti, C.M. Grimm, and K.G. Smith. 2008. The Red Queen Effect: Competitive Actions and Firm Performance. *Academy of Management Journal* 51 (1): 61–80.

Iivari, M., P. Ahokangas, M. Komi, M. Tihinen, and K. Valtanen. 2016. Toward Ecosystemic Business Models in the Context of Industrial Internet. *Journal of Business Models* 4 (2): 42–59.

Jansson, N., P. Ahokangas, M. Iivari, M. Perälä-Heape, and S. Salo. 2014. The Competitive Advantage of an Ecosystemic Business Model: The Case of Oulu Health. *Interdisciplinary Studies Journal* 3 (4): 282–294.

Kelly, Kevin. 2016. *The Inevitable: Understanding the 12 Technological Forces That Will Shape Our Future*. New York: Viking and Penguin Books.

Le, T.T., and M. Tafardar. 2009. Business Ecosystem Perspective on Value Co-Creation in the Web 2.0 Era: Implications for Entrepreneurial Opportunities. *International Journal of Entrepreneurial Venturing* 1 (2): 112–130.

Lee Vinsel, and Andrew Russell. Hail the Maintainers Capitalism Excels at Innovation But Is Failing at Maintenance. Online Publication. https://aeon.co/essays/innovation-is-overvalued-maintenance-often-matters-more.

Lehto, I., J. Hermes, P. Ahokangas, and J. Myllykoski. 2013. Collaboration in Cloud Businesses – Value Networks and Ecosystems. *Communications of the Cloud Software* (ISSN 2242- 5403). Discussion paper.

Letaifa, S.B. 2014. The Uneasy Transition from Supply Chains to Ecosystems – The Value- Creation/Value-Capture Dilemma. *Management Decision* 52 (2): 278–295.

MacArthur, D.E., and Waughray, D. 2016. *Intelligent Assets. Unlocking the Circular Economy Potential*. Rapport de la fondation Ellen MacArthur.

Magretta, J. 2002. Why Business Models Matter. *Harvard Business Review* 80: 86–92.

Massa, L., and C.L. Tucci. 2014. Business Model Innovation. In *The Oxford Handbook of Innovation Management*, ed. M. Dodgson, D.M. Gann, and N. Phillips, 420–441. Oxford: Oxford University Press.

Moore, J.F. 1993. Predators and Prey: A New Ecology of Competition. *Harvard Business Review* 71: 75–86.

———. 1996. *The Death of Competition: Leadership & Strategy in the Age of Business Ecosystems*. New York: Harper Business.

Osterwalder, A., Y. Pigneur, and C.L. Tucci. 2005. Clarifying Business Models: Origins, Present and Future of the Concept. *Communications of the Association for Information Science* 16 (1): 1–25.

Prahalad, C.K., and V. Ramaswamy. 2004. *The Future of Competition: Co-Creating Unique Value with Customers*. Boston: Harvard Business Press.

Rong, K., G. Hu, Y. Lin, Y. Shi, and L. Guo. 2015. Understanding Business Ecosystem Using a 6C Framework in Internet-of-Things-Based Sectors. *International Journal of Production Economics* 159: 41–55.

Rothschild, M. 1990. *Bionomics: Economy as Ecosystem*. New York: Henry Holt and Company.

Schladofsky, W., J. Mitic, A.P. Megner, C. Simonato, L. Gioppo, D. Leonardos, and A. Bröring. 2016. Business Models for Interoperable IoT Ecosystems. In *International Workshop on Interoperability and Open-Source Solutions*, 91–106. Cham/Chicago: Springer.

Westerlund, M., S. Leminen, and M. Rajahonka. 2014. Designing Business Models for the Internet of Things. *Technology Innovation Management Review* 4 (7): 5.

Ziouvelou, X., and F. McGroarty. 2017. Business Models for Crowd-driven IoT Ecosystems: A Review. *International Journal of Computer & Software Engineering* 2: 121.

———. 2018. A Business Model Framework for Crowd-driven IoT Ecosystems. Special Issue: Rise of the Business Ecosystems: Business Models, Structures, Processes, and People, *International Journal of Social Ecology and Sustainable Development (IJSESD),* forthcoming.

Ziouvelou, X., P. Aleksandrou, C.M. Angelopoulos, O. Evangelatos, J. Fernandes, N. Loumis, F. McGroarty, S. Nikoletseas, A. Rankov, T. Raptis, A. Ståhlbröst, and S. Ziegler. 2016. Crowd-Driven IoT/IoE Ecosystems: A Multidimensional Approach. In *Beyond the Internet of Things: Everything Interconnected*, ed. J.M. Batalla, G. Mastorakis, C.X. Mavromoustakis, and E. Pallis. Cham: Springer Publishers.

Zott, C., R. Amit, and L. Massa. 2011. The Business Model: Recent Developments and Future Research. *Journal of Management* 37 (4): 1019–1042.

5

How Business Value Is Extracted from Operational Data: A Case Study

Zsolt Ugray, David Paper, and Jeffrey Johnson

1 Introduction

In an era when data is generated at an exponentially increasing rate, business opportunities arise when actionable knowledge is extracted from data collected by organizations using advanced analytics methods. The increasing volume, velocity, and variety of data (Big Data), along with the growing capabilities of computational devices and the increasing sophistication of algorithms, techniques, and tools to analyze them give new prospects for organizations to innovate their business models and to devise ways to apply their technologies and knowhow to generate and implement processes to create value for customers and to capture some of value as their profits (Teece 2010; Zott et al. 2011). Firms that are able to adapt dynamically to their changing business and economic environments have a better chance to increase or maintain their competitiveness. The challenge for all organizations is to notice the emerging opportunities,

Z. Ugray (✉) • D. Paper • J. Johnson
Jon M. Huntsman School of Business, Utah State University, Logan, UT, USA
e-mail: Zsolt.Ugray@usu.edu; David.Paper@usu.edu; Jeffrey.Johnson@usu.edu

A. Aagaard (ed.), *Digital Business Models*,
https://doi.org/10.1007/978-3-319-96902-2_5

to choose the right ones that fit their strategy directions, and to allocate or acquire the resources to capitalize on them.

In this chapter, we observe how a young and fast-growing US company goes through phases toward building new revenue and profit streams by organically growing innovative digital business models. The process starts with collecting operational data and building unique data sets. Data initiatives within the company aim to utilize the unique data to build analytical capabilities (digital technology enablers) to serve customers better. Finally, it moves toward monetizing the analytical capabilities by offering services in an attempt to capture a share of the value unlocked from its unique data. Throughout the process, we observe how additional value to customers is created by better services, how internal processes are made more effective and efficient, and how the firm's employees develop new skills and capabilities.

We chose the qualitative case study methodology to explore in depth the details of value generation and capture of one organization. While our findings are not generalizable in the sense of traditional quantitative study methodologies, the rigorous methodology we followed gives confidence to credibility and transferability of our findings and trustworthiness in the experiences uncovered (Lincoln and Guba 1985). Our study provides empirical support (not obtainable at this granularity with other methodologies) to quantitative analysis and theory validation. In summary, this case study contributes to the understanding of how innovative digital business models develop inside a company that utilizes the benefits of novel digital technologies and its unique data.

We begin with a literature review, continue with research design, and end with an empirical report on how members of the organization view the data initiatives undertaken toward uncovering the value in the data by employing data analytics.

2 Literature Review

We have organized the literature review into the following sections: Business Models, Big Data, Creating Value, Customer Experience, Data Experts, and Leadership. It reflects relevant categories and areas of research from the extant literature.

2.1 Business Models

Business models describe firms' frameworks around their efforts to create and deliver value to customers, the ways firms convince customers to pay for their offerings, and their systems to seize some the value and turn it into profits. They are conceptual rather than financial models of firms' operations (Teece 2010). In essence, business models describe organizations' plans to turn advantages in technologies, knowhow, along with tangible and intangible assets, into a stream of profits (Teece 2018). While there is the lack of a commonly used definition of what business models are, a survey of the business model literature by Zott et al. (2011), and El Sawy and Pereira (2013) suggests that there are common themes in the research into business models. Business models are a new unit of analysis, they are a system-level view of how business operate, firms' activities are crucial parts of the analysis, and the explanation of how value is created by firm activities is just as important as the process of capturing value. The definition we use above from Teece (2010, 2018) incorporates all basic and crucial ideas and components of what is generally meant by business models. This definition describes the concept of business models and what distinguishes them from the related albeit different ideas of business strategy, business concepts, revenue models, and economic models.

The increasing importance of digital technologies that has emerged in past decades has led to the emergence of digital business models where the underlying digital technologies are at the core of the value creation and delivery processes (Remane et al. 2017). El Sawy and Pereira (2013) argue that as digital platforms have become more common and accessible, business models have become more digital, and firm capabilities have become more modular, it has become possible for businesses to create and capture value by creating novel offerings on a shoestring budget.

The spread of digital ecosystems has had a transformational effect in traditional industries and businesses as well. Deconstructing business models that rely on existing products and services and then modifying them and applying new configurations is becoming more common (Remane et al. 2017). If an organization can devise new, fully digital business models then new profit streams, aligning with the digital era, can be realized. An example of attempts to form modern theories for business models is the development of the idea of sensing business models (Lindgren and Aargaard 2014). The proliferation of physical and artificial (among them many digital) sensors, augmented with biological sensors, a real-time monitoring, analysis, and updating of business process variables becomes a reality that can increase the effectiveness of business models. Incorporating persuasive technologies into business model innovations makes it possible to support sustainable behaviors on the part of all stakeholders in a business (Aargaard and Lindgren 2015).

Sousa and Rocha (2018) investigate the importance of skills as parts of the intangible assets that are necessary components of business models, especially digital business models, in the delivery of sustainable profit streams to firms. They point to the emerging role if information technology (IT) as a major source for specialized skillsets. Internet of Things, cloud technology, Big Data, mobile technologies, artificial intelligence, and robotics, all of them digital technologies, are some of the areas identified where a mix of unique skills become necessary to succeed in building a novel digital business model for successful disruptive businesses. There are three major types of skills identified, innovation, leadership, and management, and skill development is found to have a significant relationship with job levels.

2.2 Big Data

Data is flowing, it seems, from everywhere. People are generating and consuming data from sources such as YouTube, Facebook, Twitter, Instagram, and Snapchat. Organizations are tracking customer movements with smartphones (Bertolucci 2013a; YouTube Statistics 2014), capturing customer preferences with embedded devices, gaining insights from uploaded images and videos (Gantz and Reinsel 2012), and collecting oceans of data from cable boxes, retail checkouts, credit card transactions, and call center logs (Nichols 2013). This data deluge is aptly named Big Data and is formally defined as "a new generation of technologies and architectures, designed to economically extract value from very large volumes of a wide variety of data by enabling high-velocity capture, discovery, and/or analysis" (Gantz and Reinsel, p. 9).

Historically, very large databases were at the gigabyte (GB) level (Ji et al. 2012). Present-day thinking views Big Data as representing massive amounts of data at the terabyte (TB) level (Ji et al.). In the future, technological advance will change the perspective of Big Data as representing data at the petabyte (PB), exabyte (EB), or even zettabyte (ZB) levels. Big Data is going to continue to get bigger at an exponential rate (Brands 2014). Gantz and Riensel (2012) predict that the "digital universe"—a measure of all the digital data created, replicated, and consumed annually—of Big Data will grow from 130 EB to 40,000 EB (40 trillion GB) by the year 2020. Even without considering such growth, organizations are experiencing coping issues with the data they already collect (McAfee and Brynjolfsson 2012; Paper et al. 2015).

Then "the primary goal of big data analytics is to help companies make more informed business decisions by enabling data scientists, predictive modelers, and other analytics professionals to analyze large volumes of transaction data, as well as other forms of data that may be untapped by conventional business intelligence (BI) programs" (Martinek and Stedman 2014, p. 1).

2.3 Creating Value

Organizations manage vast amounts of data, but few are able to actualize value (Bell 2013). Reasons include the inability to fully understand "their" data, failure to create viable insights from data, investments in data warehousing (or other data-related endeavors) that never mesh with business processes, and complicated analytics environments that do not connect with business value (Barton and Court 2012).

One of a handful of exceptions is Amazon, which tracks customer history to align customer preferences ("How Amazon Uses the Wish List" 2011). Amazon relies on this data to align with customer preferences, segment customers, and create better customer loyalty. Another is Euclid (a Silicon Valley startup), which created software that uses smartphone WiFi signals to monitor customer movements and augment customer profiles (Bertolucci 2013b). Data collected enables customer tracking of location inside or outside a store, length of time in store, and frequency of visiting a store. It also provides information on return customers, how much customers spend, and customer loyalty over time. A third exception is Qualtrics (www.qualtrics.com), which enables clients to collect, analyze, and act on the online customer voice for market research, customer satisfaction and loyalty, product and concept testing, employee evaluations, 360-degree reviews, brand, and website feedback purposes (Brustein 2014).

Early adopters are already harnessing value from the analysis of Big Data (Davenport and Harris 2010), which is pushing organizations to consider analytics and Big Data initiatives to remain competitive (Manyika et al. 2011). However, sifting through the hype is not easy. Franks (2012) augments the three Vs of Big Data—variety, velocity, and volume—with veracity and value. According to Franks, value is the most important, and it is often overlooked. Big Data initiatives are so complex because of the tremendous volume of data, speed with which it is generated (velocity), and the variety of different types of data sources. Veracity (genuineness) is occasionally added to the three Vs to emphasize the importance of the trustworthiness of data. Adding value to the mix is critical because dealing with the four other Vs is meaningless without it (Franks). Lee et al. (2014) argue that focusing on all of volume, velocity, variety, veracity, and value offer "a powerful strategic resource for uncovering unforeseen patterns and developing sharper insights about customers, businesses, markets, and environments" (p. 1).

Value creation hinges on several factors, including the customer experience, data experts, and leadership. Each area is presented in turn.

2.4 Customer Experience

In total, 70% of Big Data is created and consumed via digital television, social media, devices over the Internet, online shopping, and in-store shopping (Gantz and Reinsel 2012). However, organizations have barely tapped the potential value because such data tends to be unstructured (Barton and Court 2012; Frank 2012; Gantz and Reinsel; Markham et al. 2015; Warren et al. 2015). The reason is that very few methodologies exist to directly analyze unstructured data (Frank). As a result, organizations attempt to structure it without mapping to a tested methodology, which inevitably results in lost meaning and value. Frank suggests collecting some Big Data and starting to analyze it; continue by focusing on a quick win to prove the data's value. A simple method like this not only enables value creation, it aids in identifying procedural mistakes before moving on to much bigger projects. Moreover, proving the value of the data with a small project mitigates the anxiety of business executives because it is perceptually less risky and costly.

An enhanced customer experience is measured by customer satisfaction, loyalty, and retention. Analysis of Big Data allows more refined customer segmentation (Manyika et al. 2011), which leads to better understanding of customer desires (Gantz and Reinsel 2012). Loyalty and retention are also enhanced because more information can be gleaned about customer behavior in general. Understanding customers (through Big Data analytics) should also facilitate a more strategic fit with current and potential product and service offerings (Manyika, et al.). Once Big Data can be leveraged to enhance the customer experience, business executives can rely on their heuristic ability to make informed decisions based on what the data reveals (Shah et al. 2012).

For value creation to happen, business executives must be able to glean business process information from their data. That is, they must be able to understand what the technical analyst provides relative to solving business problems and enhancing business processes that ultimately provide customers with what they want. For instance, the ability to tag customer images in real time might allow insights into what customers really want and enjoy (Gantz and Reinsel 2012). However, business executives must be able to extract data that has business purpose. A major problem is that data experts may not understand business processes and/or how to translate what they extract from the data into something palpable for a business decision-maker. Succinctly, "big data is big business" (Parise et al. 2012, p. 1). The next section delves into the relationship between data and businesspeople.

2.5 Data Experts

Business executives are experts in business processes, but typically not in data analytics. Since talented data experts (people who are adept, trained, and experienced in manipulating, organizing, and analyzing data sets) thrive in environments that encourage freedom to experiment, explore, and question the status quo (Davenport and Patil 2012), executives must be able to identify, nurture, and retain data experts who possess such talent. They also ought to cultivate an environment that empowers such people to leverage Big Data and its analysis to cut cost, enhance performance, and create value (Banerjee et al. 2013; Bell 2013; Davenport 2013; Davenport and Harris 2010; Davenport and Patil 2012; Manyika et al. 2011; Ross et al. 2013; Santaferraro 2013).

The best data experts are very scarce and are attracted to organizations that encourage ideas about markets, market trends, and new ways to create value from Big Data (Marchand and Peppard 2013). As a result, a key factor in garnering Big Data value is the ability to attract and retain the best data experts while cultivating a creative, exhilarating, and comfortable Big Data environment. Such ability requires executives to be adaptable, flexible, and supportive of Big Data talent, which may not match current management practices and experiences.

2.6 Leadership

Brynjolfsson et al. (2011) suggest that companies using data and business analytics to guide decision-making are more productive and experience higher returns on equity than companies that do not. Yet business executives may be slow to embrace analytics-based decision-making principles because they see it as a threat to their ability to make good decisions based on their deeply held intuition (Bell 2013). It is a natural reaction to resist what is not understood and a challenge to their decision-making acumen (Bell). However, business executives can still trust their instincts while working with data experts to provide empirical and analytical evidence to support their decisions (Banerjee et al. 2013). Their focus should be on what they know about business and how to align business processes with data analytics initiatives (Harriott 2013; Stodder 2013).

Data analytics cannot replace intuition and innate heuristics reasoning (McAfee and Brynjolfsson 2012). Yet leadership in the Big Data era requires leaders to be even more creative (Barton and Court 2012), interactive with data experts (Davenport 2013; Davenport and Patil 2012;

Santaferraro 2013), focused on developing business-relevant data analytics implementations (Barton and Court 2012), and engaged in creating a culture that rewards data-oriented solutions (Banerjee et al. 2013). Value is derived from data by skilled people. Leaders should thereby cultivate a culture that encourages and rewards ideas derived from the analysis of data (Davenport and Harris 2010).

Leading organizations advocate a new breed of executive—a chief data officer—to better deal with the challenges of Big Data (Lee et al. 2014). Such organizations have discovered that seemingly data problems are actually business problems (Krishnan 2014; Lee et al. 2014). The focus should be on creating and sustaining effective business models and processes with the support of Big Data as well as aligning data, IT, and business models with strategic initiatives (Lee et al. 2014). Analytics should be about "focusing on the most relevant data for actionable insights ... [and how] ... generated data can add value to their business" (Merett 2015, p. 1). Many data analytics initiatives emanate from business model and business process challenges such as increasing sales and efficiencies, and improving operations, customer service, and risk management (Beal 2015).

Only about 4% of organizations are able to align the right people, tools, data, and intentional focus to leverage Big Data for improved business processes, services, and products (Wegener and Sinha 2013). A major reason is the failure to invest prudently in data-savvy people, quality data, state-of-the-art tools, and business processes and incentives that support analytical decision-making (Wegener and Sinha). Consequently, successful leaders in the Big Data era must be able to create and implement strategies for collecting and organizing data that aligns with value-creating business processes (Liu 2015; Milliken 2015; Parise et al. 2012), acquire tools that leverage data analytics (Martinek and Stedman 2014), and secure and retain excellent data experts (Davenport 2013). Specifically, strategies should include securing experienced data experts, creating a team dedicated to creating data insights (Lin 2014), creating (or adapting) business models and business processes to support analytical decision-making, championing initiatives that embrace quality and consistent data stored in an easy to access manner, and investing in state-of-the-art Big Data analytics tools.

3 Research Design

We chose the case study methodology for our research. Consistent with Dube and Pare (2003) and Pare (2004), case study research is viable when the phenomenon under study is broad and complex, when a holistic, in-depth investigation is warranted, where the existing body of knowledge is insufficient to permit causal inferences, and when a phenomenon cannot be studied outside its context. Exploring the value proposition of data analytics within a firm's context meets these criteria.

Case study research design should follow a rigorous, step-by-step methodology (Dube and Pare 2003; Pare 2004). We accomplished this by outlining our research design beginning with a clearly defined research question, continuing with the articulation of research methodology, unit of analysis, case profile, data collection, data analysis, and ending with an empirical report.

Additionally, the research design (encompassing research methodology, unit of analysis, data collection and analysis, and empirical report) should unfold in a logical, clear, and simple manner (Pare 2004). We follow these guidelines in our implementation of the case study research.

3.1 Research Question

Defining an appropriate research question is critically important in a research study (Yin 2014). The research question should clearly and simply articulate the purpose of the research and ensure that it can be completed in a timely and scientifically relevant manner (Pare 2004). In the spirit of Pare, our research question follows:

> *How do data analytics initiatives add value (perceived and/or tangible) in organizations and contribute to digital business model innovations?*

3.2 Methodology

Case study research is appropriate when existing theoretical knowledge of phenomena is limited, few studies exist (Benbasat et al. 1987; Eisenhardt 1989), and understanding complex social phenomena is desired (Yin

2014). As such, case study research can capture holistic real world context and richness in a business setting (Gummesson 2000; Yin 2014) by addressing how and/or why phenomena occur without requiring control of behavioral events (Cavaye 1996; Gable 1994; Yin 2014). Since our research goal is to capture how organizations garner value from data analytics, case study research is appropriate.

Consistent with Dube and Pare (2003), we followed a rigorous case study methodology by clearly articulating design issues, data collection methods, and data analysis techniques. Dube and Pare advise case researchers to "identify clear research questions" (p. 627) in the design phase, "provide detailed information with respect to data collection methods" (p. 627) in the data collection phase, and "provide clear descriptions of the analytical methods and procedures" (p. 627) in the data analysis phase. We followed these guidelines.

3.3 Unit of Analysis and Case Selection

The unit of analysis must be related to the research question and expected results of the study (Yin 2014). We chose a single company (headquartered in the Intermountain West area of the United States) for our research for three reasons. First, we focus on the unique experiences of a company. With this bounded case (Yin 2014), we were able to gain a fundamental understanding of how the value of data analytics is perceived and measured in a concrete organizational setting. Second, through informal conversations with one of our subsequent interview subjects (prior to embarking on formal data collection) we were able to discern that the organization analyzes a large volume of its data to develop innovative new digital business models, add value to business processes, improve efficiencies, and provide excellent customer service. These are all interesting components when it comes to answering our research question. Third, since gaining entry into an organization requires trust and availability, we relied on an established relationship with a high-level manager, the chief information officer (CIO), inside the organization. He was willing to meet us informally to discuss our research agenda. His past experiences with the researchers naturally established trust. He helped us define an interview schedule with key data experts and managers within the organization.

3.4 Case Profile

N-ergy Solutions (a pseudonym chosen to mask the company name) is a privately held utility billing service organization that provides utility management and billing services to properties across the United States. Its solutions greatly reduce operating costs for property owners (both individual and business) and promote conservation of electricity, gas, and water resources while maintaining excellent customer service. Utility billing services include utility and ancillary billing, metering equipment installation and maintenance, conservation products and services, as well as periodic (daily, weekly, or monthly) meter reads allowing for leak detection and asset integrity. Products such as utility expense management, vacant billing and cost recovery, and resident payment processing augment the company's offering and show to customers that the organization is also committed to helping its clients reduce and recover the cost of utilities. To complete the full suite of solutions, N-ergy Solutions offers energy procurement, data exchange, contract management, and due diligence services.

During the past several years, N-ergy Solutions has doubled the number of its employees about every other year, growing from 300 to 600 employees in two years and then again from 600 to 1200 employees by the end of a four-year cycle. N-ergy Solutions has embarked on several analytics initiatives, many of them building on the success of previous ones. Some examples of these initiatives are shown in Table 5.1.

Table 5.1 Analytics initiatives

Migration from worksheet-based analytics to relational database enabled analytics to data warehouse developments
Moving from ad hoc analysis to automated report generations to customizable reports utilizing both third-party tools and tools developed in house
Performing analytics for the purpose of utilities budget forecasting for clients
Forecasting utility costs based on commodity market futures
Development of advance warning systems to flag potential late payments
Real-time bill payment tracking
Automated aggregation of internal business processes with similar characteristics
Development of advance warning systems to flag delayed internal processes
Enhanced predictive capabilities garnered from effective partitioning of databases
Preparation of benchmarking reports to compare groups of items (properties, bills, providers) to similar items and historical trends, both for clients and internal business process monitoring

Most recently, the organization has been experimenting with analytics incorporating external weather data. This can help clients better manage energy usage based on weather conditions: it is used to better explain why utility costs are higher or lower rather than just anecdotal explanations about weather being hotter or colder than usual. This has significantly increased the accuracy of forecasts and monthly cash flow budgeting for clients.

3.5 Data Collection

Interviews were used as the primary means to gather evidence in support of our research question: "Interviews are an essential source of case study evidence" (Yin 2014, p. 113). Dasgupta (2015) suggests that key informants (subjects) should be identified prior to going for field study and that they should be able to "answer questions related to the organization's technological initiatives and various technological decisions" (p. 153). Data collection thereby focused on interviews with four subjects jointly identified by our contact person (the CIO), who at the beginning of this study held the title of vice president of information technology), and the researchers. We were also provided with internal documents to enrich our understanding of the organization as well as a link to the company website. Consistent with Yin, we created a stream of semi-structured interview questions that maintain a "consistent line of inquiry" (p. 110) related to the research question to encourage "guided conversations rather than structured queries" (p. 110) and promote fluid interactions with subjects. Each researcher independently created questions based on the literature and past experience with qualitative research. Researchers then met to discuss the list of questions. In this meeting, we refined and consolidated our independent ideas into a final set of mutually agreed upon questions prior to the first interview. Consistent with Creswell (1998), the list of interview questions, our data gathering instrument, evolved with each interview. That is, "Our questions change[d] during the process of research to reflect an increased understanding of the [phenomenon]" (p. 19).

The CIO (the highest-level contact at the company, also our Respondent 1 (R1) in the interviews) was initially approached at a professional meeting. A subsequent conversation solidified an agreement to allow us to visit the company and conduct interviews. The CIO was instrumental in setting up interviews with key people involved with data-oriented initiatives. The interview subjects included a reporting team leader, a software development team leader, and the firm's database administrator (DBA). The CIO also agreed to be an interview subject. The four subjects interviewed provided a variety of perspectives that included upper and middle management, business process and data experts, and viewpoints from within and outside the IT department.

Two of the researchers were present to administer interviews to the subjects. Two subjects were initially identified by our initial acquaintance, the CIO. These two subjects recommended an additional interview subject. Interview duration ranged from 45 to 90 minutes. Interviews began with the formal semi-structured interview questions, but we encouraged subjects to discuss relevant ideas as the process unfolded. Additional questions were added to the formal set of questions as they emerged from subject interviews.

We recorded each interview, took extended notes which were added to a research journal, and documented the environments and impressions of each visit. The recordings were transcribed and verified within a few days of the interviews. To facilitate reflection and analytical insight (Pare 2004), reflective remarks were "directly entered into the interview transcripts within brackets" (252). Researchers subsequently met to compare notes, discuss, and summarize the content of the interviews and their subjective impressions. Transcriptions were further reviewed, verified, and then coded and analyzed. By strictly adhering to this process, we maintained a verifiable "chain of evidence" (Yin 2014, p. 127).

Data triangulation involved several sources, including formal interviews, informal conversations between interviews, company documents, field notes from the research journal, information from the company website, and a final debriefing between the CIO and the researchers. Creswell (1998) advocates that researchers should " keep a journal during the research study" (p. 121) to improve recall accuracy of events. Journal notes were useful because of the occasional time elapsed between the interviews, transcribing, and the coding activities. We also often consulted our notes before other discussions with respondents, and before and during meetings with each other to discuss emergent ideas. Researchers met several times to collaborate, collate, and compare findings from interview transcripts, and consolidate the data with company documents, field notes, ideas, and website information.

As a final point of the data collection process, we debriefed the CIO after data analysis and the initial report write-up, to verify that our understanding and interpretation of the interviews were accurate. The debriefing completed data triangulation. These data triangulation efforts served to validate data collection and to inform the data analysis (presented in Section 3.6). The final debriefing was essential to provide corroborating evidence to our findings (Creswell 1998). We asked the CIO to read two write-ups—a five-page brief and a draft of the full case study—for accuracy and validity. He informed us that the documents were accurate (with a few exceptions that he personally noted and we corrected). Cross-verification from several data sources (Patton 2002), executed in adherence with sound case study principles, provides confidence that our efforts triangulated on the research question.

3.6 Data Analysis

The dominant mode of analysis (Dube and Pare 2003) embraced by the researchers was to work through the data from the " ground up" (Yin 2014, p. 136). This approach encourages researchers to sift through the data to identify patterns, gain insights, and find useful concepts (Yin). Following the ground up analytical approach, three major findings emerged.

After the first interview, the researchers individually pored through the transcript; identified important themes and coded these themes; met several times to discuss emergent insights into the themes; and collated themes into three broad categories. Consistent with Pare (2004), coding allowed the researchers to reduce the data to three categories (findings). Following such an analytic path led the researchers farther into the data and allowed us to validate and refine emergent insights (Yin 2014).

The three categories found as the driving forces behind the use of data analytics are: (1) better client service; (2) internal process improvement; and (3) data expert-driven technological progresses. Figure 5.1 graphically depicts the three emergent forces as they contribute to the data analytics initiatives. The "better client service" driving force refers to the situations when clients (customers) of the organization push for data analytics. That is, clients ask the organization to provide some form of analytics as either a part of or the billing service or as a corollary information service to inform the customers about certain aspects relevant to the billing services. The "internal process improvement" force is at work when data analytics facilitates improvements (e.g. improved efficiencies, cost savings, and better customer service) to existing business processes within the organization. The "data expert-driven technological progresses" force is discernible when data analytics prompts internal "techies" (data experts) to keep up with leading edge technologies. That is, the organization's technical staff strive to continually learn and improve their own skills in relation to data analytics initiatives with which they have been involved. They do this in parallel with introducing newer and more effective tools and techniques to the analysis processes they are working on.

The three emergent categories of driving forces from the first interview informed the three subsequent interviews by compelling the researchers to refine the interview instrument to probe respondent perceptions of possible drivers of data analytics initiatives. After each of the subsequent

Fig. 5.1 Getting the big data analytics ball rolling, with the three driving forces

interviews, we followed the same analytic approach as the first interview: individually poring through the transcripts; identifying important themes and coding these themes; discussing emergent insights into the themes; and collating the themes into broader categories. We found that the previously identified three categories of driving forces consistently emerged from the themes of interview data. Subsequently, each succeeding interview allowed us to refine our perceptions. Such thorough analysis permitted us to probe deeper than just the current state of the organization's data analytics initiatives. A combination of maintaining copious field notes (journal), coding, reflective remarks, emergent insights, researcher contemplations, and following an established analytic path facilitated the emergence of a set of driving forces related to data analytics from the data. As the process unfolded, we were able to delve deeper into our data to gain a profound understanding of how data analytics initiatives create value for the organization and how they contribute to the innovations in the business models toward developing new revenues and profit streams.

The interviews with respondents helped us understand how the company views, supports, and invests in analytics initiatives. Our initial perception was that analytics served as a cost reduction, enhanced decision-making, and was a value creation tool. However, the reality is that big data is unstructured and its initial analysis was customer-driven and on an ad hoc basis. At this point, N-ergy Solutions navigated data analytic initiatives in a sea of data stored in databases, files, and other media without a strategic plan to create value from the existing business processes. At the start, N-ergy Solutions did not formally dedicate many resources to Big Data and analytics. At first, it started to provide data solutions to clients on an ad hoc basis. These solutions included providing aggregate data based on the utility bills processed for customers along with trends and similarities with similar properties and clients in the industry. Slicing and dicing the data along with easily interpretable visualizations were further services that were initially produced on an ad hoc basis and then provided as value-added services often for a fee. It was at this time that managers in the organization recognized the potential of data analytics as a means of value creation. Service improvements and standardization were subsequent steps that opened up opportunities to monetize the new services and to make an innovative step in the evolution of the firm's business model.

4 Empirical Report

The empirical report (narrative) was naturally shaped through our data collection and analysis. First, "we let the voices of our informants speak and carry the story through dialogue" (Creswell 1998, p. 20). Second, we "formulate[d] and compose[d] early and throughout" (Yin 2014, p. 195) the research process. Third, we let the literature review inform the research topic, interview questions, and general understanding of the phenomenon. Fourth, we maintained a chain of evidence by developing a case study database (Pare 2004) consisting of field notes (journal), company documents, interviews in raw form, narratives (documents containing respondent citations and ideas from the raw transcripts), and a final debriefing meeting with the CIO to verify and corroborate our findings.

The process began with an initial meeting with the CIO of the organization. The CIO agreed to participate and arranged an onsite interview. He provided his insights based on interview questions, gave suggestions as to whom we should contact for additional interviews, offered to make contact with potential respondents, and agreed to make appropriate introductions. With our contact's assistance, we were able to secure three additional interviews—a technical department head (second interview), a DBA (third interview), and non-technical department head (fourth interview). Respondents were coded as R1, R2, R3, and R4 respectively.

Conceptualization of the three driving forces behind the evolution of data analytics into something that is essential for a new digital business model—client, internal business processes, and technical motivation—naturally emerged from the data. As a result, we use these three categories as a means to organize the subsequent narrative.

4.1 Better Client Service

R1 strongly suggested that data initiatives are client driven. "We very rarely say 'no' to a client [data-oriented] request … but we first have to understand … [client] … requirements … then, depending on the scope of that project … is it cost effective for us to do so from within our current service contract that we have with the client."

Clients tend to request data solutions without practical experience. R1 stated: " talking to ... clients ... I don't think they actually knew what they wanted ... And so [clients] said 'we need this' and they sent us the documentation and then we'd ask questions and they wouldn't know the answers, and back and forth ... our emerging understanding of Big Data and analytics [drives what we do for clients]." Apparently, both client and provider were learning about Big Data and analytics as initiatives unfolded.

Based on the collected interview data we believe that Big Data and analytics were so new to the organization that managers were struggling to grasp what to do. However, the organization knew that clients were excited about Big Data because they were asking for Big Data solutions. The organization's view was to provide these solutions when (and if) requested by the client. R1 stated: "Only what they [clients] ask us." R2 added that client requests take the form "Hey we are getting this can you do it for us?" At the time, the organization did not formally offer Big Data and analytics solutions; rather it offered solutions at the request of its clients. R4 supported this assertion: "We're a client-driven company, so if the clients want faster [data] reports, want[s] bigger report[s], then we ... have to do it."

R2 further illustrated how clients' drove data requests: " right now we do static reports ... the next step will be ad hoc so [clients] would be able to go in and take a cube into Excel and do whatever they do with that." R2 continued: "[clients] use [our data analytics] to have a deeper understanding of what is actually happening with their data because they can slice it however they want without having to request it from us so it gives them a greater freedom to ... look at the data." However, R2 elucidated that there were limitations to what the organization could provide to clients in terms of Big Data: "SQL server 2008 generates an .xls file so it can't export anything more than sixty-four thousand rows into Excel, so we are limited by the size of data sets ... which means we ... do our analysis [for] one [client] at a time ... we are limited at the moment as far as what we can give [our clients]."

Another problem was that the organization was still learning about big data and analytics and how to leverage it. R2 expounded: "We are learning as we go." R3 pointed out: "we are in the process of trying to figure out how to deal with [data analytics]." R3 provided an example of a client request: "Okay, give me a data dump and I'll just do it in Excel." Although in this case the organization was not providing analytics, it was providing data so the client could perform his own analytics. Client "push" for data analytics helped the organization prioritize. R3 stated: "Usually the highest priorities here are … from the clients, so … if a client says, 'Hey, I need information on the last six months in my bill', [our response is] what does a client want to see?" R3 continued: "the biggest success … not only for clients to be able to see [what they want] at a glance, all of their utility data for a month, but for us to be able to … do … quality control internally, because that's the information clients want to look at."

Finally, big data and analytics requests from clients not only drove what the organization provided, but also helped it learn what it should do for them and future clients. R3 stated: "What is relevant? What do they [clients] really need to look at? And we could put something together that we send out that's easy for a [client] that's not specialized [in 'Big Data'] to make sense of." R3 continued: "if we've done as much as we can with the information we have, then it's easier for us to be ready when … management is already supporting us … combine[d] with what's happening to a client, it might get bumped up that priority list."

R1 summarized: "We consider ourselves as 'reactive' to Big Data because we only react to client request rather than proactively pursuing Big Data initiatives for value." R1 continued: "We look for ways to 'lock in' customers [clients] for longer contracts. We try to make our products 'sticky.' That is, we want to find ways to keep our customers for a minimum of two years. If we can lock them in for two years, we believe that they tend to stick with us for at least three to five years beyond the initial two-year timeframe."

4.2 Internal Process Improvement

R1 related how he conceptually visualized Big Data: "We get involved with 'data initiatives' that involve business analytics or business intelligence that are beyond standard SQL queries and database applications. We probably don't do Big Data like other organizations. We are new to this idea ... We focus on business needs first and try to prioritize our data projects from 'low' to 'high' involvement. We also are careful when investing in new technology because we are relatively new to this and are very limited in new resources."

Our emerging understanding of the company's stance, and the nuanced differences among stakeholders with various points of view within the company, were strengthened and expanded in the fourth interview. Some illustrative quotes from R4 (the non-technical department head) follow:

> So, I don't know that ... anyone in management is [saying], 'Hey ... we need some business intelligence,' like we need some data analytics, but they may say something like, 'Well, what percent of the bills that we pay are late fees?'

> Well, I think ... My real wish list would be, and I don't even know if there is a technical term for it, but basically, an Excel pivot table on the database.

The above responses from R4 indicate an acknowledgement that analytics capabilities were desired, coupled with a reluctance to attach a trendy name (such as Big Data or data analytics) to that need.

The organization relied heavily on data, but the focus was on support for internal business processes. R1 stated: "it doesn't have to be ... huge numbers of terabytes ... it's more of ... doing the kind of analysis like data mining ... [for] reporting services." R1 continues: "a big name [client] ... require[s] a lot of different data and looking at that data a lot of different ways." Internal business processes therefore were still geared toward supplying clients with data and data analysis. R3 states: "the kind of data focus at [the organization] is more of a byproduct of our core, which is processing the bills accurately and paying them on time." R3 continued: "accuracy for our processing [is] ... well above ninety-nine percent ... when you look from the perspective of a hundred thousand bills or two hundred thousand bills ... that's a substantial number." It appears that accurate data was more of a focus than data analytics at this point.

As the organization grew, it was beginning to adjust internal business processes accordingly. R1 stated: "we process about 130,000 utility bills a month … that's anywhere from 6–8000 bills a day … we're probably looking at about anywhere between 500 gigs and a terabyte of growth a year." The size of data processing may not have been in the Big Data realm at this point, but the organization was growing so rapidly that management realized internal processes would have to be modified soon. R1 continued: "Late fees on … utility bills can be quite pricey … so when it deals with a process of how we can improve our process internally … we are looking at that on several different data levels. But it really depends on the process you're trying to improve." R1 provided an internal business process improvement example: "[the] late fee process … sometimes … can take longer than expected … and so by eliminating … days [from the process] … we can get the bill earlier, then it shortens that length of time we are spending on the bill … so that gives us a little more of a window … and we've dropped our late fee percentage by about 3 percentage points." However, R1 pointed out that process improvement was daunting: "there are many processes that touch the core data so they all need to be rewritten." R3 stated: "When you [are] processing a hundred thousand bills every month … you have to go into some sort of [data] reporting or analytics."

R2 offered a different perspective: "We have an entire founding process that we are trying to enhance … [the] process of paying the providers, they see a number of enhancements that can be made. But without data to back it up I am not sure what to do … the challenge is convincing management that it's a necessity not a want."

An issue with analytics related to internal process improvement was education. R1 stated: "whenever there's [an] internal process … that you can do better … data analytics can take place [to support improvement]." However, R1 realized "there's a lot of hype that goes to 'Big Data', so it is a part of continual education."

R1 summarized: "It's very cool to predict things, but it's still hard to pay for. The challenge is to find a way to make money from the analytics that we do while still offering clients excellent service."

4.3 Data Expert-Driven Technical Progress

R2 (the technical department head) led the reporting team. He corroborated R1's assessment of management's attitude toward adopting new technology. However, his attitude was less enthusiastic about the conservative stance toward adoption.

I've talked with [R1] a couple of times … he is hesitant because he still sees that [adopting new technology] as something shiny and so he is not sure about the Return on Investment (ROI) and so he has given me the permission to go ahead and go through the process for a single entity here and build the data warehouse, do the Extract, Transform, and Load (ETL), build the cube to see what kind of data we can get out of it … so we are in the middle of that process; we are gathering requirements and figuring out how to design the warehouse. That's where we currently are.

R2 continued: "There are a few people that really push for it and I've talked to a couple of them as well so they kind of … from a non-IT perspective I am trying to feed them the visions of … so that they can put some pressure also on [R1] and some other people."

Clearly, R2 is referred to a political process that must be navigated when moving into new technologies (in this case big data and analytics). Our analysis suggests that attaching a value proposition to a data initiative proved useful.

R3 (the DBA) shed light on the internal, technical staff members' desire to move ahead with more or better analytics technology, as illustrated in the following exchange:

Researcher question: "So you say you anticipate that you will be moving to a data warehouse. What advantages do you see? Why will you do that?"

R3 responded:

> There are several advantages that we will see with that. First is that data is going to be ready for reporting. We don't have to do all these extra steps to filter data out or anything like that. They will be more ready for reporting. Faster speed. And probably more unified in a way because the problem with our database, we have a lot of columns that we inherit from [the] legacy database. And we started using them but they've been repurposed, so the name is not really what they are. And for inexperienced developers, the ones

> who just started, they have no clue what that does. And once in a while there's like ten different ways to retrieve one field, and they're all correct. Depends on who the client is, what they want to see, what they do not want to see. And so [the] data warehouse will take care of all that. There will be no confusion. Data will be scrubbed before it comes out. So in essence you're going to have the same data to work with. Instead of trying to figure out, OK should we put a flag in here to say don't show this don't show that.

R4 stated: "We're a client-driven company, so if the clients want faster reports, want bigger report[s], then we … have to do it. And the data warehouse will take care of all that … Data will be scrubbed before it comes out." R4 continued: "the client wasn't happy [with the requested report, so] that's the reason we bought a new server … $50,000 to get the report server." To satisfy clients, the organization invests in technology. However, it attempts to do so as efficiently as possible. R2 stated: "what can our clients do with the data? … Can they reduce their utility bills? … How can we make ourselves more efficient? … What are the technical things that are successful? … What does a client want to see? … So … probably the biggest success … not only for our clients to be able to see … all their utility data for a month, but for us to be able to … do a quality control internally … What is relevant? What do [clients] really need to look at?" R2 continued with an example: "Do I pull the Cube file from all of our three thousand clients and check their data … or … Can I pull one giant file with all of that data where I can pivot off of that or graph off that?"

R1 added the business perspective to technical motivation:

> A key to successful long-term data analytics is keeping our best technical employees. If employees get better through experience they are worth more. If we can pay them more, we will. If we can't then we're sending their value to other employers. Our experience is that IT people leave after two years and three months. If we can keep them until three years, they settle in and we can keep them five more years. I've only had two employees leave with between three and eight years of service. We entice the best people by offering interesting projects (like analytics), and higher salary. We don't [normally] send employees to certification classes. I'll pay for the certifications that you pass, but not for the ones you fail. Finally, the latest tech is in startup companies. We don't always have the latest technology, but we offer great benefits, a great place to live, and opportunity to advance for our best prospects.

5 Conclusions

Our findings with N-ergy Solutions suggest that the transition from a traditional way of doing business, even it involves working with digital data, to a more data-driven way of doing business is neither automatic nor easy. It takes motivation and will to overcome inertia enough to start the ball rolling. Client demand, internal pressure to improve processes, and employees' desire to stay current and continuously update their technological skills constitute the three dominant forces that combine to initiate motion toward the transition and the development of the new revenue generating models. Meanwhile, the company's main goal is to strive to serve its current client base at the highest possible level while concurrently moving ahead with a more data-driven approach to its internal business processes. Both of these objectives help to keep existing customers and acquire new ones based on capabilities and reputation. They are also tightly coupled with the need to improve the technical skills and knowhow possessed by the data experts. Managers' attitudes toward supporting the personal improvement of the technical staff, along with their appreciation of the fact that experimenting with novel technologies is crucial for the future growth of the company are also key facets. It is a combination of all of these driving forces that made it possible to move toward innovation in digital business models that will start to provide new profit streams for the company.

We initially set out to investigate the value proposition offered by the new digital technologies of big data and analytics; that is, whether and how big data analysis adds perceived and/or tangible value in organizations. Certainly, clients of N-ergy Solutions who ask for analytic services do so because they not only perceive but also actually realize the value in such services. Similarly, internal process improvement is undertaken because of the observation of existing troubles and monetary losses. Their reduction and elimination contributes to the bottom line. Employees also see value in keeping up with the state of their art that both benefits them personally and contributes to the success of their employer.

References

Aagaard, A., and P. Lindgren. 2015. The Opportunities and Challenges of Persuasive Technology in Creating Sustainable Innovation and Business Model Innovation. *Wireless Personal Communications* 81 (4): 1511–1529.

Banerjee, A., T. Bandyopadhyay, and P. Acharya. 2013. Data Analytics: Hyped Up Aspirations or True Potential? *Vikalpa* 30 (4): 1–11.

Barton, D., and D. Court. 2012. Making Analytics Work for You. *Harvard Business Review* 90: 79–83.

Beal, V. 2015. Big Data Analytics. http://www.webopedia.com/TERM/B/big_data_analytics.html.

Bell, P. 2013. Creating Competitive Advantage Using Big Data. *Ivey Business Journal* (May): 1–5.

Benbasat, I., D.K. Goldstein, and M. Mead. 1987. The Case Research Strategy in Studies of Information Systems. *MIS Quarterly* 11 (3): 369–386.

Bertolucci, J. 2013a. Your Smartphone As Big Data Analytics Tool. *InformationWeek*, January 7.

———. 2013b. Big Data in 2014: 6 Bold Predictions. *InformationWeek*, December 23.

Brands, K. 2014. Big Data and Business Intelligence for Management Accountants. *Strategic Finance* 96 (6): 64–64.

Brustein, J. 2014. How an Online Survey Company Joined the $1 Billion Club. *Businessweek*. http://www.bloomberg.com/news/articles/2014-09-24/how-qualtrics-turned-online-surveys-into-a-1-billion-business.

Brynjolfsson, E., L.M. Hitt, and H.H. Kim. 2011. Strength in Numbers: How Does Data-Driven Decision Making Affect Firm Performance? *Social Science Research Network* (April).

Cavaye, A.L.M. 1996. Case Study Research: A Multi-faceted Research Approach for IS. *Information Systems Journal* 6 (3): 227–242.

Creswell, J.W. 1998. *Qualitative Inquiry and Research Design: Choosing Among Five Traditions*. Thousand Oaks: Sage.

Dasgupta, M. 2015. Exploring the Relevance of Case Study Research. *Vision* 19 (2): 147–160.

Davenport, T.H. 2013. Keep Up with Your Quants. *Harvard Business Review* 91 (July–August): 120–123.

Davenport, T.H., and J.G. Harris. 2010. *Analytics at Work: Smarter Decisions, Better Results*. Boston: Harvard Business School Press.

Davenport, T.H., and D.J. Patil. 2012. Data Scientist: The Sexiest Job of the 21st Century. *Harvard Business Review* 90 (October): 70–76.

Dube, L., and G. Pare. 2003. Rigor in Information Systems Positivist Case Research: Current Practices, Trends, and Recommendations. *MIS Quarterly* 27 (4): 597–635.

Eisenhardt, K.M. 1989. Building Theories from Case Study Research. *Academy of Management Review* 14 (4): 532–550.

El Sawy, O.A., and F. Pereira. 2013. Digital Business Models: Review and Synthesis. *Business Modelling in the Dynamic Digital Space: An Ecosystem.* Ch2, Springer Briefs in Digital Spaces. doi: https://doi.org/10.1007/978-3-642-31765-1_2

Franks, B. 2012. *Taming the Big Data Tidal Wage: Finding Opportunities in Huge Data Streams with Advanced Analytics.* Hoboken: Wiley.

Gable, G.G. 1994. Integrating Case Study and Survey Research Methods: An Example in Information Systems. *European Journal of Information Systems* 3 (2): 112–126.

Gantz, J., and D. Reinsel. 2012. The Digital Universe in 2020: Big Data, Bigger Digital Shadows, and Biggest Growth in the Far East. *IDC Analyze the Future* 3: 1–16.

Gummesson, E. 2000. *Qualitative Methods in Management Research.* Thousand Oaks: Sage.

Harriott, J. 2013. A Leader's Guide to Incorporating Big Data Across the Organization. *Marketing Insights* (Spring): 34–41.

How Amazon Uses the Wish List to Drive a Better Customer Experience. 2011. http://jlwatsonconsulting.typepad.com/my-blog/2011/06/how-amazon-uses-the-wish-list-to-drive-a-better-customer-experience.html.

Ji, C., Y. Li, W. Qiu, Y. Jin, Y. Xu, U. Awada, and K. Li. 2012. Big Data Processing: Big Challenges and Opportunities. *Journal of Interconnection Networks* 13 (3 & 4): 1–19.

Krishnan, K. 2014. 10 Mistakes Enterprises Make in Big Data Projects. http://www.ibmbigdatahub.com/blog/10-mistakes-enterprises-make-big-data-projects.

Lee, Y., S. Madnick, R. Wang, F. Wang, and H. Zhang. 2014. A Cubic Framework for the Chief Data Officer: Succeeding in a World of Big Data. *MIS Quarterly Executive* 13 (1): 1–13.

Lin, P.P. 2014. What CPAs Need to Know About Big Data. *The CPA Journal* (November): 50–55.

Lincoln, Y., and E.G. Guba. 1985. *Naturalistic Inquiry*. Newbury Park: Sage Publications.

Lindgren, P., and A. Aagaard. 2014. The Sensing Business Model. *Wireless Personal Communications* 76: 291–306.

Liu, Y. 2015. Big Data and Predictive Business Analytics. *Journal of Business Forecasting* 33 (4): 40–42.

Manyika, J., M. Chui, B. Brown, J. Bughin, R. Dobbs, C. Roxburgh, and A. Hung-Byers. 2011. *Big Data: The Next Frontier for Innovation, Competition, and Productivity*, 1–3. New York: McKinsey Global Institute.

Marchand, D.A., and J. Peppard. 2013. Why IT Fumbles Analytics. *Harvard Business Review* 91 (January–February): 104–112.

Markham, S.K., M. Kowolenko, and T.L. Michaelis. 2015. Unstructured Text Analysis to Support New Product Development Decisions. *Research-Technology Management* 58 (2): 30–38.

Martinek, L., and C. Stedman. 2014. Big Data Analytics Definition. http://searchbusinessanalytics.techtarget.com/definition/big-data-analytics.

McAfee, A., and E. Brynjolfsson. 2012. Big Data: The Management Revolution. *Harvard Business Review* 90 (October): 61–68.

Merett, R. 2015. Where are Big Data and Analytics Heading in 2015? http://www.cio.com.au/article/559668/where-big-data-analytics-heading-2015/.

Milliken, A.L. 2015. Transforming Big Data into Supply Chain Analytics. *Journal of Business Forecasting* 33 (4): 23–27.

Nichols, W. 2013. Advertising Analytics 2.0. *Harvard Business Review* 91 (March): 60–68.

Paper, D., Z. Ugray, and J. Johnson. 2015. Mega Data Value Creation: A Roadmap to Success. *Journal of Information Technology Cases and Application Research* 16: 3–4 119–126.

Pare, G. 2004. Investigating Information Systems with Positivist Case Study Research. *Communications of the AIS* 13: 233–264.

Parise, S., B. Iyer, and D. Vesset. 2012. Four Strategies to Capture and Create Value from Big Data. *Ivey Business Journal* (July/August). http://iveybusinessjournal.com/publication/four-strategies-to-capture-and-create-value-from-big-data/.

Patton, M.Q. 2002. *Qualitative Research and Evaluation Methods*. Thousand Oaks: Sage.

Remane, G., A. Hanelt, R.C. Nickerson, and L.M. Kolbe. 2017. Discovering Digital Business Models in Traditional Industries. *Journal of Business Strategy* 38 (2): 41–51.

Ross, J.W., C.M. Beath, and A. Quaadras. 2013. You May Not Need Big Data After All. *Harvard Business Review* 91 (December): 90–98.

Santaferraro, J. 2013. Filling the Demand for Data Scientists: A Five-Point Plan. *Business Intelligence Journal* 18 (4): 13–18.

Shah, S., A. Horne, and J. Capella. 2012. Good Data Won't Guarantee Good Decisions. *Harvard Business Review* 90 (April): 23–25.

Sousa, M.J., and A. Rocha. 2018. Skills for Disruptive Digital Business. *Journal of Business Research*. https://doi.org/10.1016/j.jbusres.2017.12.051.

Teece, D.J. 2010. Business Models, Business Strategy and Innovation. *Long Range Planning* 43: 172–194.

———. 2018. Business Models and Dynamic Capabilities. *Long Range Planning* 51: 40–49.

Warren, J.D., K.C. Moffitt, and P. Byrnes. 2015. How Big Data Will Change Accounting. *Accounting Horizons* 29 (2): 397–407.

Wegener, R., and V. Sinha. 2013. *The Value of Big Data: How Analytics Differentiates Winners*. Atlanta: Bain & Company.

Yin, R.K. 2014. *Case Study Research: Design and Methods*. Thousand Oaks: Sage.

YouTube Statistics. 2014. http://www.youtube.com/yt/press/statistics.html.

Zott, C., R. Amit, and L. Massa. 2011. The Business Model: Recent Developments and Future Research. *Journal of Management* 37 (4): 1019–1042.

6

Digital Business Model Innovation: Implications for Offering, Platform and Organization

Johan Simonsson and Mats Magnusson

Digitalization can enable manufacturing companies to pursue new strategies where various services are bundled with products to support the customer in a larger part of his business and operations, often referred to as servitization. Such a transition is of interest for original equipment manufacturers (OEMs) for several reasons, for instance as it targets a larger part of the customer business and builds closer customer contact. This chapter explores a number of fundamental challenges related to digital business model innovation and how it affects, for example, innovation, platform strategies and organization, based on a case study from the Swedish company Husqvarna.

J. Simonsson • M. Magnusson (✉)
IPD, School of Industrial Engineering and Management, KTH Royal Institute of Technology, Stockholm, Sweden
e-mail: josimon@kth.se; matsmag@kth.se

A. Aagaard (ed.), *Digital Business Models*,
https://doi.org/10.1007/978-3-319-96902-2_6

1 Introduction

Digitalization is a common theme in recent management literature as well as in academic articles. A main reason for this interest is that digitalization can have a major impact on business models by enabling a transformation of not only company operations and offerings, but also how companies interact with customers. Digitalization has frequently been found to facilitate a servitization transition in manufacturing companies, under which different services complement earlier product offerings in order to support the customer in a broader way (Lenka et al. 2017; Coreynen 2017; Porter and Heppelmann 2014).

A servitization approach can, for example, support a closer interaction with the customer base and generate new revenue streams, but there are also several challenges for manufacturing companies aiming for such a transition as new capabilities are needed (Ulaga and Reinartz 2011). This chapter explores some of the key challenges for manufacturing companies striving to innovate their business models supported by digitalization.

This chapter is based on a single case study with senior managers at the Swedish company Husqvarna, with the aim of understanding the challenges facing manufacturing companies in their move into more digital business models. Altogether four key challenges were identified; relating to (1) having a more holistic customer value approach, (2) the need to establish new capabilities to support a new business model, (3) managing the tension between speed and platform focus in offer development and (4) changes in different parts of the organization.

2 Exposition of Theory

It is commonly understood that digitalization is already affecting companies and entire industries in a series of different ways. The World Economic Forum, for example, states that "the digital revolution is already transforming companies and even entire industries" (World Economic Forum 2016, p. 4). Several studies show that managers in companies across several industries are well aware that digitalization will affect them substantially. A recent global study by MIT Sloan management review and Deloitte shows that 90% of the responding managers and executives in the survey "anticipate that their industries will be disrupted by digital trends to a great or moderate extent" (Kane et al. 2016, p. 1). Consequently, there is a need to understand in more depth exactly what this impact will look like, and how managers can prepare for the expected disruptions of their businesses.

2.1 Digitalization

Many scholars have for a long time reported that new technologies often facilitate changes in products and processes and thereby reshape business models or even entire industries (Porter and Millar 1985; Porter and Heppelmann 2014, 2015; Björkdahl 2009). Digitalization is a fairly recent technological concept, and is currently frequently reported as an enabler for various changes in company operations, offerings and the overall competitive landscape, for example (Rymaszewska et al. 2017; Porter and Heppelmann 2014; World Economic Forum 2016). Gartner defines digitalization as "the use of digital technologies to change a business model and provide new revenue and value producing opportunities" ("Gartner IT Glossary," n.d.). A similar logic is provided by Hsu (2007, p. 1), who states that digitization has an "almost infinite potential to connect persons, systems, processes, enterprises, products, and services." This implies that digitalization induces transformation rather than supporting and developing traditional ways of working (Treutiger et al. 2017). This view is shared by Matt et al. (2015, p. 1), who state that digitalization may affect large parts of the organization by impacting "products, business processes, sales channels, and supply chains." In particular, it is noted that digitalization in manufacturing companies often leads to an increased emphasis on services, an aspect that arguably requires particular attention from management.

2.2 Servitization

As highlighted above, digitalization is a multi-faceted concept that induces changes in many parts of the organization. "It can manifest as an automated supply chain; a new distribution or customer engagement platform; a virtualized or dematerialized product; or a strategic shift from product-based to service-based offerings" (Bughin and Zeebroeck 2017, p. 3). Digitalization is thus commonly seen as an enabler of servitization (Lenka et al. 2017). It is becoming more common that manufacturing companies shift from a product only focus to a strategy where products and services are bundled in various combinations. This approach is commonly called servitization (Vandermerwe and Rada 1988; Parida et al. 2014), and is described as a shift from a "focus from goods, technology and manufacturing to services, intangible resources, co-creation of value and relationships" (Windahl and Lakemond 2010, p. 15). Some scholars refer to this shift as "service infusion in manufacturing" or "servitization of manufacturing" (Kindström and Kowalkowski 2014, p. 2). Other similar terms used are Product Service Systems (Barquet et al. 2013) or Integrated Product Service Offerings (Lindahl et al. 2014). An increased focus on services also means that the relationship with the customer changes, from being transactional in nature to becoming more relational and long term (Windahl and Lakemond 2010).

2.3 Business Model Transformation

As companies increasingly pursue servitization strategies enabled by digitalization, creating new customer offerings based on combinations of products and services, related business models change as well. Teece (2010) states that a business model describes the design or architecture of the value creation, delivery and capture mechanisms employed. Hence, when companies make changes to the way they operate, these changes are frequently also reflected in their business model(s). This is also often true for manufacturing companies aiming to use digitalization as an enabler for a transition into offering services in addition to their product offering (World Economic Forum 2016). One potential effect of new service offerings is that they can generate new revenue streams, but digitalization may also be a key to substantial cost savings. It may also be challenging to get a new business model right. However, companies that are first to market may not fully understand in advance the customer demands, customer willingness to pay or the cost structure and capabilities needed to deliver the offer (Teece 2010), but have to face substantial uncertainty in the development and launch of new service offerings.

2.4 Organization Transformation

Digitalization is a current global megatrend and companies across several industries are well aware of the disruptive power of this change. Companies are thus rarely struggling with understanding the importance of digitalization, rather they are struggling with how to implement a digitalization strategy (Bughin and Zeebroeck 2017; Berger 2016). The technology enabling digitalization is in most cases quite well known and already available or even implemented. Consequently, it is not the technology in itself that constitutes a problem. Rather, the challenges are related to business models and how to organize and attract the right competencies (World Economic Forum 2016; Treutiger et al. 2017). Traditional manufacturing companies often have an organization structure which is organized along different product lines. To succeed with a servitization approach, companies instead need to organize for collaboration across functions in an "end to end manner" (Treutiger et al. 2017, p. 5). The digital agenda should also be driven by top management (Kane et al. 2015). "Most companies, however, are constrained by a lack of resources, a lack of talent, and the pull of other priorities, leaving executives to manage digital initiatives that either take the form of projects or are limited to activities within a given division, function, or channel" (Kane et al. 2016, p. 2).

2.5 Aim of the Study

As described above, the servitization-driven transition of manufacturing companies is still in its infancy and it is important to further understand its inherent challenges. A key question for managers is thus to identify the related key challenges for organizations, in order to find out what factors they should primarily focus on. This chapter aims to address this broad and difficult issue, in order to improve our understanding of the fundamental challenges manufacturing companies are facing in a servitization transition. More specifically, this chapter intends to identify key challenges to existing business models when digitalization is used to drive a servitization approach. The coming sections first explore how different managers view the transition into servitization. Thereafter, the empirical observations are grouped into a number of main categories of challenges, and finally these challenges are discussed.

3 Research Setting

3.1 Husqvarna Group

Husqvarna Group was founded in 1689, and has a long history of developing innovative and leading products within many different product areas. Husqvarna Group is today organized into three divisions: Husqvarna, Construction, and Gardena. The company has during its long history been able to successfully shift focus many times and move into new and profitable product areas, leading to its current business and product portfolio that includes, for example, chainsaws, trimmers, power cutters, and watering products. The group is in a leading position on the global market for robotic lawn mowers. Generally Husqvarna Group promotes a shift to battery powered products. Another major industry trend where Husqvarna Group is increasing its focus is digitalization, and the company has in recent years invested in the development of different offers based on this. Two successful examples are Gardena Smart System and Husqvarna Fleet Services. The former supports the passionate gardener with automatic watering and lawn care, for example, and the latter connects the fleet of customer-owned machines (Husqvarna branded or others) to the cloud and enables fleet owners to keep track of, for example, the usage and position of their fleet assets.

The studies at Husqvarna Group were performed in the Construction division, which is a global leader in machinery, diamond tools and related accessories used in the construction and stone industries. It has been reported that the construction industry has not yet seen the same level of innovation in process and product as many others, and that there is a great potential "for improving productivity and efficiency thanks to digitalization, innovative technologies and new construction techniques" (Gerbert et al. 2016). There is also a growing understanding of the changes that digitalization will bring to the construction industry. A study by the Association of German Chambers of Commerce and Industry (DIHK) with the title "Digitization in the Construction Industry" states that as many as 93% of the companies in the study agreed with the statement that "digitization will influence every one of their processes." The same study also reports that digitalization is still in its early stages in the construction industry and that less than 6% of construction companies make full use of digital planning tools (Roland Berger 2016).

3.2 Methods Used

The empirical observations in this chapter are based on a single case study in one company. The chosen company has a long tradition as a manufacturer of products, but has in recent years with increased efforts started to invest in a transition with the aim of offering more services and solutions. Today it can be seen as a leader in this kind of transition among comparable companies.

There are two sources of information for the empirical results presented here. A firm-internal survey was performed, with ten individuals assigned to different initiatives related to service offer development. The respondents were asked to rank a number of pre-defined statements, but also to add their own ideas, about what hampers a transition into service offers. Moreover, they were asked to describe, in their own words, the underlying reasons for the observed problems and how these could be overcome. Furthermore, a total of eight semi-structured interviews were undertaken with managers and directors within sales and product management. These interviews were recorded and the answers were analyzed together with the results from the survey. The results from the survey and the interviews displayed high levels of agreement and jointly indicated four main areas constituting key challenges. These are described more thoroughly below, and representative quotes from both the survey and the interviews have been used to illustrate them more in detail.

4 Results and Analysis

4.1 Servitization at Husqvarna Construction

Husqvarna Construction has built a leading position globally based on strong product values, such as performance, ergonomics and reliability. A product-centric approach has for a long time been the main focus of this division and a very strong and competitive product line has been developed. However, as customers could be further supported by various services, an increased emphasis has been put on developing a portfolio of solutions that include financing, service contracts and fleet management using connected products. The respondents in the survey and in the interviews presented many reasons why a servitization approach is of interest for Husqvarna and why they believe it should remain a focus in the future. A key reason is a growing demand from customers not only for good products, but also for these products to be supported by services and solutions that go beyond the values provided when the product is put into immediate use. This need clearly emerges from the interview data, or as it was put by one of the interviewees:

- *Customers will expect that [offering services and solutions] from us.*

The new competitive battle is moving up the value chain and is revolving more around service solutions instead of just product offerings, which are becoming more similar. Companies that are not able to follow this development and compete in terms of different service solutions as well will face the risk of becoming pure commodity suppliers (Coreynen et al. 2017; Reinartz and Ulaga 2008). This risk was pointed out by a respondent from Husqvarna:

- *There is risk that we otherwise become a commodity supplier.*

Increased customer satisfaction was listed as a main driver of future growth and increased revenue streams. Customer value can be increased as products become more integrated and customized (Coreynen et al. 2017). A key to this is increased customer satisfaction, which to a large extent builds a long-term relationship (Cenamor et al. 2017). This understanding was also found in the study, namely that customers will be loyal to companies they feel can help solve more of their daily problems and issues. This helps customers to be more productive and data from the services helps manufacturers to further tailor offerings and products, creating a positive spiral of customer satisfaction and trust. This was clearly expressed by one of the respondents:

- *We solve more problems. The customer will be more productive. That will build more trust.*

A strong internal benefit of servitization is the possibility to develop better products as more data about how the products are actually used become available. Increased knowledge on how the products are actually used in the field will be beneficial to internal product development. As more and more products are connected to the surrounding world, the better data there will be for research and development (R&D) departments (Porter and Heppelmann 2015). This tendency was expressed by one respondent:

- *Data from the products will also help us understand the customer and make it possible to enhance both our products and our services. Different kinds of service offers will enhance both the product line and the service offerings.*

4.2 Challenges

There are numerous compelling reasons for manufacturing companies to embrace a servitization approach, but this also creates new challenges for a company with a product-oriented legacy. A clear focus on products and product performance has served many companies well for a long time, and that has in a good way fulfilled the demand from the customers. As a result, many of the processes at manufacturing companies have become very product oriented, for example in product development and in sales processes. Different product lines are developed by different people, sometimes with limited coordination between the lines. Different product managers are mainly measured on the performance of their own product lines and not on the performance of others. This has created what in many companies is commonly referred to as a silo structure (Treutiger et al. 2017). This compartmentalized way of working leads to fragmentation and renders development, taking into account end-to-end activities, even more challenging.

Holistic Customer Value Approach

With a shift from product focus to a service focus follows a need not only to understand (as before) the product features of importance but also which other services could be of interest and benefit to the customers. Consequently, it becomes more important also to analyze other parts of the customer business, beyond where the product is being used or serviced. To be able to develop new services, one must first understand this new setting and demands, and this stands out as a major difference from when only product features are in focus, as highlighted by one of the interviewees:

- *The people benefiting from a service offer could be the workshop staff, the person that pays the bills, the finance people. Some we don't have much contact with today.*

It is important to underscore that although services are often regarded as a substitute for products, this may actually be misleading, as servitization does not necessarily decrease the importance of products. One reason for this is that preferences differ among customers, and there will most likely often be some customers that are not interested in different service solutions but prefer to work in the traditional way: that is, they want to buy a product and pay for it up front. The other reason why products will continue to be important is that they still remain a crucial piece of the offering even when customers buy a solution. In these cases, the products turn into an enabler of the offered solution and will continue to affect the total business case for the offering. Products will remain important, but are only one (major) piece of the overall solution.

Altogether, this development can be summarized in a quote from one of the respondents:

- *Products will continue to be important, but service offers will be more important over time.*

The literature offers ample examples of why a servitization approach is of interest, not the least for manufacturing companies (Tongur and Engwall 2014). However, from identifying the potential of servitization in terms of customer benefits to realizing it as new service solutions is a difficult step because it requires new ways of working, or as put by Burton et al. (2017, p. 5), "developing effective NSD [new service development] processes is a key challenge outlined in extant literature." To some extent this issue is simply brought about by a lack of attention: in heavily engineering-driven firms, innovation still tends to be synonymous with new products or manufacturing processes (Kindström and Kowalkowski 2014). Another issue is that there is also an apparent lack of knowledge about how to perform service innovation in product-centric firms (Ostrom et al. 2010).

Offer Delivery

Another challenge emerging from the observations is that a servitization approach frequently challenges several parts of the current business model. The interviews showed that there is a concern about how the company will be able to deliver on its new promises. The interviews underlined the need to have the necessary processes and procedures in place to be able to fulfill the new customer expectations, as revealed in this quote from one of the interviewees:

- *When you buy a product and it breaks it is your problem. But to deliver on a service offer you need to have certain capabilities, you need to be high-performing as there is a promise on downtime.*

With the sales of different solutions where product lines and services have been bundled come new challenges related to business follow-up. The importance of both products and service receiving the correct recognition was underlined by respondents, as future priorities might otherwise be affected:

- *It's maybe good to bundle products and services, but both parts need to get the right credit. For the customer it does not matter how we divide the value, but internally it is important that we need to understand that both parts are important.*

The delivery of an offering is one key part of a business model (Teece 2010). It is also known that different capabilities are needed in the delivery process of a service (Kindström and Kowalkowski 2014). A major management question then becomes how one can understand the capabilities that are needed to provide a service, and in particular the costs that will be incurred to realize these underpinning capabilities.

Platform Versus Speed and Autonomy

To share components, subsystems, subproducts and solutions as much as possible is a well-known approach within Husqvarna Construction. The basic reasons for this are that costs can be saved and speed to market increased when different elements can be shared across a range of products. In general, a product platform strategy reduces costs as components are shared between product lines, while at the same time it limits the degree of freedom for engineers who are developing the products, as they have to use standardized interfaces, components and systems. Currently some of the product lines at Husqvarna Construction have limited interdependencies with other products and can therefore be developed quite independently. With a stronger emphasis on services it is likely that this will change. Many service offers will imply similarities between all products, for example in terms of digital components and systems. An example could be fleet management that is designed to keep an overview of an entire fleet of products, requiring similar information from all products in that fleet. Such a solution requires that all products communicate in a structured way and that a common approach is used for connectivity, and consequently also that a common platform approach is applied. The interviews highlighted this challenge by pointing towards a tradeoff between autonomy and platform strategy. Autonomy, and sometimes also speed to market, for one product line may be restricted by an overarching connectivity strategy, or as one respondent put it:

- *Platforms are good, but will make things slower.*

At the same time, the interviewees stressed the importance of speed to market for service solutions, as there may be substantial first-mover advantages due to network externalities and lock-in effects:

- *There will be a lock in effect—similar to software in computers.*
- *When more customer products are connected to our services it will be more difficult for them to switch supplier.*

Summarizing the above, we note that servitization puts increased demands on the use of product platforms in order to enable certain types of service development, but also new demands in terms of development speed. To some extent these two demands may also be conflicting, resulting in a challenging tradeoff that needs to be managed deliberately by someone with an overview of the development of both products and services.

The empirical observations also point to the fact that it is not primarily the technology part of various services that will be the challenging component of new service offerings. In fact, a representative quote from one of the respondents about the new technology was that:

- *It [digital technology] is new to us, but not to the world.*

Or, as found in the literature, "[d]igital fluency, however, doesn't demand mastery of the technologies. Instead, it requires the ability to articulate the value of digital technologies to the organization's future" (Kane et al. 2015).

What emerges from our study is that the challenge consists of managing the tension between on the one hand increased development speed and the related need of autonomy to move rapidly, and on the other hand the use of a platform approach, which in the long run allows for efficient and rapid creation of new offerings but initially requires a comprehensive effort that often takes a long time. Existing knowledge related to platforms states that product platforms can be used to generate increased product variety, keep costs related to production and inventory down, and shorten time to market (Gawer and Cusumano 2014). However, even though platforms have many advantages once they have been established, putting in place a new platform is often difficult and burdensome. This is particularly important for platforms designed to support servitization, as these have to span a wide range of relevant product areas and thus need to be included in many product roadmaps.

Organization

A transition into service offers is also likely to drive a change in the current organization. The empirical study revealed that key organization challenges were found to relate to innovation, sales and product management.

Extant research not only informs us that services require a different approach to innovation activities, but also that companies which regard servitization to be important frequently struggle with service innovation (Kindström and Kowalkowski 2014). The respondents in this study also pointed to a number of other organizational challenges. One pointed towards the increased need for cross-functional innovation activities:

- *For service offers there could be services only valid for my products but most maybe would span all product groups. I will need to rely on a more cross-functional approach.*

The interviews also pointed to the fact that there needs to be a larger degree of local and customer interaction, but at the same time a need for central facilitation and coordination, as highlighted by these quotes:

- *We must a have a general umbrella for the conditions, but with local adaptations.*
- *There needs to be a separate function with a holistic view on how we could change, but then involvement is needed from every function.*

The interviews also pointed at some important changes needed for the sales organization. Current discussions with customers primarily revolve around product performance, features and to some degree price. With services, salespeople have to explain the benefit and value of a service, maybe without anything practical to showcase. These concerns were put forward by the respondents as follows:

- *Not selling the specification of the product but the specification of the service.*
- *The customers then don't care too much about the technical aspects, but more about the cost and the value.*
- *When you sell a power cutter it's about features, when you sell services it is something you cannot touch.*

The changes indicated above arguably have far-reaching consequences for the sales organization and the sales process. First of all it points to the difficulty of selling something less tangible than a physical product, something which may have implications as the customer most likely will then be more critical about what the value of the purchase actually is. In order to handle this, salespeople will need to understand the customer's value-creating processes much more in detail, in order to be able to convincingly argue for the value (and price) of the service. This has implications for the competence that is needed in order to sell. Most likely, training will be needed to prepare the salesforce for the changed situation.

It may also be that there are other contacts alongside the customers, as the understanding of what value a service brings about is not necessarily easily understandable for purchasing. This may also lead to a longer and more iterative sales process, as expressed by one of the interviewees:

- *There may be other persons seen as responsible at the customer when you sell services. It's probably a longer process and other persons to approach.*

With the above in mind, we can see that service offers definitely constitute a driver for a break-up of the silo approach (Kane et al. 2015). A service offer may depend on several products to be of value, so a silo approach of product management will most likely not work very well:

- *It will have to break the silo thinking.*

From the above, it is seen that a fundamental change implied by servitization is the way it alters the sales process and in turn what type of sales organization and competence is are required.

5 Discussion and Conclusions

The study at Husqvarna revealed four key challenges for a transition towards services: (1) having a more holistic customer value approach, (2) the need to establish new capabilities to support a new business model, (3) managing the tension between speed and platform focus in offer development and (4) changes in different parts of the organization. These challenges are schematically outlined in Figure 6.1.

Apart from the apparent necessity for organizations to use digitalization as a means towards servitization to attend to each of the specific challenges, there is also a need to attend to their interrelationships. Arguably, all challenges need to be taken into account in order to allow for a successful business model transformation, and based on the comprehensive nature of the challenges their joint handling ought to be a top management priority. The business model is obviously something that every business needs as this describes how value is created, delivered and captured in a company (Teece 2010).

In the move towards new business models it is key to first understand which services the customer base actually has an interest in. For manufacturing companies this may mean that there is a need to look beyond maximizing product performance and start to understand how different services actually offer value for customers. However, all possible service offers should not be developed. Developing and offering more advanced services is likely to require that more (advanced) capabilities are in place

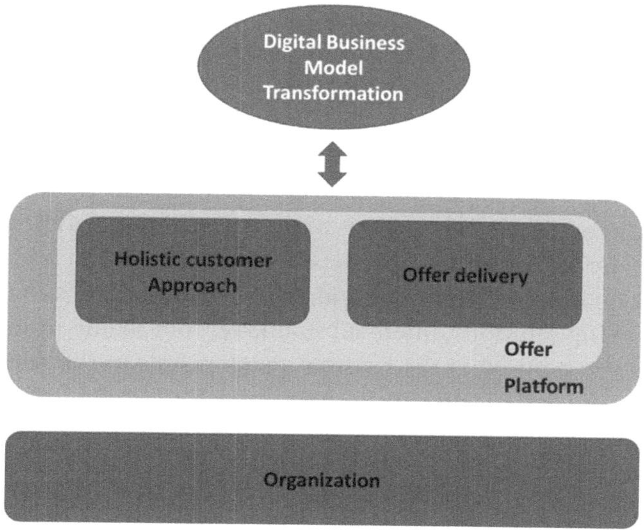

Fig. 6.1 Key challenges on the road towards digital business model transformation

than if more basic offers are to be sold. The study at Husqvarna underlined the importance of being able to deliver on promises. Consequently, in order to keep customer trust, all value ambitions must be supported with necessary capabilities. If a company aims for advanced integrated solutions, for example, it will need to "develop competences within system integration (to design and integrate systems composed of hardware, software and services) and operational services (to maintain, operate and renovate a product throughout its operational life cycle), and sometimes also business consulting and financing" (Windahl and Lakemond 2010). The importance of pairing the ambition with the needed capabilities is underlined by the fact that some companies have had to withdraw from specific service initiatives—a process that Kowalkowski et al. (2017) refer to as de-servitization.

The platform challenge is closely related both to the need for a more holistic customer approach and to the challenge of delivering services. A platform, once in place, can have positive effects on product variety offered to the market, reduce costs and shorten development time (Gawer and Cusumano 2014). A platform strategy is important as it constitutes a key to support increased variety and yet reduces cost and time to market. The challenge here is primarily how companies can establish platforms in a rapid and flexible manner, especially when they should support a wide range of products and related services.

The findings also underline that organizations will need to become increasingly complex, as many parts of the organization are affected at the same time by servitization. This sets a high demand on achieving the fruitful integration of knowledge and activities. It is clear from the literature that selling solutions differs substantially from selling products. The interviews also pointed to the fact that many people in the salesforce are very technically skilled and may in many cases have been hired because of their product-related competence. The findings underline what has been stressed in previous studies, namely that sell services is different from selling products (Ulaga and Reinartz 2011) and that incentives and follow-up metrics are, in many cases, still product centered (Shah et al. 2006; Reinartz and Ulaga 2008). Another major change is that product management needs to work in a different way. Instead of being silo based, the organizational design needs to allow for handling new value streams in the organization, where different products may support the same service. This also further stresses the importance of platform thinking for service offers. If a service is to rely on information from products, the products need to adhere to a common platform strategy.

5.1 Managerial Implications

The findings in this chapter provide a number of managerial implications. A digitally induced servitization approach will challenge the existing business model, and to cope with this companies need to make several important decisions that affect fundamental parts of them. One first implication is the need to understand which possible services could accompany the earlier product offerings, and more importantly to decide how advanced the services are that the company desires to offer to the market, as these services must be supported by the correct level of capabilities to ensure successful delivery. Hence, the ambition level of offerings needs to be aligned with the available capabilities, otherwise the servitization intentions risk failure. Another managerial implication is the establishment of a platform approach that can support the servitization approach across product platforms. Different products need to be related to the same services in a structured and consistent way. A delicate challenge is to support the servitization with a platform that can enable structure and speed once established, without losing speed to market while it is being developed. A fourth managerial implication is that the organization needs to change in many aspects, from how the offers are developed to how they are sold. The above challenges are likely to have a great effect on the company and need to be dealt with in a careful manner. As they cut across many earlier ways of working they may encounter substantial resistance, implying a need for support from top management.

5.2 Future Research

As this case study merely identifies and explores a number of challenges on the road towards the digital transformation of a business model, and in particular relates it to servitization, there are of course several areas for future research that will add important knowledge to this field. One key area is understanding how the customer value of services can be captured in an effective manner, and in connection with this how new service offerings should be priced. Traditional manufacturing companies are very used to setting prices for manufactured goods but are normally less used to pricing various service offerings. Another interesting area for future research previously underlined by Kindström and Kowalkowski (2014) is how to manage service innovation in high variety product companies. Current innovation activities are mainly driven internally from R&D, but these activities need to be moved closer to the customer when the offer changes from products to service solutions. This poses significant challenges to companies, in particular in relation to the use of a platform development approach.

References

Barquet, Ana Paula Bezerra, Maicon Gouvea de Oliveira, Carolina Román Amigo, Vitor Pinheiro Cunha, and Henrique Rozenfeld. 2013. Employing the Business Model Concept to Support the Adoption of Product-Service Systems (PSS). *Industrial Marketing Management* 42 (5): 693–704. https://doi.org/10.1016/j.indmarman.2013.05.003.

Björkdahl, Joakim. 2009. Technology Cross-Fertilization and the Business Model: The Case of Integrating ICTs in Mechanical Engineering Products. *Research Policy* 38 (9): 1468–1477. https://doi.org/10.1016/j.respol.2009.07.006.

Bughin, Jacques, and Nicolas Van Zeebroeck. 2017. The Best Response to Digital Disruption. *MIT Sloan Management Review* 58 (4): 80–86.

Burton, Jamie, Vicky M. Story, Chris Raddats, and Judy Zolkiewski. 2017. Overcoming the Challenges That Hinder New Service Development by Manufacturers with Diverse Services Strategies. *International Journal of Production Economics* 192: 29–39. https://doi.org/10.1016/j.ijpe.2017.01.013.

Cenamor, J., D. Rönnberg Sjödin, and V. Parida. 2017. Adopting a Platform Approach in Servitization: Leveraging the Value of Digitalization. *International Journal of Production Economics* 192: 54–65. https://doi.org/10.1016/j.ijpe.2016.12.033.

Coreynen, Wim, Paul Matthyssens, and Wouter Van Bockhaven. 2017. Boosting Servitization through Digitization: Pathways and Dynamic Resource Configurations for Manufacturers. *Industrial Marketing Management* 60: 42–53. https://doi.org/10.1016/j.indmarman.2016.04.012.

Gartner IT Glossary. n.d. http://www.gartner.com/it-glossary/digitalization. Accessed 6 Sep 2018.

Gawer, Annabelle, and Michael A. Cusumano. 2014. Industry Platforms and Ecosystem Innovation. *Journal of Product Innovation Management* 31 (3): 417–433. https://doi.org/10.1111/jpim.12105.

Gerbert, Philipp, Santiago Castagnino Christoph Rothballer, and Andreas Renz. 2016. Shaping the Future of Construction a Breakthrough in Mindset and Technology. *World Economic Forum (WEF)*. https://www.bcgperspectives.com/Images/Shaping_the_Future_of_Construction_may_2016.pdf. Accessed 6 Sep 2018.

Hsu, Cheng. 2007. Scaling with Digital Connection: Services Innovation. *Conference Proceedings – IEEE International Conference on Systems, Man and Cybernetics*, 4057–5061. https://doi.org/10.1109/ICSMC.2007.4414260.

Kane, Gerald C., Doug Palmer, Anh Nguyen Phillips, David Kiron, and Natasha Buckley. 2015. Strategy, Not Technology, Drives Digital Transformation. *MIT Sloan Management Review & Deloitte* 57181: 27. https://doi.org/http://

www2.deloitte.com/content/dam/Deloitte/cn/Documents/technology-media-telecommunications/deloitte-cn-tmt-strategy-not-technology-drive-digital-transformation-en-150930.pdf.

———. 2016. Aligning the Organization for Its Digital Future. *MITSloan Management Review*, no. 58180: 1–29.

Kindström, Daniel, and Christian Kowalkowski. 2014. Service Innovation in Product-Centric Firms: A Multidimensional Business Model Perspective. *Journal of Business & Industrial Marketing* 29 (2): 96–111. https://doi.org/10.1108/JBIM-08-2013-0165.

Kowalkowski, Christian, Heiko Gebauer, Bart Kamp, and Glenn Parry. 2017. Servitization and Deservitization: Overview, Concepts, and Definitions. *Industrial Marketing Management* 60: 4–10. https://doi.org/10.1016/j.indmarman.2016.12.007.

Lenka, Sambit, Vinit Parida, and Joakim Wincent. 2017. Digitalization Capabilities as Enablers of Value Co-Creation in Servitizing Firms. *Psychology and Marketing* 34 (1): 92–100. https://doi.org/10.1002/mar.20975.

Lindahl, Mattias, Erik Sundin, and Tomohiko Sakao. 2014. Environmental and Economic Benefits of Integrated Product Service Offerings Quantified with Real Business Cases. *Journal of Cleaner Production* 64: 288–296. https://doi.org/10.1016/j.jclepro.2013.07.047.

Matt, Christian, Thomas Hess, and Alexander Benlian. 2015. Digital Transformation Strategies. *Business and Information Systems Engineering*. https://doi.org/10.1007/s12599-015-0401-5.

Noke, Hannah, and Mathew Hughes. 2010. Climbing the Value Chain: Strategies to Create a New Product Development Capability in Mature SMEs. *International Journal of Operations & Production Management* 30 (2): 132–154. https://doi.org/10.1108/01443571011018680.

Ostrom, A.L., M.J. Bitner, S.W. Brown, K.A. Burkhard, M. Goul, V. Smith-Daniels, H. Demirkan, and E. Rabinovich. 2010. Moving Forward and Making a Difference: Research Priorities for the Science of Service. *Journal of Service Research* 13 (1): 4–36. https://doi.org/10.1177/1094670509357611.

Parida, Vinit, David Rönnberg Sjödin, Joakim Wincent, and Marko Kohtamäki. 2014. A Survey Study of the Transitioning towards High-Value Industrial Product-Services. *Procedia CIRP* 16: 176–180. https://doi.org/10.1016/j.procir.2014.01.019.

Porter, Michael E., and James E. Heppelmann. 2014. How Smart, Connected Product Are Transforming Competition. *Harvard Business Review* (November): 64–89. https://doi.org/10.1017/CBO9781107415324.004.

Porter, Michael E., and James E. Heppelmann. 2015. How Smart, Connected Products Are Transforming Companies. *Harvard Business Review*. https://doi.org/10.1017/CBO9781107415324.004.

Porter, Michael E., and Victor E. Millar. 1985. How Information Gives You Competitive Advantage. *Harvard Business Review* 63 (4): 149. https://doi.org/10.1038/bdj.2007.481.

Reinartz, Werner, and Wolfgang Ulaga. 2008. How to Sell Services More Profitably. *Harvard Business Review* 86 (5): 1–9. www.hbr.org.

Roland Berger. 2016. Digitalization in the Construction Industry. https://www.rolandberger.com/sv/Publications/pub_digitization_of_the_construction_industry.html?country=null.

Rymaszewska, Anna, Petri Helo, and Angappa Gunasekaran. 2017. IoT Powered Servitization of Manufacturing – An Exploratory Case Study. *International Journal of Production Economics* 192: 92–105. https://doi.org/10.1016/j.ijpe.2017.02.016.

Shah, Denish, Roland T. Rust, A. Parasuraman, Richard Staelin, and George S. Day. 2006. The Path to Customer Centricity. *Journal of Service Research*. https://doi.org/10.1177/1094670506294666.

Teece, David J. 2010. Business Models, Business Strategy and Innovation. *Long Range Planning* 43 (2–3): 172–194. https://doi.org/10.1016/j.lrp.2009.07.003.

Tongur, Stefan, and Mats Engwall. 2014. The Business Model Dilemma of Technology Shifts. *Technovation* 34 (9): 525–535. https://doi.org/10.1016/j.technovation.2014.02.006.

Treutiger, Johan, Jonas Andrén, Lokesh Dadhich, and Tove Kjellén. 2017. Four Key Questions to Consider for Successful Digital Transformation. http://www.adlittle.com/en/insights/prism/four-key-questions-consider-successful-digital-transformation.

Ulaga, Wolfgang, and Werner J. Reinartz. 2011. Hybrid Offerings: How Manufacturing Firms Combine Goods and Services Successfully. *Journal of Marketing* 75 (6): 5–23. https://doi.org/10.1509/jmkg.75.6.5.

Vandermerwe, Sandra, and Juan Rada. 1988. Servitization of Business: Adding Value by Adding Services. *European Management Journal* 6 (4): 314–324. https://doi.org/10.1016/0263-2373(88)90033-3.

Windahl, Charlotta, and Nicolette Lakemond. 2010. Integrated Solutions from a Service-Centered Perspective: Applicability and Limitations in the Capital Goods Industry. *Industrial Marketing Management* 39 (8): 1278–1290. https://doi.org/10.1016/j.indmarman.2010.03.001.

World Economic Forum. 2016. Digital Transformation of Industries: Digital enterprise. http://reports.weforum.org/digital-transformation/wp-content/blogs.dir/94/mp/files/pages/files/digital-enterprise-narrative-final-january-2016.pdf. Accessed 6 Sep 2018.

7

Service Markets: Digital Business Models and International Expansion

Robert Wentrup and Patrik Ström

1 Introduction

The growth of the Internet is radically changing the way firms operate (Tiessen et al. 2001; Yip and Dempster 2005; Pezderka and Sinkovics 2011). Although the role of the Internet has already been analyzed from an internationalization perspective (Samiee 1998; Petersen et al. 2003; Arenius et al. 2005; Sasi and Arenius 2008; Sinkovics et al. 2013), little has been written about the spatial impacts of internationalization for pure Internet firms, or so-called online service providers (OSPs) (Satta et al. 2014).[1] The

[1] We apply the term 'Online Service Provider' (OSP), which has become an accepted term in research (Taddeo and Floridi 2015). An OSP is as a firm that provides services for users over the Internet. Examples of online services are social media (e.g. Facebook), games (e.g. Angry Birds), or information (e.g. Dictionary.com), and are digitized services. We want to emphasize that OSPs should not be confused with manufacturing and service firms using the Internet as a sales channel.

R. Wentrup (✉) • P. Ström
Centre for International Business Studies (CIBS), School of Business, Economics and Law, University of Gothenburg, Gothenburg, Sweden
e-mail: robert.wentrup@handels.gu.se

A. Aagaard (ed.), *Digital Business Models*,
https://doi.org/10.1007/978-3-319-96902-2_7

question of whether the growth of the Internet and the rising service economy require a reassessment of traditional internationalization logic has been raised by business scholars (Axinn and Matthyssens 2002; Forsgren and Hagström 2007). Studies have shown how the Internet can enable and enhance export performance, and can be used as a sales channel (Sinkovics et al. 2013; Petersen et al. 2003; Arenius et al. 2005; Gabrielsson and Gabrielsson 2011). Previous research has also analyzed the internationalization strategies for Internet start-ups (Loane et al. 2004; Loane 2005; Forsgren and Hagström 2007; Kuivalainen et al. 2012). It is an intersection where economic geography offers a conceptual contribution and understanding of spatial dynamics through the focus on context (Gertler 2003; Storper 2009). The contextual setting is the form of cultural and institutional aspects, and how knowledge is being translated helps us to understand the uneven spatial distribution of economic activity as seen in the internationalization of OSPs. Though the Internet and the digitization of business enable a rapid and networked-based internationalization process, little is known about how this translates into location and offline presence decisions in the internationalization process for OSPs (Alcácer et al. 2016; Brouthers et al. 2016).

For example, the world's largest OSP, Facebook, has more than 2 billion users spread across the globe. Until a few years ago it had few international offices despite its large online user base, but today it has expanded its offline presence with 42 offline offices outside the USA (Facebook 2018).[2]

At the same time, the Facebook case is also unusual. Most firms never get an equal international traction and spread in viral effects to become global. Many do not even survive more than a few months. For example, a UK-based study showed that only 50% of London start-ups survived more than three years (Nilsson 2017). Wentrup (2016) showed that most Swedish Internet firms concentrated their international activity to near markets, and few were active in Asia and Latin America. Similarly, (Kim 2003) argued that American Internet firms choose a regional expansion.

[2] The number of international offline offices increased substantially between 2016 and 2017—from 37 to 42.

The rationale behind the spatial distribution is often complex, and we find that the theoretical contributions concerning the motives for offline presence are limited in the international business (IB) literature for OSPs and other Internet-related firms. The speed of customer acquisition can be explained by the theory of network effects (Rochet and Tirole 2003, 2006, 2014), but these firms' need for offline presence remains a rather unexploited topic. OSPs often fall into the category of "born global" firms, hence firms that internationalize early after inception and have a large part of their sales outside their domestic markets (Oviatt and McDougall 1994; Gabrielsson and Gabrielsson 2011). Yet, despite being such a geographically laden term, theory concerning location aspects of born globals is surprisingly thin.

This chapter addresses the reflection and criticism of many scholars that we cannot explain location and space-oriented aspects of internationalization for digital businesses on the basis of existing IB theories. Given the increasing importance of OSPs in the global economy, and more firms becoming Internet dependent, this is a growing concern in international business. Location and space-oriented aspects of these firms are important since they tell us where foreign direct investment (FDI) will be placed and where in the geography business activity, job creation, and innovation will emerge. By scrutinizing the internationalization and locational decisions of Internet-dependent firms we will know more about the places that will be the winners and losers in a progressively technology-impregnated society, where context facilitates connections across regions and the global marketplace (Storper 2009; Strom and Wentrup 2016). The contribution of this chapter is to bring more clarity to internationalizing OSPs' motives for international offline presence and to enhance our understanding of the determinants for the international scalability of digital business. Our research question (RQ) is:

RQ: What makes a digital business model internationally scalable?

In the chapter, we present a longitudinal single case study of the Swedish OSP Truecaller (www.truecaller.com). We have followed Truecaller over a period of more than seven years. Truecaller offers an online service consisting of a global phone directory, and has acquired more than 100 million users worldwide as of December 2017. Truecaller's international journey is paradoxical and intriguing, as it has a large and wide international audience of users, but its engagement in offline presence appears geographically restricted. Our contribution is a longitudinal, in-depth firm study in an area that is often rather closed for research. We bring some useful concepts to the IB literature on this rather new industry and species of firm, interconnected with how insights on new spatial dynamics emerge in the online economy, and in how the firm is handling the external environment.

The rest of the chapter is structured in the following way. First, a literature review is undertaken drawing on international business and economic geography theory. Second, the method is outlined. Third, the case study is presented. Finally, the results are analyzed and both managerial and theoretical implications are posited and conclusions drawn.

2 Literature Review

2.1 Geographical Proximity and Locational Advantages as Motives for Offline Presence

Localization and spatial dynamics of Internet firms and clusters is not a new field in economic geography (Zook 2002a, b; Warf 2013; Bryson et al. 2013). This research points to the strong agglomeration effects in the Internet sector. Internet start-ups tend to concentrate to a restricted set of global North cities with high Internet penetration rates, high supply of financial resources, well-educated human "talent," and clusters of technology firms (Graham 2010; Graham et al. 2015). These are places where OSPs can profit from economies of localization and urbanization. Being physically close to skilled labor and the buzz is something that is considered critical for localization patterns in knowledge-intensive service industries, including the Internet sector (Storper and Venables 2004; Pratt 2008; Trippl et al. 2009). Localization is thus affected by the necessity for face-to-face contact with clients (Gertler 2003). But whereas economic geography theory gives us a good view of where Internet firms are born and flourish, it often falls short when analyzing the motives behind international expansion. Combining economic geography and international business is seen to be a viable theoretical aim for understanding the issues that exist with the internationalization of coordination across different geographical levels (Buckley and Ghauri 2004).

A possible theoretical bridge between the economic geographers' view and IB theorists' view is therefore Dunning's eclectic paradigm, which proposes three specific and interdependent "advantages" for firms in an international setting (Dunning 1977, 1998, 2001, 2003, 2004). Location is depicted as one of these advantages, alongside ownership advantages and internalization. The so-called "L" in Dunning's OLI framework is particularly relevant for this chapter and refers to the extent to which firms choose to locate value-adding activities outside their national boundaries. Location-specific advantages could mean low cost of labor, but also access to customers, expert networks, or capital. These location-specific advantages are thus asset-based determinants for firms to establish on international markets. Dunning (1977, 1998) pointed to four different motives for FDI investments of multi-national enterprises(MNEs): resource seeking (e.g. resources are not available at home); market seeking (to exploit the possibilities granted of larger markets), efficiency seeking, and strategic asset seeking (e.g. access to new technology). The eclectic paradigm framework does not provide any explicit answer as to whether MNEs are becoming more or less dependent on foreign offline presence as a consequence of increased digitalization, but shows the increase of relational assets and networks in the knowledge-driven economy in order to build and sustain competitiveness (Dunning 2001, 2003). Today's large OSPs such as Facebook, Google, and Truecaller are relatively new-born knowledge-intensive service firms. Most of them are also much smaller in terms of employees, albeit not necessarily smaller in terms of geographic customer spread, and tend to keep offline presence to a restricted level in knowledge-intensive global cities on international markets. Therefore the strategic seeking asset argument as a motive for international offline presence appears the strongest one.

A contingency of such a development, that is less market-seeking than strategic asset-driven internationalization, will inevitably lead to a strong concentration of FDIs to knowledge-intensive global cities, which in turn will reinforce a cementation of a hierarchical structure in an Internet-dependent economy (Gorman 2002; Wentrup et al. 2016; Graham et al. 2015).

2.2 Offline Presence as Means to Shorten Psychic Distance on International Markets

Johanson and Vahlne's Uppsala Model (UM) from 1977 suggests that the motives for offline presence depend on the need to lower the geographical and psychic distance to a specific market. Offline presence should be seen as a contingency of incremental commitment to an international market and the unwillingness of the firm to remain an outsider on the international market. The UM accentuates the increasing learning and commitment of the firm in the internationalization process. Firms choose locations, which are either geographically and/or, socio-culturally close to their home markets where they learn and develop networks (Johanson and Vahlne 1977, 1990, 2003, 2006 2009; Vahlne and Johanson 2013). The UM stresses the need for the firm to reduce psychic distance, that is the linguistic and socio-cultural barriers, in order to reduce the liability of foreignness (Håkanson and Ambos 2010; Ojala 2015; Schu et al. 2016). As an effect firms tend to choose markets where both geographical and psychic distance are low (Johanson and Vahlne 1977; Andersson 2004, 2011). In the eyes of an OSP observer, UM's empirical base is biased towards large Swedish manufacturing MNEs, which grew internationally during the late twentieth century. The UM was also criticized in the early 1990s as it could not fully explain why some firms, often small and medium-sized enterprises, turned out to be "born global" firms (McKinsey 1993; Moen 2002; Andersson 2004; Oviatt and McDougall 2005), hence having a global focus from the outset. Born global firms often enter far-distant markets early in their internationalization in an ad hoc manner, using networks, joint ventures, and other forms of partnerships, which thus contradicts the UM. Together with the network approach (Tikkanen 1998; Moen et al. 2004), the international new ventures theory (INV) (Madsen and Servais 1997; McDougall 1989; Oviatt and McDougall 1994, 2005; Jones and Coviello 2005, Gabrielsson and Gabrielsson 2011) and the born globals discourse, a new wave of IB theory emerged, suggesting that firms can move more freely across geographical borders and that the key determinant for offline presence is not necessarily geographic distance but the access and mobility of entrepreneurs' networks.

In the later versions of the UM model, the construction and coordination of local networks are progressively accentuated as a way to reduce and bridge both psychic and geographical distance and lower the liability of outsidership (Vahlne and Johanson 2013). Johanson and Vahlne (2009) and Vahlne and Johanson (2013) consider that outsidership refers more to relation and network specificity than to country specificity. The network approach to internationalization has been developed in order to explain how companies use business networks to internationalize (Coviello and Munro 1995; Chen and Chen 1998; Tikkanen 1998; Moen et al. 2004). Networks have been especially important for the internationalization of service firms to allow them to combine the competitive advantages of the home market and the host market (Rusten and Bryson 2010; Ström and Schweizer 2011). This network perspective is also central to Internet-dependent firms, but from another angle. Yamin and Sinkovics (2006) argue that firms relying too much on online networks are not fully engaged in learning about the foreign market, and are prone to fall into the "virtuality trap" as a negative outcome of not investing in foreign market knowledge enough to become locally embedded. In a similar vein, Wentrup (2016) posits that by managing the "online–offline balance," that is by making a balanced commitment to both offline and online space, this virtuality trap can be overridden. Wentrup (2016) points to the relative dependence on offline resources in the business models for OSPs. For example, it is highlighted that business-to-business (B2B) oriented OSPs are generally more regional and place-dependent than business-to-consumer (B2C) oriented OSPs.

Nevertheless, the limitations of the network-based IB theory in light of the internationalization of OSPs are twofold. First, it accentuates the long and slow process of network building in order to create trust and commitment (Sasi and Arenius 2008). This stands in contrast to the rapid internationalization of OSPs, in which a market entry can be made swiftly into the online space without any pre-constructed networks. Second, it overemphasizes offline as opposed to online networks in the early phase of internationalization. The Internet can enable speed via peer-to-peer (P2P) technology platforms in online network building by connecting consumers to each other (Puschman and Are 2016). To our knowledge, this has not yet been put forward as a mechanism for internationalization.

Viral marketing, e-wom, has recently gained attention among marketing academics (Ho and Dempsey 2010; Lindgreen et al. 2013) but such P2P technologies with transcendent spatial capacity have not been directly analyzed from the internationalization perspective. The Internet's network mechanisms such as online communities are able to shorten spatial distances for both users and firms and can enable firms to disassemble the value transformation chain, giving them flexibility in resource allocation decisions and thus geographical spread (Ball et al. 2008). Studies have shown that technology-intensive service firms have greater geographical flexibility than labor-intensive service firms because of the possibility of separating back office and delivery (Erramilli 1990; Philippe and Léo 2011). According to Grabher et al. (2008), codevelopment creates new modes of online copresence, and the Internet plays a fundamental role as a knowledge-producing platform.

2.3 Insufficient Theoretical Explanations for OSPs' Spatial Internationalization Paths

We argue that these mechanisms need to be integrated into the IB literature given their growing importance for firms. The literature is less clear on the question whether Internet-based phenomena such as viral marketing, online networks, and online codevelopment mean that OSPs are not bound to the same geographical trajectories and spatial configurations as manufacturing firms. It should be mentioned that neither the born globals discourse, the UM, nor the eclectic paradigm has used OSPs as its empirical base. We find that economic geography highlights the concentration of the Internet sector into a few cities in the global North where there is an abundance of knowledge and capital intensive industries, but tells us little about the OSPs' international offline networks (Alvstam et al. 2016.). Dunning's eclectic paradigm that can outline motives is still relevant, but pays little attention to geographically transcending Internet technology. The UM and its gradual discourse falls short of explaining how OSPs have been able to reach 100 million users across the globe within a few years. The born globals theory and INV, on the other hand, can to a certain extent explain rapid growth and the ad hoc geographic pattern, but in terms of mode of entry these discourses do not yet consider technology-constructed modes of entry and how these potentially affect the need for offline presence. The motives that pure Internet-dependent firms have for establishing in the offline space remains unanswered in the literature.

3 Method

3.1 Data Selection and Data Collection

An important element for ensuring coherence in this chapter was the selection process of the case study company that could be representative for a digital business model. It has proved to be a fruitful way of combining economic geography and more management-oriented studies (Clark 1998; Bathelt and Gertler 2005) and makes it possible to describe phenomena more richly in a spatial and temporal context (Yin 2009). As underlined by Eisenhardt (1989), the selection of an appropriate population controls extraneous variation and helps to define the limits for generalizing the findings. We chose to study Truecaller for three main reasons. First, the firm fits the definition of an OSP well. It provides an online service only accessible over the Internet. Second, Truecaller's internationalization process seemed complex to us in terms of its rapid online international expansion, but also in terms of its geographical pattern. In general, Swedish firms are near-market oriented (Norway and Germany are Sweden's largest export markets), but in Truecaller's case India is the largest market, followed by many markets in the Middle East. This research mystery (Alvesson and Kärreman 2007) inspired us to look into the particulars of the Truecaller case. Additionally, Truecaller's staff were basically all concentrated in Stockholm in Sweden, and hence there was little international offline presence to balance its strong online presence. The third reason was accessibility to the firm; one of the authors of the chapter had pre-knowledge of Truecaller in the capacity of a former employee at Business Sweden—the Swedish Trade and Invest Council. This gave us access to a unique dataset—a database with comments and logs from the meetings between Truecaller and Business Sweden (2009–2017), which brought useful insights into the internationalization process.

We have used four main data sources (see Table 7.1). Both formal and informal interviews were held with the Truecaller staff, and mainly with the two cofounders, Nami Zarringhalam and Alan Mamedi. In total, 13 formal and informal interviews were undertaken. We used a semi-structured interview form in which we noted all questions beforehand, but let the interviewees express themselves freely and expand on the questions without any interruption. This method was used in earlier studies of internationalization by Crick and Jones (2000) and Andersson (2011). The interviews (60–90 minutes long) were recorded and transcribed. For validity purposes, the analysis and results of the interviews were sent to and subsequently approved by the interviewees. As mentioned above, data logs of Truecaller's activities with Business Sweden between 2009 and 2017 were collected and analyzed. Furthermore, we collected internal data from Truecaller regarding their international user base, and we analyzed more than 60 media articles written between 2009 and 2017.

Table 7.1 Data sources for the case study

Data source for the case study	Description	Time period
Formal interviews with the founders and executive managers from the case company	Nami Zarringhalam, CEO and cofounder (2); Priyam Bose, Director & Head Global Developer Relations; Ted Nelson, Chief Commercial Officer at Truecaller; Kari Krishnamurthy, VP of Brand & PR Strategy; Deepak Juin, a "Truecaller ambassador" in India	2010–2017
Informal interviews	Nami Zarringhalam, CEO and cofounder (2); Alan Mamedi (2), CEO and cofounder and, Tomas Bennich, business advisor to Truecaller	During Le Web (international Internet forum in Paris) December 2011, December 2012, December 2013
Publications and press articles about the case companies	Mainly Swedish industrial press accessible online during 2012–2017, approximately 60 articles	2012–2017
Databases	Business Sweden's database containing more than 50 logs and longer comments about meetings with Truecaller	2009–2017

3.2 Limitations of the Case Study

Aligned with best practice in qualitative research (Yin 2009; Eisenhardt 1989; Tracy 2012; Alvesson and Kärreman 2011), we want to give the reader a transparent view of the empirical material. We acknowledge the limited sample size of a single case study. It can be debated whether such a single case study is generalizable—and critics often point to its inherent inability to meet standard scientific criteria for research (Mariotto et al. 2014). We argue that it is an example of force that could have transferability (Flyvbjerg 2011) and thus could add to the knowledge base of internationalization and localization motives for Internet-dependent firms.

This research has been conducted on a firm undergoing rapid technological development. The firm has grown alongside the rapid growth of global Internet users, from 1 billion in 2005 to more than 3.5 billion in 2017 (ITU 2017). It is challenging to develop theory for "moving targets" like this, but with the longitudinal approach of this case study we are able to capture the firm's international trajectory over a sufficiently long period of time to draw theoretical conclusions from it.

4 Case: Truecaller

4.1 Global Online Ambition, but Offline Urban Concentration

Truecaller (registered as True Software AB) was founded in 2009 by the Stockholm-based engineers Alan Mamedi and Nami Zarringhalam. The Truecaller founders had a global ambition from the company's inception, which is aligned with the born globals discourse (Madsen and Servais 1997; Andersson 2011). They were determined to create an international company. This entrepreneurial born global attitude is supported by studies about the managers' ambition in cases of internationalizing Internet firms (Gabrielsson and Gabrielsson 2011; Arenius et al. 2006; Shneor 2012; Wentrup 2016). Users share their phone contacts in their mobile phones via a common platform. The business model is based on advertisement fees and a freemium model; that is, people can use the basic service for nothing and have the option to pay for more advanced services. As of December 2017 the app has more than 100 million users and 3 billion numbers in its database, which manifests the magnitude of network effects (Rochet and Tirole 2003; Puschman and Are 2016) via e-vom and viral marketing (Ho and Dempsey 2010; Lindgreen et al. 2013). Truecaller has approximately 85 employees and a modest turnover. Internally, Truecaller is an international microcosm with employees from 45 different nationalities, which confirms their international ambition. Half of the employees do not speak Swedish, and English is the corporate language. The philosophy of the company is to attract top international students to Sweden without requiring that they speak Swedish. This strategy also helps when working with international users. According to the founders, their multi-cultural and multi-lingual staff serves to decrease "foreignness," which is aligned with the UM argument about lowering psychic distance when approaching new markets (Johanson and Vahlne 2009). The mix of top students with an international background would have been harder to achieve in smaller peripheral cities in Sweden, according to Truecaller, which further motivates their choice to establish their offline presence in a large city.

Truecaller's headquarters are located in Stockholm's city centre, and most of the staff work in this office. As shown in the literature review, both the online and the offline concentration on certain geographic places are typical characteristics in the Internet sector. Knowledge-intensive Internet firms seek locations where their brand name will have strong signaling effects, and where they can find competent labor, financial resources, and capitalize on knowledge spillover effects, and thus take advantage of these externalities through their offline location (Gertler 2003; Bryson et al. 2013; Zook 2002a; Graham et al. 2015). Studies in economic geography clearly indicate the role of agglomeration in knowledge-intensive business services (Zook 2002b; Bryson et al. 2013; Beyers 2012; Rusten and Bryson 2010; Cuadrado-Roura 2013). Connections to global networks are also vital through travel or information technology (IT) (Faulconbridge 2008). Stockholm is primarily advantageous as a location for attracting financial capital, according to Truecaller. Truecaller has also decided to remain and develop the office in Stockholm, and has not chosen to establish any additional offices elsewhere in Sweden. The argument about concentrating in one offline location in a large city has been put forward in previous studies concerning Stockholm's dominance as the geographical Internet pole in the Swedish online sector ecosystem (Jansson 2008, 2011; Skog et al. 2016). The case of Truecaller therefore brings additional evidence to propositions about stark agglomeration effects in the Internet sector.

In retrospect, the springboard for Truecaller's internationalization is a bit paradoxical. The founders were determined to reach a global online spread, but at the same time they wanted to concentrate their offline presence on a delimited geographical area in order to capitalize on a multi-cultural labor pool and access to capital. The offline presence did not seem to be at the top of the agenda for the founders in the initial phase.

4.2 Data Model-Based Market Prioritization and Online Collaboration as International Mode of Entry

Truecaller developed their own data model for prioritizing international markets. In short, the data model is based on data such as population, mobile penetration, mobile numbers per capita, existing phone directory, and gross domestic product. With the help of the model, Truecaller can calculate the expected number of new users and turnover for a given numbers of hours invested in online marketing activities, which in turn determines how their marketing resources should be allocated. Initially, Truecaller imported available national phone directories into its system, but the amount of data was not sufficient and its quality was low. Consequently, they developed a collaborative model, in which the users upload content into the application, referred to as crowdsourcing. This became a critical shift in their business model and also came to trigger the network effects that are typical for successful platforms (Rochet and Tirole 2003; Puschman and Are 2016). The agreement with the user is that if the user shares their phone book they obtain access to a global phone book. This collaborative behavior is in line with Boulaire and Cova (2013) and Grabher et al.'s (2008) idea of community-driven development. Truecaller works closely with its local "ambassadors" in the international markets to ensure the spread of awareness of the service. With regard to the literature of liability of foreignness (Johanson and Vahlne 2009; Vahlne and Johanson 2013), the ambassadors can be seen as a means to lower the distance both in the online and the offline sphere. In this way Truecaller is bridging a potential green-field offline presence, with Truecaller ambassadors as proxies to international markets. The ambassadors work in both offline and online spaces, serving as the eyes and ears in the local market and reporting on news and events related to Truecaller's business. Often they are students with a special interest in online services who often see their collaboration with Truecaller as something valuable on their CV and a way to obtain professional experience. They also participate in offline marketing events wearing the "Truecaller hoodie," a sweatshirt with the Truecaller logo. This offline marketing material becomes the first step towards an offline presence. From an internationalization perspective, the ambassadors can be seen as local networks lowering the liability of foreignness as a way to penetrate international markets, and they are thus partly supported by the UM (Johanson and Vahlne 2009; Vahlne and Johanson 2013). The ambassadors differ from how traditional business partners, or distributors, are normally understood in the IB literature for two main reasons: they mainly operate in the online sphere and they are not economically compensated. Yet they serve as their eyes on the market and as anchoring points in both the online and offline geography, and are the absorbers of local knowledge and vehicles for local market commitment.

We can summarize by positing that there are coinciding events that provoke a set of hybrid motives for Truecaller's offline presence: the growing online network; the collaboration with the local ambassadors; and entanglement of strategic partnerships with Google's local partners in India. These combined events push Truecaller to engage in the offline space in order to shorten geographic and psychic distance to the market. Yet the engagement arises late in the internationalization process, and with a certain resistance. The default attitude of the founders is "online first." Commitment to the offline location and geography seem to remain a secondary priority until the point when the online–offline asymmetry appears too disturbing. We thus find a constant asymmetry between the leading online presence and the lagging offline presence.

5 Analysis

5.1 Computer Screen Internationalization, but the Offline Catches Up

We have depicted some distinct phases in Truecaller's spatial internationalization path: the data model-based market prioritization, followed by online market entry and viral growth via P2P technology marketing mechanism and the online collaboration with the local ambassadors. This leads to an online–offline asymmetry, which eventually triggers a need for offline presence. The motives are grounded in both market-seeking and strategic asset-seeking. As a complement to Yamin and Sinkovic's (2006) virtuality trap and Wentrup's (2016) online–offline balance, the online–offline asymmetry is a useful theoretical concept to explain why Internet-dependent firms are motivated to enter the offline space. We consider the online–offline asymmetry as a typical state for B2C-oriented OSPs. In Truecaller's case it handles 100 million users from five offline offices, and this scenario would be unsuitable in sectors such as manufacturing or retail because of the burden of complex supply chains.

Truecaller's internationalization process is steered by the evolution of its online growth, which in turn is nurtured by the growth of online communities and codevelopment with the online users. If the virality yields a growth in Truecaller's online user base, this serves as an indication of market prioritization for the managers. The managers have an "online first" attitude in the internationalization process. We therefore call their internationalization behavior "computer screen internationalization" and it is characterized by emphasizing a data model for market prioritization (as opposed to professional networks), a dependence on online marketing mechanisms (e.g. e-vom and online communities), and a weak commitment to the offline presence. If an online market reaches sufficient traction, the managers decide to commit more online marketing resources and to assign an online and local ambassador to strengthen the online community. The whole process and the commitment-building are managed in the online space from the headquarters, rather than offline in the geographical market. In Truecaller's case their "ambassadors" and their user community constitute the market network. The difference with regard to the network-oriented UM discourse (Johanson and Vahlne 1977; Tikkanen 1998; Moen et al. 2004) is that the creation of the online networks is swift and less time-consuming than network theory claims it to be. Moreover, the online networks have a low formal level and are often initiated by the users.

Our findings partly support Boulaire and Cova's (2013) theory about the increasing importance of consumer communities. The online community as a form of mode of entry has theoretical support in Grabher's et al. (2008) and Rusten and Bryson's (2010) propositions that hybrid or online communities with knowledgeable users have a direct impact on firms' internationalization patterns, as well as in Ström and Ernkvist's (2012, 2018) theory of codevelopment as a facilitator in the internationalization process. Users and loosely formalized partner networks contribute to rapid internationalization and thus blend into the firm's international business operations. Truecaller's crowdsourcing element in the internationalization process is an example of the theory that consumption shifts from an individual to a collective action, as proposed by Grabher et al. (2008).

The internationalization process for Truecaller contradicts the UM model and the born globals discourse, which stress an incremental internationalization process and the use of existing networks of the entrepreneur when selecting a market. The Truecaller founders had no intention, no network, nor any relations to India beforehand—some markets "just happened" to fit their online service (Shneor 2012). Whereas the born globals and INV literature stress the importance of the entrepreneur's existing international network, Truecaller was not dependent on pre-built international networks at the beginning of its internationalization process. The networks were created in an ad hoc way—for example from incoming requests from existing users via the online medium. Consequently, the importance of being an insider in the relevant entrepreneurial networks, as suggested by Vahlne and Johanson (2013), seems to be limited in the internationalization process for OSPs, at least in the initial stage. Instead the case firm is heavily dependent on fast-growing online networks for steering the internationalization process. In a computer screen style of internationalization, local ambassadors could serve as proxies to compensate for the lack of insidership on the local market.

5.2 Hybrid Set of Motives for Offline Presence to Limit the Online- Offline Asymmetry

As mentioned above, the offline presence is considered late, if at all, in the internationalization process, and remains moderate. In the first years, Truecaller tried to limit the geographical and psychic distance by focusing on recruiting people with diversified international backgrounds, and by collaborating online with both the users and the ambassadors. In parallel, the online community grew fast and the company engaged in strategic partnerships with Internet key players in both India and the USA. These elements make the geographical online–offline asymmetry disturbing. Consequently, the need for offline presence becomes too important to ignore, which forces a commitment to it.

Strategic asset-seeking remains the most important motive for an offline presence for Truecaller. Our findings support Dunning's reasoning regarding the increasing importance of the strategic asset-seeking argument as a central element in the internationalization process, and not least for the localization of the firm. The example of how Truecaller's offline location decision was affected by Google's offline presence in both the USA and in India is an example of this. Instead of the "following the customer" argument for internationalization, Truecaller wants to shorten the psychic and geographical distance to its strategic partners. The prioritization of the strategic asset-seeking argument over the market-seeking argument leads to a hesitant and ephemeral internationalization process with a low commitment level to offline presence. The offline presence is tried, but abandoned swiftly, if the online growth does not take off, as manifested in Truecaller's offline attempts in Brazil, China, and the United Arab Emirates. These fast market entries and exits are well aligned with our understanding of computer screen internationalization. We are inclined to support Shneor's (2012) claim that there is no real predetermined geography orientation at the outset, and that instead the online uptake steers the internationalization process. The reiterating mindset of Truecaller is that the online space should always precede the offline. The internationalization is monitored in real time, and managed from the headquarters' computer screens. From a geographical perspective, it becomes clear that the internationalization process differs from the

UM model in various aspects. Initially, geographical and psychic distances do not seem to be particularly relevant when making a service available online. The lack of pre-determination in the geographical prioritization in combination with computer screen internationalization leads to frequent changes and a certain short-sightedness in the commitment building process. As a consequence Truecaller relies on few offline offices in its internationalization process, despite achieving wide geographical coverage of online users.

Overall, though, the offline presence does not seem to be a priority for Truecaller. The firm is convinced that it can manage without for a long time in new markets. At the same time Truecaller is aware that the offline presence signals a significantly strong dependence on specific dynamics existing in a set of limited locations. These locations create anchoring points for business development and are thus bridging the contextual specificities that are connected to centers for technological and business model development, skilled labor, finance and the distribution of existing users.

The internationalization for Truecaller primarily takes place in online space and there is a considerable time lag between online and offline presence. As illustrated in our internationalization flow model (Fig. 7.1), the firm is enmeshed in both the online and the offline realms. The existence

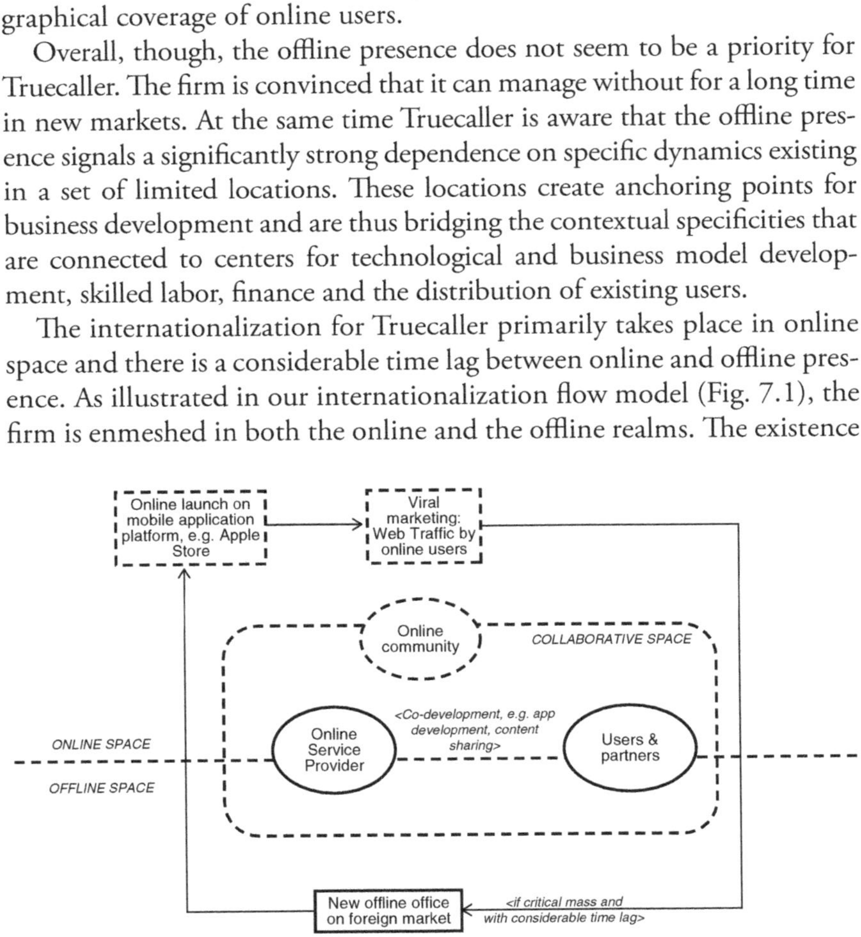

Fig. 7.1 Online internationalization flow model—a hybrid spatial internationalization pattern. (Authors' model)

of an online realm has support from Zott et al.'s (2000) theory of the online markets and from Yamin and Sinkovics (2006). Our arguments add a new spatial dimension to the UM and born globals theories in that they are primarily based on the idea of an offline space with brick and mortar offices and not online spaces.

6 Conclusions and Implications

6.1 Theoretical Implications

With more than 100 million users worldwide, Truecaller is an intriguing example of a digital business model with international scalability potential. Truecaller only has four international offices in addition to its Stockholm headquarters. These are all located in knowledge-intensive global cities close to the "buzz." It is not mainly the market-seeking but the strategic asset-seeking argument that is the primary motive for Truecaller's offline presence. Geographical proximity to online market titans such as Google and Facebook are clear motives for offline presence for Truecaller in San Francisco and Delhi. As shown, the relevance of the offline catches up as the number of online users grows. OSPs such as Truecaller do not seem to need international offices during their first years of operation, nor until they reach a certain critical mass of users. However, as the online community grows large and becomes more local, the stronger the case for offline presence: the online–offline asymmetry finally triggers the offline presence.

A couple of theoretical implications deserve careful attention. First, the shift from offline to the online space is obvious. Today, the online world has become a permanent and important feature for business operations and in contemporary society (Graham 2009). The need to include the online spatial dimension into theory building about internationalization is crucial. The online–offline asymmetry concept helps us to advance the theory that and understand how the offline and the online move differently in time and space, but show that they still remain connected. The theoretical understanding of context shows that even "footloose" activities are in need of anchoring points and spatial presence at some point.

Without the capacity to facilitate this development, sustained economic growth seems to be highly questionable. Understanding of context (Gertler 2003; Storper and Venables 2004) thus depends on the interaction between online and offline presence in order to compensate for outsidership and instead create relational capacity through loosely defined networks (Dunning 2001, 2003). Second, codevelopment and viral marketing within virtual communities stimulate a convergence between producer and user that also impacts the spatial configuration of the operations and the spatial dynamics or the firm's development process (Ernkvist and Ström 2018). This signifies the emergence of a collaborative approach to internationalization, where the OSP may reach out to users in order to facilitate the internationalization process.

6.2 Determinants for International Scalability for Digital Business Models

Based on the literature review and the case study we propose a few determinants that we think are critical in order to increase the chances for international scalability for digital businesses:

B2C-oriented Business Model If we look at the most successful firms in the digital business they have B2C-driven business models: Google, Facebook, Apple, Amazon, Dropbox, Twitter, and Spotify are all examples. Some of these are so-called double-sided platforms, which generate revenues from other firms through advertisement, for example Google and Facebook. Nevertheless, the business models are consumer driven, so they need many users in order to attract advertisers. The digital business models with a B2B character are generally more glued into the offline geography and therefore more difficult to scale.

User Engagement: Collaborative Approach The Truecaller case is a typical example of codevelopment and entanglement of users into a business model in the online space. Truecaller users share information and content across borders. The users themselves, or the content they provide, tend to become the actual product or commodity in the business model. The more engaged and embedded the users are, the more difficult it is for them to leave the application. There are many examples of how user engagement-driven digital businesses have scaled internationally, and Truecaller is one of them.

Local Offline Dependence The more offline-dependent the digital service is to local adaptations the more difficult it is to rapidly scale internationally. When studying Swedish OSPs, Wentrup (2016) found that case firms such as Klarna and iZettle were to a large degree dependent on local legal compliance in order to launch their services. This compliance criterion slowed down the process and made internationalization more complicated. In Truecaller's case there are not many local compliance regulations to adapt to, which makes international scalability easier.

Human Resource Intensiveness In general, we argue that the less human resource-dependent the business model is, the easier it is to scale internationally. Recruitment is a slow and complicated process. Even for typical emblematic digital businesses in the sharing economy, such as Uber, it has been proved that once there is a dependence on human resources it takes time to adapt to new regulations on new markets. At the same time, in order for digital businesses to become attractive for local markets, offline and online adaptions is needed, and only staff with local knowledge and networks are capable of making such adjustments and ensuring that the firm becomes an insider in the new market, both in the online and the offline space.

Time-to-market The last determinant we want to highlight is the time-to-market factor, and this is a consequence of the previous two. It is logical that the more dependent the business model is on offline local context compliance and human resource intensiveness, the longer it will take to enter a new market. This does not necessarily mean that international scalability is hindered, but there is a risk that it will take a longer time and hence become more cumbersome and costly. In the case of Truecaller we have seen that the online time to market was rather quick, but that the company progressively made adaptions to the local context and also assessed the online–offline asymmetry as being too disturbing just to rely on an online presence.

6.3 Managerial Implications

With the concept of "computer screen internationalization" we imply there is a business risk in relying too much on an online strategy and on loose informal networks for entering a foreign market. This risk is also accentuated with the "virtuality trap" (Yamin and Sinkovics 2006). In Truecaller's case it seems that there is almost too much trust in the online. The downside of such an approach could be that local markets are not fully understood and engaged. Tacit knowledge, which is often critical in knowledge-intensive business, might not be captured. Without an offline presence there is also a risk that online marketing and low-control modes of entry could easily take a negative turn and create a bad company reputation. This would imply that the location is becoming more important for the firm as the internationalization process continues. IT can strengthen the managerial commitment to the location and to a certain extent reduce outsidership or lack of network presence. Yet from a managerial perspective it would facilitate more learning of the market dynamics, which is difficult to obtain only through online market presence.

The internationalization process for OSPs requires managers to be proactive and innovative in order to compete in the international arena. The online market sees market leaders come and go quickly. An example of this phenomenon is the rise and fall of several web browser firms over the past decade (The Economist 2013). The challenges is therefore to find "stickiness" in the online service or, in other words, to retain web traffic and users (Zott et al. 2000) and create sustainable brand loyalty. A way to increase this loyalty and to avoid the online trap is to adapt the online service to the local cultural setting systematically and to invest in local online communities. An offline presence could be a transcendent element in this process, and is needed to sustain a market position. Ideally, it should be considered early in the process, also in the digital businesses.

6.4 Concluding Remarks

This chapter shows that the offline space matters even for the most digital of firms. Companies with B2C-oriented business models, with low local market adaptation needs and low human resource intensiveness, have the chance to scale internationally rather fast in the online space, but the online–

offline asymmetry cannot be neglected. The firm needs to make investments in the offline space in order to sustain competitiveness. As seen in the Truecaller case, the offline space catches up with the online space, and over time the firm increases its entanglement in the local market's offline space.

For mangers it is important not to rely too much on "computer screen internationalization." Early online traction could be a good indicator for market potential, but the firm needs to develop a strategy enabling early commitment to local markets in both the online and offline space by engaging with local users, and by making sure the staff understand and adapt to the international markets' prerequisites.

Acknowledgements The authors want to express gratitude to the interviewed cofounders and managers of Truecaller for sharing their experiences regarding internationalization.

Appendix

Table 7.2 Truecaller's top markets per active users

Country	Top countries (Active users) 2013	Country	Top countries (Active users) 2017
India	48.31%	India	66,20%
Lebanon	11.78%	Egypt	9,10%
United States	5.73%	Nigeria	2,40%
Jordan	4.66%	Kenya	2,30%
Egypt	3.96%	Jordan	1,90%
Sweden	3.87%	Israel	1,60%
Kuwait	3.49%	South Africa	1,30%
Saudi Arabia	3.21%	Iraq	1,20%
United Kingdom	0.88%	USA	1,10%
Nigeria	0.84%	Morocco	1,00%
Iraq	0.83%	Lebanon	0,90%
United Arab Emirates	0.66%	Pakistan	0,90%
Germany	0.63%	Ghana	0,80%
Syria	0.56%	Turkey	0,50%
Oman	0.47%	Sweden	0,50%
Israel	0.41%	Tunisia	0,50%
South Africa	0.40%	Saudi Arabia	0,40%
Canada	0.39%	UK	0,40%
Russia	0.39%	Italy	0,40%
Denmark	0.38%	Bangladesh	0,40%
		Other markets	6,10%

References

Alcácer, Juan, John Cantwell, and Lucia Piscitello. 2016. Internationalization in the Information Age: A New Era for Places, Firms, and International Business Networks? *Journal of International Business Studies* 47 (5): 499–512.

Alvesson, Mats, and Dan Kärreman. 2007. Mystery Empirical Constructing Matters in Theory Development. *Academy of Management Review* 32 (4): 1265–1281.

———. 2011. *Qualitative Research and Theory Development*. London: Sage.

Alvstam, C.-G., Patrik Ström, and R. Robert Wentrup. 2016. Heterogeneous Economic Space in a Global Archipelago: An Economic Geography Perspective of Emerging Markets. In *Handbook of Research on Emerging Markets*, ed. Hermant Merchant. Cheltenham: Edward Elgar Publishers.

Andersson, Svante. 2004. Internationalization in Different Industrial Contexts. *Journal of Business Venturing* 19 (6): 851–875.

———. 2011. International Entrepreneurship, Born Globals and the Theory of Effectuation. *Journal of Small Business and Enterprise. Development* 18 (3): 627–643.

Arenius, Pia, Viveca Sasi, and Mika Gabrielsson. 2005. Rapid Internationalisation Enabled by the Internet: The Case of a Knowledge Intensive Company. *Journal of International Entrepreneurship* 3 (4): 279–290.

Arenius, Sasi V., and M. Gabrielsson. 2006. Rapid Internationalisation Enabled by the Internet: The, Case of a Knowledge Intensive Company. *Journal of International Entrepreneurship* 3: 279–290.

Axinn, Catherine N., and Paul Matthyssens. 2002. Limits of Internationalization Theories in an Unlimited World. *International Marketing Review* 19 (5): 436–449.

Ball, David A., Valerie J. Lindsay, and Elizabeth L. Rose. 2008. Rethinking the Paradigm of Service Internationalisation: Less Resource-Intensive Market Entry Modes for Information-Intensive Soft Services. *Management International Review* 48 (4): 413–431.

Bathelt, H., and Meric S. Gertler. 2005. The German Variety of Capitalism: Forces and Dynamics of Evolutionary Change. *Economic Geography* 81 (1): 1–9.

Beyers, William B. 2012. The Service Industry Research Imperative. *The Service Industries Journal* 32 (4): 657–682.

Boulaire, Christèle, and Bernard Cova. 2013. The Dynamics and Trajectory of Creative Consumption Practices as Revealed by the Postmodern Game of Geocaching. *Consumption Markets and Culture* 16 (1): 1–24.

Brouthers, Keith D., Kim Dung Geisser, and Franz Rothlauf. 2016. Explaining the Internationalization of Ibusiness Firms. *Journal of International Business Studies* 47 (5): 513–534.

Bryson, John R., Peter W. Daniels, and Barney Warf. 2013. *Service Worlds: People, Organisations and Technologies. Service Worlds: People, Organisations and Technologies*. London: Routledge.

Buckley, Peter J., and Pervez N. Ghauri. 2004. Globalisation, Economic Geography and the Strategy of Multinational Enterprises. *Journal of International Business Studies* 35 (2): 81–98.

Chen, Homin, and Tain-Jy Chen. 1998. Network Linkages and Foreign Location Direct Choice Investment. *Journal of International Business Studies* 29 (3): 445–467.

Clark, Gordon L. 1998. Stylized Facts and Close Dialogue: Methodology in Economic Geography. *Annals of the Association of American Geographers* 88 (1): 73–87.

Coviello, Nicole E., and Hugh J. Munro. 1995. Growing the Entrepreneurial Firm Networking for International Market Development. *European Journal of Marketing* 29 (7): 49–61.

Crick, Dave, and Marian V. Jones. 2000. Small High-Technology Firms and International High-Technology Markets. *Journal of International Marketing* 8 (2): 63–85.

Cuadrado-Roura, Juan R. 2013. *Service Industries and Regions, Growth, Location and Regional Effects*. Berlin: Springer.

Dunning, John H. 1977. Trade, Location of Economic Activity and the Multinational Enterprise: A Search for an Eclectic Approach. In *The International Allocation of Economic Activity*, ed. B. Ohlin, P.O. Hesselborn, and P.M. Nijkman, 395–418. London: Macmillan.

———. 1998. Location Enterprise : The Multinational Neglected. *Journal of International Business Studies* 40 (1): 45–66.

———. 2001. The Eclectic (OLI) Paradigm of International Production: Past, Present and Future. *International Journal of the Economics of Business* 8 (2): 173–190. https://doi.org/10.1080/13571510110051441.

———. 2003. Relational Assets, Networks and International Business Activity. In *Alliance Capitalism and Corporate Management: Entrepreneurial Cooperation in Knowledge Based Economies*, ed. J.H. Dunning and G. Boyd, 1–23. Singapore: John Wiley & Sons.

———. 2004. An Evolving Paradigm of the Economic Determinants of International Business Activity. In *Managing Multinationals in a Knowledge*

Economy: Economics, Culture, and Human Resources, 3–27. Amsterdam: Elsevier.

Eisenhardt, K.M. 1989. Building Theories from Case Study Research. *Academy of Management Review* 14 (4): 532–550.

Ernkvist, Mirko and Patrik Ström. 2018. Differentiation in Digital Creative Industry Cluster Dynamics: The Growth and Decline of the JAPANESE Video Game Software Industry. *Geografiska Annaler: Series B, Human Geography* 100 (3): 263–286. https://doi.org/10.1080/04353684.2017.1423506.

Erramilli, M. Krishna. 1990. Entry Mode Choice in Service Industries. *International Marketing Review* 7 (5): 50–62.

Facebook. 2018. Facebook Newsroom. Available at: http://newsroom.fb.com/company-info. Accessed 7 Jan 2018.

Faulconbridge, James R. 2008. Negotiating Cultures of Work in Transnational Law Firms. *Journal of Economic Geography* 8 (4): 497–517.

Flyvbjerg, Bent. 2011. Case Study. In *The Sage Handbook of Qualitative Research*, 301–316. Thousand Oaks: Sage.

Forsgren, Mats, and Peter Hagström. 2007. Ignorant and Impatient Internationalization?: The Uppsala Model and Internationalization Patterns for Internet-Related Firms. *Critical Perspectives on International Business* 3 (4): 291–305.

Gabrielsson, Mika, and Peter Gabrielsson. 2011. Internet-Based Sales Channel Strategies of Born Global Firms. *International Business Review* 20 (1): 88–99.

Gertler, M.S. 2003. Tacit Knowledge and the Economic Geography of Context, or The Undefinable Tacitness of Being (There). *Journal of Economic Geography* 3 (1): 75–99.

Gorman, Sean P. 2002. Where Are the Web Factories: The Urban Bias of E-Business Location. *Tijdschrift Voor Economische En Sociale Geografie* 93 (5): 522–536.

Grabher, Gernot, Oliver Ibert, and Saskia Flohr. 2008. The Neglected King: The Customer in the New Knowledge Ecology of Innovation. *Economic Geography* 84 (3): 253–280.

Graham, Mark. 2010. Neogeography and the Palimpsests of Place: Web 2.0 and the Construction of a Virtual Earth. *Tijdschrift Voor Economische En Sociale Geografie* 101 (4): 422–436.

Graham, Mark, Stefano De Sabbata, and Matthew A. Zook. 2015. Towards a Study of Information Geographies: (Im)mutable Augmentations and a Mapping of the Geographies of Information. *Geo: Geography and Environment* 2 (1): 88–105.

Håkanson, Lars, and Björn Ambos. 2010. The Antecedents of Psychic Distance. *Journal of International Management* 16 (3): 195–210.

Ho, Jason Y.C., and Melanie Dempsey. 2010. Viral Marketing: Motivations to Forward Online Content. *Journal of Business Research* 63 (9–10): 1000–1006.

ITU. (International Telecommunication Union) 2017. Measuring the Information Society 2017. Geneva: ITU. Available at: https://www.itu.int/en/ITU-D/Statistics/Documents/publications/misr2017/MISR2017_Volume1.pdf. Accessed 22 Jan 2017.

Jansson, Johan. 2008. Inside the Internet Industry: The Importance of Proximity in Accessing Knowledge in the Agglomeration of Internet Firms in Stockholm. *European Planning Studies* 16 (2): 211–228.

———. 2011. Emerging (Internet) Industry and Agglomeration: Internet Entrepreneurs Coping with Uncertainty. *Entrepreneurship and Regional Development* 23 (7–8): 499–521.

Johanson, Jan, and Jan-Erik Vahlne. 1977. The Internationalization Process of the Firm—A Model of Knowledge Development and Increasing Foreign Market Commitments. *Journal of International Business Studies* 8 (1): 23–32.

———. 1990. The Mechanism of Internationalisation. *International Marketing Review* 7 (4): 2651339010137414.

———. 2003. Business Relationship Learning and Commitment in the Internationalization Process. *Journal of International Entrepreneurship* 1: 83–101.

———. 2006. Commitment and Opportunity Development in the Internationalization Process: A Note on the Uppsala Internationalization Process Model. *Management International Review* 46 (2): 165–178.

———. 2009. The Uppsala Internationalization Process Model Revisited: From Liability of Foreignness to Liability of Outsidership. *Journal of International Business Studies* 40 (9): 1411–1431.

Jones, Marian V., and Nicole E. Coviello. 2005. Internationalisation: Conceptualising an Entrepreneurial Process of Behaviour in Time. *Journal of International Business Studies* 36 (3): 284–303.

Kim, Daekwan. 2003. The Internationalization of US Internet Portals: Does It Fit the Process Model of Internationalization? *Marketing Intelligence & Planning* 21 (1): 23–36.

Kuivalainen, Olli, Sami Saarenketo, and Kaisu Puumalainen. 2012. Start-up Patterns of Internationalization: A Framework and Its Application in the Context of Knowledge-Intensive SMEs. *European Management Journal* 30 (4): 372–385.

Lindgreen, Adam, Angela Dobele, and Joëlle Vanhamme. 2013. Word-of-Mouth and Viral Marketing Referrals: What Do We Know? And What Should We Know? *European Journal of Marketing* 47 (7): 1.

Loane, Sharon. 2005. The Role of the Internet in the Internationalisation of Small and Medium Sized Companies. *Journal of International Entrepreneurship* 3 (4): 263–277.

Loane, Sharon, Rod B. McNaughton, and Jim Bell. 2004. The Internationalization of Internet-Enabled Entrepreneurial Firms: Evidence from Europe and North America. *Canadian Journal of Administrative Sciences* 21 (1): 79–96.

Madsen, Tage Koed, and Per Servais. 1997. The Internationalization of Born Globals: An Evolutionary Process? *International Business Review* 6 (6): 561–583.

Mariotto, Fabio Luiz, Pedro Pinto Zanni, and Gustavo Hermínio Salati Marcondes de Moraes. 2014. What Is the Use of a Single-Case Study in Management Research? *RAE- Revista de Administración de Empresas* 54 (4): 358–369.

McDougall, Patricia P. 1989. International Versus Domestic Entrepreneurship: New Venture Strategic Behavior and Industry Structure. *Journal of Business Venturing* 4 (6): 387–400.

McKinsey & Co. 1993. *Emerging Exporters. Australia's High Value-added Manufacturing Exporters.* Melbourne: McKinsey and Company and the Australian Manufacturing Council.

Moen, Øystein. 2002. The Born Globals. *International Marketing Review* 19 (2): 156–175.

Moen, Øystein, Morten Gavlen, and Iver Endresen. 2004. Internationalization of Small, Computer Software Firms: Entry Forms and Market Selection. *European Journal of Marketing* 38 (9/10): 1236–1251.

Nilsson, Patricia. 2017. London Start-ups Are Most Likely to Fail. *Financial Times*. Available at: https://www.ft.com/content/e3c745c4-88d8-11e7-afd2-74b8ecd34d3b. Accessed 3 Feb 2018.

Ojala, Arto. 2015. Geographic, Cultural, and Psychic Distance to Foreign Markets in the Context of Small and New Ventures. *International Business Review* 24 (5): 825–835.

Oviatt, Benjamin M., and Patricia P. McDougall. 1994. Toward a Theory of International New Ventures. *Journal of International Business Studies* 25 (1): 45–64.

———. 2005. Defining International Entrepreneurship and Modeling the Speed of Internationalization. *Entrepreneurship: Theory and Practice.* 29: 537.

Petersen, Bent, Lawrence S. Welch, and Peter W. Liesch. 2003. The Internet and Foreign Market Expansion by Firms. *IEEE Engineering Management Review* 31 (4): 81–88.

Pezderka, Noemi, and Rudolf R. Sinkovics. 2011. A Conceptualization of E-Risk Perceptions and Implications for Small Firm Active Online Internationalization. *International Business Review* 20 (4): 409–422.

Philippe, Jean, and Pierre Yves Léo. 2011. Influence of Entry Modes and Relationship Modes on Business Services Internationalisation. *Service Industries Journal* 31 (4): 643–656.

Pratt, Andy C. 2008. Creative Cities: The Cultural Industries and the Creative Class. *Geografiska Annaler, Series B: Human Geography* 90 (2): 107–117.

Puschmann, Thomas, and Rainer Alt. 2016. Sharing Economy. *Business & Information Systems Engineering* 58 (1): 93–99.

Rochet, Jean-Charles, and Jean Tirole. 2003. Platform Competition in Two Sided Markets. *The European Economic Journal …* 1 (4): 990–1029.

———. 2006. Two-Sided Markets: A Progress Report. *The RAND Journal of Economics* 37 (3): 645–667.

———. 2014. Platform Competition in Two-Sided Markets. *Competition Policy International* 1: 990. https://doi.org/10.1162/154247603322493212.

Rusten, Grete, and John R. Bryson. 2010. Placing and Spacing Services: Towards a Balanced Economic Geography of Firms, Clusters, Social Networks, Contracts and the Geographies of Enterprise. *Tijdschrift Voor Economische En Sociale Geografie* 101 (3): 248–261.

Samiee, Saeed. 1998. Exporting and the Internet: A Conceptual Perspective. *International Marketing Review* 15 (5): 413–426.

Sasi, Viveca, and Pia Arenius. 2008. International New Ventures and Social Networks: Advantage or Liability? *European Management Journal* 26 (6): 400–411.

Satta, Giovanni, Francesco Parola, and Luca Persico. 2014. Temporal and Spatial Constructs in Service Firms' Internationalization Patterns: The Determinants of the Accelerated Growth of Emerging MNEs. *Journal of International Management* 20 (4): 421–435.

Schu, Matthias, Dirk Morschett, and Bernhard Swoboda. 2016. Internationalization Speed of Online Retailers: A Resource-Based Perspective on the Influence Factors. *Management International Review* 56 (5): 733–757.

Shneor, Rotem. 2012. Born Global Firms, Internet and New Forms of Internationalization. In *Handbook of Research on Born Globals*, ed. M. Gabrielsson and V.H.M. Kirpalani, 61–184. Cheltenham: Edward Elgar.

Sinkovics, Noemi, Rudolf R. Sinkovics, and Ruey-Jer "Bryan" Jean. 2013. The Internet as an Alternative Path to Internationalization? *International Marketing Review* 30 (2): 130–55.

Skog, Albin, Mats Lewan, Michael Karlström, Sergey Morgulis-Yakushev, Yixin Lu and Robin Teigland. 2016. Chasing the Tale of the Unicorn – A Study of Sweden's Misty Meadows. Available at: https://www.hhs.se/contentassets/eba3ab2b0b1147fc942cf5f4fb902c14/chasing-the-tale-of-the-unicorn%2D%2D-a-study-of-stockholms-misty-meadows.pdf.

Storper, Michael. 2009. Regional Context and Global Trade. *Economic Geography* 85 (1): 1–22.

Storper, Michael, and Anthony J. Venables. 2004. Buzz: Face-to-Face Contact and the Urban Economy. *Journal of Economic Geography* 4 (4): 351–370.

Ström, Patrik, and Mirko Ernkvist. 2012. Internationalization of the Korean Online Game Industry: Exemplified Through the Case of NCsoft. *International Journal of Technology and Globalization* 6: 312–334.

Ström, Patrik, and Roger Schweizer. 2011. Space Oddity – On Managerial Decision-making and Space. In *Spaces of International Economy and Management, Launching New Perspectives on Management and Geography*, ed. R. Schlunze, N. Agola, and W. Baber, 304–321. New York: Palgrave.

Strom, Patrik, and Robert Wentrup. 2016. Internationalization as Innovation Driver in Services. In *Service Innovation*. Japan: Springer.

Taddeo, M., and L. Floridi. 2015. The Debate on the Moral Responsibilities of Online Service Providers. *Science and Engineering Ethics*. Available at: http://link.springer.com/article/10.1007/s11948-015-9734-1. Accessed 10 Aug 2018.

The Economist. 2013. Chrome Rules the Web. The Economist. Printed: 10 August 2013. Available at: http://www.economist.com/news/business/21583288-what-googles-browser-has-common-queen-victoria-chrome-rules-web.

Tiessen, James H., Richard W. Wright, and Ian Turner. 2001. A Model of E-Commerce Use by Internationalizing SMEs. *Journal of International Management* 7 (3): 211–233.

Tikkanen, Henrikki. 1998. The Network Approach in Analyzing International Marketing and Purchasing Operations: A Case Study of a European SME's Focal Net 1992–95. *Journal of Business & Industrial Marketing* 13 (2): 109–131.

Tracy, Sarah J. 2012. *Qualitative Research Methods. Collecting Evidence, Crafting Analysis, Communicating Impact*. Oxford: Wiley-Blackwell.

Trippl, Michaela, Franz Tödtling, and Lukas Lengauer. 2009. Knowledge Sourcing beyond Buzz and Pipelines: Evidence from the Vienna Software Sector. *Economic Geography* 85 (4): 443–462.

Vahlne, Jan-Erik, and Jan Johanson. 2013. The Uppsala Model on Evolution of the Multinational Business Enterprise – from Internalization to Coordination of Networks. *International Marketing Review* 30 (3): 189–210.

Warf, Barney. 2013. Global Geographies of the Internet: Global E-Commerce. In *SpringerBriefs in Geography. Vol. 1*. Dordrecht: Springer.

Wentrup, Robert. 2016. The Online–Offline Balance: Internationalization for Swedish Online Service Providers. *Journal of International Entrepreneurship* 14 (4): 562–594.

Wentrup, Robert, Patrik Ström, and H. Richard Nakamura. 2016. Digital Oases and Digital Deserts in Sub-Saharan Africa. *Journal of Science and Technology Policy Management* 7 (1): 77–100.

Yamin, Mohammad, and Rudolf R. Sinkovics. 2006. Online Internationalisation, Psychic Distance Reduction and the Virtuality Trap. *International Business Review* 15 (4): 339–360.

Yin, Robert K. 2009. Case Study Research: Design and Methods. In *Essential Guide to Qualitative Methods in Organizational Research. Vol. 5*. Beverly Hills: Sage Publications.

Yip, George S., and Anna M. Dempster. 2005. Using the Internet to Enhance Global Strategy. *European Management Journal* 23 (1): 1–13.

Zook, M.A. 2002a. Grounded Capital: Venture Financing and the Geography of the Internet Industry, 1994–2000. *Journal of Economic Geography* 2 (2): 151–177.

———. 2002b. Hubs, Nodes and by-Passed Places: A Typology of E-Commerce Regions in the United States. *Tijdschrift Voor Economische En Sociale Geografie* 93 (5): 509–521.

Zott, Christoph, Raphael Amit, and J.O.N. Donlevy. 2000. Strategies for Value Creation in E-Commerce : Best Practice in Europe. *European Management Journal* 18 (5): 463–475.

8

The Impact of the European General Data Protection Regulation (GDPR) on Future Data Business Models: Toward a New Paradigm and Business Opportunities

Sébastien Ziegler, Emilia Evequoz, and Ana Maria Pacheco Huamani

1 Introduction

The entry into force of the European General Data Protection Regulation (GDPR) has deeply impacted the legal framework for Digital Business Model (DBM) not only in Europe, but also for any company that interacts with the European market. Beyond the European framework evolution, public opinion and societal pressures are forcing companies to take more seriously the duty to respect the personal data of their users and customers. A good illustration of this evolution is the crisis faced by Facebook when the public discovered that a huge volume of personal data had been used

S. Ziegler (✉) • E. Evequoz
Mandat International, Geneva, Switzerland
e-mail: sziegler@mandint.org

A. M. P. Huamani
Archimede Solutions, Geneva, Switzerland

A. Aagaard (ed.), *Digital Business Models*,
https://doi.org/10.1007/978-3-319-96902-2_8

by Cambridge Analytica to perform the political profiling of electors. Facebook lost $35 billion in market capitalization in a very short period.[1]

In this chapter, we will highlight the main implications of the GDPR on present and future DBMs. We will also present some emerging approaches and solutions applied in the context of Synchronicity, the European large-scale pilot on the Internet of Things. Finally, we will leverage these examples to sketch and outline some trends and opportunities for future privacy by design DBMs.

2 GDPR Overview

In April 2016, the European Union (EU) adopted the Regulation (EU) 2016/679 of the European Parliament and of the Council of April 27, 2016, better known as the General Data Protection Regulation (GDPR), which came into force on May 25, 2018.[2] The GDPR is the result of a long evolution and maturation of a set of norms that move beyond the traditional concept of privacy. Personal data protection is considered by the European institutions as a fundamental human right.

The notion of privacy finds its roots in antiquity, and more specifically in the Roman Republic. The initial notion was related to the boundaries between the public and private sphere.[3] This has been a recurring issue, closely associated to a recognition by political and religious authorities that individuals have the right to preserve and protect their private life.

This notion of privacy has evolved over time. In 1890, the concept of privacy was formalized by two American scholars, S.D. Warren and L.D. Brandais, who published a paper entitled "The Right to Privacy." They coined a modern definition of privacy as the right to be let alone.[4]

---

[1] http://fortune.com/2018/03/19/facebook-stock-share-price-cambridge-analytica-donald-trump/.

[2] Regulation (EU) 2016/679 of the European Parliament and of the Council of April 27, 2016 on the protection of natural persons with regard to the processing of personal data and on the free movement of such data, and repealing Directive 95/46/EC (General Data Protection Regulation) Official Journal L. 2016;119(1).

[3] Chrabonszczewski Maciej, Prywatnosc Teoria i Praktyka, Warsaw, ASPRA JR 2012, p. 32.

[4] Warren S.; Brandeis L., The Right to Privacy, Harvard Law Review, Boston, Vol. 4, No. 5. (Dec. 15, 1890), pp. 193–220. https://www.jstor.org/stable/1321160?seq=1#page_scan_tab_contents.

In Europe, the recognition of privacy as a fundamental right was accelerated by the Second World War. The development of authoritarian regimes and their impact on individual freedoms led to the international recognition of human rights and fundamental individual rights, including the right to privacy of communication and family life. This evolution has been characterized by the adoption of several international declarations and treaties, such as the Universal Declaration of Human Rights in 1948 and the European Convention on Human Rights in 1950.

These key principles have been deeply integrated into the legal framework of the European construction. A large number of European treaties have included specific references to the right to privacy and personal data protection, including inter alia:

- Treaty Establishing the European Coal and Steel Community (Treaty of Paris) in 1951;
- Treaty Establishing the European Economic Community (Treaty of Rome) in 1957;
- Treaty Establishing a Single Council and a Single Commission of the European Communities (Merger Treaty) in 1965;
- Treaty regarding the protection of individuals with regard to automatic processing of personal data of the Council of Europe (also known as Convention 108) in 1981.

As a natural consequence, the European institutions have progressively specified and detailed these privacy related rights through different secondary norms. We can mention inter alia:

- Resolution 73/22 and 74/29 in 1973–1974;
- Directive 95/46/EC on the protection of individuals with regard to the processing of personal data and on the free movement of such data (also known as European Data Protection Directive) in 1995;
- EU Regulation 45/2001 on the protection of individuals with regard to the processing of personal data by the institutions and bodies of the Community and on the free movement of such data.

This process of specifying the rights and obligations related to personal data protection has been continuous. The adoption of the GDPR constitutes the apex of this evolution. It is also characterized by an evolution from the notion of "privacy" to a more comprehensive notion of "personal data protection." The latter constitutes a substantial extension of individual rights. For instance, personal information shared by an individual on social media will not be considered any more to be private information. One could argue that the data subject has voluntarily renounced his or her right to privacy by disclosing this information on the Internet. However, the notion of personal data enables data subjects to maintain their rights to their personal data, regardless of their level of dissemination. It enables the data subject to keep control of his or her personal data.

3 GDPR Key Obligations

The GDPR enumerates key obligations that rest on the data controller in order to safeguard effective protection when processing personal data:

(1) Prior Informed Consent

A fundamental principle set by the GDPR is the duty to collect the consent of the individuals (the data subjects) before collecting and processing their personal data. There are a few exceptions that are tolerated, where consent is not required, but the rule is by default to request consent.

The Article 29 Data Protection Working Party established in its opinion on consent a comprehensive definition of informed consent. It defines consent as "a freely given, specific and informed indication of data subject agreement to processing of his or her personal data."[5] In summary, this consent must comply with several criteria:

[5] Art. 29 Data Protection Working Party, Opinion 15/2011 on the definition of consent, WP 187, Brussels, 2011.

- it must be collected prior to the collection and processing of the data;
- it must be "informed," which means that the data subject must have been clearly and transparently informed on the purpose and use of personal data;
- it must be "freely" consented and avoid any unnecessary constraint; in other words, a service provider would not be authorized to refuse a service on the pretext that the data subject is not willing to share his or her personal data if these data are not indispensable for providing the mentioned service.

Consent of the data subject under the GDPR echoes the Article 29 Data Protection Working Party definition and describes a consent as any freely given, specific, unambiguous indication of the data subject's wishes by which he or she, by a statement or by a clear affirmative action, signifies agreement to the processing of personal data relating to him or her.[6] The acceptance of the processing of the personal data by the data subject has to be clearly indicated. The GDPR embodies an open catalogue of conducts and actions which are affirmative, such as a written or oral statement or ticking a box when visiting a website. The implied or tacit consent does not constitute consent, however. Consent should apply to all undertaken processing activities,[7] to fulfill their purposes and analogically while the processing has multiple purposes.[8] The burden of proof lies with the data controller.[9] Also in this context, a declaration of consent pre-formulated by the controller should be provided in an intelligible and easily accessible form, using clear and plain language and should not include unfair terms.[10]

The GDPR invokes that consent can be regarded as freely given when a data subject is provided with an unprejudiced option to choose from and when a refusal or withdraw of consent does not cause a detrimental effect for the data subject.[11]

---

[6] Art. 4 clause (11) GDPR.

[7] Art. 6 GDPR.

[8] Recital 32 GDPR.

[9] Art. 7 clause (1) GDPR

[10] Formal requirements stated in Art. 7 GDPR and enhanced by Recital 42 GDPR.

[11] Recital 42 GDPR.

The data subject's consent renders the processing of his or her personal data lawful, and therefore places the data subject at the legal center of gravity.[12]

Nonetheless, consent should not provide a legal basis for lawful processing whenever there is an evident disproportion between the data subject and the controller.[13] For instance, children are considered as vulnerable natural persons and enjoy special protection under GDPR.[14] The "reasonable efforts" on the part of the controller are expected to verify that the consent has been given or authorized by the holder of parental responsibility.[15] The GDPR also overlays a controller with a duty to provide a notice in clear and plain language so that a child can easily understand it.[16]

Properly given explicit consent is of utmost importance when processing special categories of personal data.[17] This is an exemption to the general rule of proscription of this processing.[18] The data subject may only provide his or her explicit consent to the processing of his or her special categories of personal data for one or more specified purposes, when EU or European member state law does not interfere by forbidding a lifting of the general rule prohibition by the data subjects.[19]

(2) Data Minimization

Data minimization is one of the fundamental principles of the GDPR relating to personal data processing and a main obligation of the data controller. The GDPR defines that the collected personal data should be adequate, relevant, and limited to what is necessary in relation to the

[12] Bensoussan Alain, Henrotte Jean-François, Gallardo Marc, Fanti Sébastien, General Data Protection Regulation: Texts, commentaries, and practical guidelines, Wolters Kluwer, Belgium, 2017, p. 23.

[13] Recital 43 GDPR.

[14] Recital 75 GDPR.

[15] Art. 8 clause (2) GDPR. With regard to description of legal capacity of a child the member state's law applies – art. 8 clause (1) GDPR.

[16] Art. 12 GDPR and Recital 58.

[17] Art. 9 clause (2) (a) GDPR, enhanced by the Recital 51 GDPR on explicit consent.

[18] Art. 9 clause (1) GDPR.

[19] Art. 9 clause (2) letter (a) GDPR.

purposes for which they are processed.[20] In other words, no more than the strict minimum amount of data should be kept for relevant processing. In order to properly apply this provision, it must be intrinsically coupled with the purpose limitation principle, which allows a determination of the boundaries of necessary processing.[21] The embodiment of data minimization principle is of utmost importance when applying data protection by design and by default.[22]

The notion of data minimization can be understood as two-dimensional:

- the scope of personal data collected, processed, and stored should be limited to what is really useful and necessary;
- the period of time during which the data are kept should also be limited to what is effectively needed.

(3) Data Subject Rights

The GDPR reinforces the legal protection of data subject rights. Beyond the obligations of data controllers and processors to act with transparency, the GDPR defines a clear list of data subject rights. This catalogue encompasses inter alia the following fundamental rights:

1. the right to be informed;[23]
2. the right of access;[24]
3. the right of rectification;[25]
4. the right to erasure;[26]
5. the right to restriction of processing;[27]
6. the right to data portability;[28]

---

[20] Art. 5 clause (1) letter (c) GDPR.
[21] Art. 5 clause (1) letter (b) GDPR.
[22] Art. 25 GDPR and Recital 78 GDPR.
[23] Art. 13–14 GDPR and Recital 60–62 GDPR.
[24] Art. 15 GDPR and Recital 63–64 GDPR.
[25] Art. 16 and 19 GDPR and Recital 63–64 GDPR.
[26] Art. 17 and 19 GDPR and Recital 65–66 GDPR.
[27] Art. 18 and 19 GDPR and Recital 67 GDPR.
[28] Art. 20 GDPR and Recital 68 GDPR.

7. the right to withdrawn consent;[29]
8. the right to object;[30]
9. the right to object to automated individual decision making.[31]

The catalog of data subject rights represents armor against the abuse of personal data processing and results from the development of the protection of the fundamental rights of a natural person. The above-mentioned rights, however, can be restricted by EU or European member state law under the premises of Article 23 GDPR.[32]

3.1 Right to be Informed

The right to be informed is a fundamental principle necessary for exercising data subject rights under the GDPR. In order to collect personal data, the data controller must provide the data subject with concise and transparent information relating to the processing of his or her personal data.[33] The GDPR does not define *expressis verbis* what the collection of personal data means, but uses it in the context of the example of the operation related to information obligations resulting from Articles 13 and 14 GDPR. The collection should be understood as any kind of acquisition of personal data with a goal of further processing. The fact that the collected personal data create or do not create a data file is not important. It is also irrelevant whether a data subject provides the data by his or her own initiative or whether a data controller obtains it directly from the data subject. The important fact is the possession of data.

The information must be provided in an easily accessible form, using clear and plain language, and special care should be taken in order to provide children with easily understandable information in a written

[29] Art. 7 GDPR and Recital 42 GDPR.
[30] Art. 21 GDPR and Recital 69–70 GDPR.
[31] Art. 22 GDPR and Recital 71–72 GDPR.
[32] Art. 23 GDPR in connection with the Recital 8 and 72 GDPR.
[33] Art. 13, 14, 15 to 22 and 34 GDPR.

form, especially by electronic means (oral information is allowed only on request of the data subject).[34]

Article 13 GDPR consists of a catalogue of the indispensable information that has to be delivered to the data subject in order to fulfill the requirements of the principle of the right to be informed whenever the personal data are collected directly from the data subject. The catalogue differs if the personal data have not been obtained directly from the data subject; then the data controller must apply the catalogue of information stated in Article 14 GDPR accordingly.

When the personal data are collected directly from the data subject based on Article 13 GDPR, the controller has an obligation to provide the data subject with his or her identity as the data controller and contact details or those of his or her representative, and while applicable also those of his or her data protection officer. The data subject also has to be provided with information about the purpose of processing personal data and the legal basis or legitimate interest. This includes information about the recipients of personal data as well as the possible intention of the data controller to transfer personal data to a third country or international organization, and information about appropriate safeguards when applicable. Further, Article 13 (2) GDPR specifies that in order to assure fair and transparent data processing, the data controller has an obligation while acquiring personal data to provide the data subject with information on the period of storage of the data and the rights of the data subject: rights to access, rectification, erasure, restriction of processing, and objection, as well as the data portability right and the right to lodge a complaint.

The data subject must be informed that he or she can withdraw consent at any time when the processing is based on consent. Furthermore, while the processing is based on legal or contractual obligations in order to execute a contract, the data subject has to be informed equally of the consequences of incompliance with the fulfillment of necessary requirements.

The data subject has to be informed in case of the application of automated decision-making, including profiling. He or she can obtain meaningful information about the logic involved as well as the importance and the foreseen consequences of such processing for him or her.

[34] Art. 12 GDPR and Recital 58 and 61.

Whenever the controller plans to further process the collected data for a purpose other than the primary defined, he or she has a duty to inform the data subject before the intended processing starts.

Article 14 GDPR specifies the information that the data controller has to provide to a data subject when the personal data have not been acquired directly from that data subject. Similarly, the data controller must provide the data subject with the same catalog of information when the personal data are obtained directly from a data subject. However, what differs in this case is the obligation of the data controller to define the categories of personal data concerned,[35] and the source from which the personal data originate.[36] Moreover, the GDPR specifies a period for providing the data subject with the necessary information.[37] In principle, the data subject has to be informed within a maximum of one month after the data controller has acquired personal data. In some cases, it can be done alter, but at the latest at the time of data disclosure to another recipient.

Article 14 GDPR exempts the data controller from an obligation to provide information to the data subject in four cases. First, when the data subject already has the information; second, when the provision of such information is impossible to achieve or would require disproportionately large exertion on the part of the data controller (however, the data controller shall in such case display information publicly); third, whenever the exemption of provision of information is based on EU or member state law; and fourth, when EU or member state law specifies that the personal data must remain confidential subject to an obligation of professional secrecy. This principle had already been confirmed by the European Court of Justice in the context of processing between public administrative bodies.[38]

---

[35] Art. 14 (1) (d) GDPR.

[36] Art. 14 (2) (f) GDPR.

[37] Art. 14 (3) GDPR.

[38] CJUE Smaranda Bara and Others v. Preşedintele Casei Naţionale de Asigurări de Sănătate, Casa Naţională de Asigurări de Sănătate, Agenţia Naţională de Administrare Fiscală (ANAF), C-201/14, October 1, 2015.

The right to be informed manifests also in the event of a data breach occurrence, when the data controller has the obligation to inform a data subject when the breach is likely to result in a high risk to the rights and freedoms of natural persons, except when the conditions listed in Article 34 (3) GDPR occur.[39]

3.2 Right to Access

The data subjects have the pivotal right of requesting access to their personal data. This principle is transposed in the GDPR and was clarified by the European Court of Justice based on the application of Directive 95/46,[40] to ensure that the data subject's personal data are processed in a correct manner; in other words that the personal data regarding him or her are accurate and that they are disclosed to authorized recipients. The data subject may request information about the purpose of data processing, the period of time for which the data will be stored, the identity of the data recipient if applicable, the existence and logic of automatic data processing, and the consequences of any profiling. This right is fundamental and serves as a jumping-off point to the exercise of the other data subject rights. Nevertheless, personal data should never be retained by the data controller with the unique purpose to satisfy the potential data subject request.[41]

It is worth underlining that the data subject, once the processing of his or her personal data is confirmed by the data controller, may request a rectification or erasure of personal data concerning him or her. This right applies to past actions,[42] and the data subject right may execute it by

---

[39] Art. 34 GDPR and Recital 85 and 87.

[40] CJUE College van burgemeester en wethouders van Rotterdam versus M.E.E. Rijkeboer, C-553/07, May 7, 2009 http://eur-lex.europa.eu/legal-content/EN/ALL/?uri=ecli:ECLI:EU:C:2009:293.

[41] Recital 64 GDPR.

[42] Ibidem. (CJUE College van burgemeester en wethouders van Rotterdam versus M.E.E. Rijkeboer, C-553/07, 7th of May 2009 http://eur-lex.europa.eu/legal-content/EN/ALL/?uri=ecli:ECLI:EU:C:2009:293).

restricting further processing of his or her personal data or make an objection for further processing of personal data concerning him or her.[43]

The right of access is, however, not an absolute right and it should be counterbalanced with the rights and freedoms of the third parties and should not adversely affect them; this includes trade secrets or intellectual property rights, especially software copyrights. However, this must not be used as a base for refusal to deliver all information to the requesting data subject.[44] In this context, the scope of the data subject access right was closely examined by the Court of European Justice and confirmed the divergence between the right of access to information on personal data processed by the data controller and the right of access to administrative documents, which is not in the scope of the application data protection regulations.[45]

The data controller is obliged to provide the data subject with a copy of the personal data undergoing processing in a commonly used electronic form. The copy is delivered free of charge. If further copies are requested the data controller may demand administrative fees.

In cases where the controller processes "a large quantity of information" about the data subject, he or she may require the data subject to specify the information or processing activities at issue in the request.

3.3 Right to Rectification

The right to rectification obliges the data controller to facilitate the exercise of the data subject's right to correct, rectify, or complete the personal data concerning him or her. The data controller should have an implemented mechanism facilitating the submission of the data subject's request, which should be at no cost and should include the possibility of exercising the data subject's right of access, rectification, or erasure of personal data, or the right to object to the processing of personal data.[46]

---

[43] Art. 15 GDPR.

[44] Recital 63 GDPR.

[45] CJEU – Joined cases Y.S v Minister voor Immigratie, Integratie en Asiel, C-141/12; Minister voor Immigratie, Integratie en Asiel v M. and S., C-372/12, July 17, 2014.

[46] Art. 16 GDPR and Recital 59 GDPR.

The data controller shall rectify such data without undue delay and at the latest within one month, and especially state the reasons if the controller does not foresee complying with the data subject request. Moreover, the duty of informing any recipient of the personal data of the rectification of data lies with the data controller.[47]

3.4 Right to be Forgotten

The right to be forgotten was raised on the ground of Article 12 (b) of the repealed Directive 95/46 and was then renamed by the GDPR as the right to erasure. This right has been confirmed by the European Court of Justice in the ruling Google Spain SL v. Costeja,[48] where as a result the data subject could claim from the data operator, the Google search engine, the right to remove links from its index concerning personal data of an Internet user and to prevent access to the data in future. The court ruling specifies that "even initially lawful processing of accurate data may, in the course of time, become incompatible with the directive where those data are no longer necessary in the light of the purposes for which they were collected or processed. That is so in particular where they appear to be inadequate, irrelevant or no longer relevant, or excessive in relation to those purposes and in the light of the time has elapsed." The GDPR transposes the list of conditions enumerated by the European Court of Justice and states them as a ground on which the right of erasure can be demanded.[49] Other grounds apply in case of data subject consent withdrawal and consequently when there is no legal basis for the processing, and also when the data subject objects to the processing if the conditions of the Article 17 (1) (c) GDPR are met. In the case of unlawful processing the data subject may also request an erasure concerning personal data. However, it is worth underlining that the GDPR does not clarify on whom the onus falls for demonstrating the unlawfulness of processing.[50]

---

[47] Art. 19 GDPR.

[48] CJEU, Google Spain SL v. Costeja, C-131/12, May 13, 2014.

[49] Art. 17 (1) (a) GDPR.

[50] Further on this: P. Litwinski editor in P. Litwinski, P. Barta, M. Kawecki, Rozporzadzenie UE w sprawie ochrony osob fizycznych w związku z przetwarzaniem danych osobowych i swobodnym przepływem takich danych. Komentarz, Warsaw, C.H. Beck 2018, p. 402.

Another applicable ground exists when EU or member state law imposes a legal obligation to erase the personal data of the concerning data subject.

The last is applied when the data were collected in relation to the offer of information society services addressed directly to a child.[51] This legal basis is echoing and emphasizing by the recital 65 GDPR, stating *expressis verbis* that a data subject has a right to have his or her personal data erased where the data subject has given his or her consent as a child and is not fully aware of the risks involved in the processing and later wants to remove such personal data from the Internet.

The data controller has an obligation to erase personal data without undue delay, and if the data was publicly disclosed the data controller must inform controllers who are processing the personal data about the data subject's request for erasure.[52] Furthermore, the controller has an obligation to communicate the right to erasure to any recipient to whom the personal data was communicated.[53]

The right of erasure is not an absolute right and can be overridden by the necessity of processing which occurs when exercising the right of freedom of expression and information and the right to history, consisting of archiving purposes in the public, scientific, statistical, or historical interests and purposes. Public interest may also override the right of erasure, especially when such processing is regulated by EU or member state law or is carried out in the domain of public health. The right to be forgotten may also be refused when the processing is necessary for the establishment, exercise, or defense of legal claims.[54]

3.5 The Right to Restriction of Processing

The GDPR empowers the data subject rights by giving him or her the right to restriction of personal data processing carried out by the data controller. This right may be raised only when one of the four legal bases occurs.

---

[51] Art. 17 (1) (f) in relation to art. 8 (1) GDPR and recital 65 GDPR.

[52] Art. 17 (1) and 17 (2) and recital 66 GDPR.

[53] Art. 19 GDPR.

[54] Art. 17 (3) GDPR.

First, the restriction of processing applies whenever the data subject contests the correctness of the personal data and the period of its verification by the data controller. Second, whenever the processing is unlawful but the data subject does not want to apply the right to erasure. Third, when the data controller does not require the collected data any more for the defined purpose of processing but they are necessary for the data subject in relation to concerning his or her legal claims. Fourth, the restriction of processing applies equally for the period of verification of the existence of the legal basis to override the data subject request, when the data subject exercise his right to object to processing of personal data concerning him or her based on Article 21 (1) GDPR.[55] There is an onus on the data controller to provide the data subject with the information when he or she has acquired restriction of processing before the restriction of processing is lifted.

The handling of the restricted processing should be limited to undertaking storage related actions and with the data subject's consent or for purposes covering public interest of utmost importance or for the purpose of soliciting and defending legal claims.

The burden of notifying any recipient of personal data whose processing has been restricted lies with the data controller.[56]

3.6 Right to Data Portability

Data portability allows the data subject to receive personal data which have been provided to a controller. Two categories of data are considered as being provided to the data controller; first, where the processing is based on the consent (i.e. for processing of special categories of data of the data subject),[57] or it is necessary to perform a contract to which the data subject is a party, and second where the data subject provides the data indirectly by using the services or devices that retrieve the data, such as activity logs and providing geographical location.

[55] Art. 18 GDPR and recital 67 GDPR.

[56] Art. 19 GDPR.

[57] Art. 9 GDPR.

The data subset must be retrieved in a structured, commonly used, and machine-readable format in order to be able to transmit it to another controller, and it must be conducted without any restraint on behalf of the data controller who initially extracts the data. The data portability rule is related only to the personal data, but in the case of pseudonymized data the data subject may request his or her data from the data controller, and by doing so he or she must provide additional information enabling his or her identification.[58]

This right is closely related to the data subject access right. It is also in line with a goal to foster the Single Digital Market strategy and enhance competition between EU countries.[59] The Article 29 Working Party specifies further that the controller that receive the data must ensure that the data transmitted is relevant and not excessive in relation to the purpose of its processing.[60] The receiving controller becomes the new data controller and must comply with the principles relating to the processing of personal data,[61] and provide a data subject with the required information in a timely manner.[62] The transmission of data results in the applicability of a new data controller's obligations toward the respect of the data subject rights and it extends to third-party rights if his or her data are included in the transmitted dataset.[63]

3.7 The Right to Withdraw Consent

The definition of consent has been presented in depth in the GDPR overview section of this chapter. We will now shed light on the right to withdraw consent that results from Article 7 (3) GDPR. The consent can be withdrawn at any time by the data subject. The data controller must facilitate the exercise of the right to withdraw consent, which should be as easy as to obtain the consent of the data subject. The withdrawal of the

[58] Art. 11 (2) GDPR.

[59] Article 29 Working Party Guidelines on the right to portability, 12.13.2016, p. 3.

[60] Article 29 Working Party Guidelines on the right to portability, 12.13.2016, p. 6 ss.

[61] Art. 5 GDPR.

[62] Art. 13 and 14 GDPR.

[63] Art. 20 (4) GDPR and 6 (1) (f) GDPR.

consent does not have retroactive effects and thus does not affect the lawfulness of the personal data processing before the consent withdrawal.

It is worth mentioning that the withdrawal of the consent may be expressed as conditional, timely, or territorially limiting; for example, it may concern only partial processing of the personal data. The data controller always bears the burden of proof in relation to the lawfulness of personal data processing based on the data subject's consent.

3.8 The Right to Object

The data subject has the right to object to the processing of personal data concerning him or her when it is carried out in the public interests or the legitimate interest of the data controller or third party at any time on grounds that relate to his or her particular situation. The GDPR does not specify what the term "particular situation" means. One can construe that the situation must have changed since the time of the collection of the personal data, and also the data subject must demonstrate that this change will adversely impact his or her situation. In this case the onus to demonstrate it lies with the data subject. This right can be overridden by the data controller if he or she demonstrates compelling legitimate interest or the necessity to establish, exercise, or defend legal claims.[64]

The right to object may be also raised by the data subject to oppose the processing of his or her personal data for the purpose of direct marketing at any time without fulfilling any particular conditions.

The right to object can be applied when the data subject's particular situation stands as a ground when the personal data is to be processed for historical or scientific research or statistical purposes in the public interest.[65] This right can be overridden in opposition to the necessity for the performance or task to be carried out for reasons of public interest by the data controller.

The data controller has the obligation to inform a data subject of his or her right to object at the latest moment of the first communication with the last one.

[64] Art. 21 (1) and Recital 69 GDRP.

[65] Art. 21 (6) and 89 (1) GDPR.

3.9 The Right to Object to Automated Decision-Making

The right to object to automated decision-making, including profiling, derives from the right of access.

The data subject may refuse the automated processing of personal data concerning him or her whenever this processing leads to a decision which affects or produces legal effects on him or her. The GDPR stipulates three exceptions if the processing is authorized by EU or member state law, or if it is necessary to execute a contract between data subject and data controller or whenever the processing is based on the data subject's explicit consent.[66] In all three cases suitable measures to safeguard the data subject's rights and freedoms and legitimate interest are incumbent and have to be implemented by the controller or laid down by law in the case of authorization by EU or member state law. In this context, the member states may make reference to the pre-existing document issued by the Council of Europe that serves as a cornerstone for this regulation. The Council of Europe issued a Recommendation of the Committee of Ministers to member states on the protection of individuals with regard to the automatic processing of personal data in the context of profiling,[67] and this serves as a basis for interpretation of these requirements.

When the automated decision-making or profiling is based on the necessity to execute a contract between a data subject and a data controller, or whenever it is based on the data subject's explicit consent of the data subject, it is incumbent on the data controller to implement other necessary measures. The controller shall guarantee minimum rights to the data subject, such as the right to obtain human intervention in order to express his and her point of view or to obtain explanations of the decision reached after such assessment and to challenge the decision.[68] Scholars criticize the too narrow scope of protection in this provision, as it applies

[66] Art. 22 (2) GDPR and recital 71 GDPR.

[67] Recommendation CM/Rec(2010)13 of the Committee of Ministers to member states on the protection of individuals with regard to automatic processing of personal data in the context of profiling; 11.23.2010; http://194.242.234.211/documents/10160/10704/Recommendation+2010+13+Profiling.pdf.

[68] Art. 22 (4) Recital 71 GDPR.

only in cases when the automated decision or profiling produces legal effects or significantly affects the data subject.[69] Article 13 GDPR also narrows down the obligation of providing a data subject with meaningful information about the logic involved as well as the significance and the envisaged consequences of processing while applying the automated decision-making process or profiling.

The catalogue of rights established under the GDPR empowers the data subject's position with regard to his or her personal data processing conducted by the data controller or by the third party involved in the data processing. Although scholars decry some of the adopted concepts and language used in the description of the rights as vague and as causing confusion,[70] one may agree on the general realization of the GDPR objectives as stated in the GDPR Preamble. By this approach, however, the goal to provide naturals persons in all member states with the same level of equally enforceable rights and the same obligations and responsibilities for controllers and processors is deemed achievable.[71]

(4) Security

The GDPR imposes an obligation of implementation of the appropriate technical and organizational measures to ensure security while processing personal data. This obligation is imposed both on controller and processor. The regulation provides a non-exhaustive list of appropriate measures, including adherence to an approved code of conduct or an approved certification mechanism.[72] In furtherance of an evaluation of the appropriateness of required security efforts, a measure must be given supplementary conditions, in order to minimize the occurrence of risks inseparably connected with processing.[73]

---

[69] Sandra Wachter, Brent Mittelstadt, Luciano Floridi; Why a Right to Explanation of Automated Decision-Making Does Not Exist in the General Data Protection Regulation, International Data Privacy Law, Volume 7, Issue 2, May 1, 2017, pp. 76–99, https://doi.org/10.1093/idpl/ipx005.

[70] Christopher Kuner, Dan Jerker B. Svantesson, Fred H. Cate, Orla Lynskey, Christopher Millard; The language of data privacy law (and how it differs from reality), *International Data Privacy Law*, Volume 6, Issue 4, November 1, 2016, pp. 259–260, https://doi.org/10.1093/idpl/ipw022.

[71] Recital 13 GDPR.

[72] Art. 32 (1) and 32 (3) in relation to Art. 40 and 42 GDPR.

[73] Art. 32 (2) GDPR emphasized by Recital 83 GDPR.

The GDPR introduces a proactive approach toward the security of personal data by also implementing a concept of privacy by design, which was developed in Canada as a safeguard mechanism to be applied before processing personal data.[74]

(5) Cross-border transfer limitations

The GDPR imposes an obligation on data controllers to check and ensure that personal data are transferred only to countries and entities that can guarantee an equivalent level of data protection to Europe. The European Commission can recognize countries that provide equivalent level of protection through what the GDPR names "adequacy decisions." Otherwise, strict rules apply that limit the possibility of transferring personal data to countries that do not provide an equivalent level of protection.

(6) Effectiveness of penalties and worldwide impact

Companies that do not respect the GDPR are exposed to massive fines, up to 4% of their worldwide turnover. This constitutes a massive legal and financial risk. Another element that characterizes the GDPR is its universality in terms of geographic scope. Any company collecting and/or processing data from European residents is exposed to the GDPR penalties. This innovative aspect constitutes a game changer and has led many non-European companies to anticipate and actively prepare for the entry into force of the GDPR.

4 Impact on Data Business Models

While the GDPR seems to limit the collection and transfer of personal data, the EU has adopted a clear strategy toward an integrated European digital single market.[75] It intends to overcome the current national

---

[74] Wiewiorowski Wojchiech, 'Privacy by Design' as a paradigm for privacy protection, in Internet, Prawno – Informatyczne problemy sieci, portal I e-uslug, edited by Wiewiorowski Wojciech and Szpor Grazyna, CH Beck, Warsaw, 2012, p. 13.

[75] https://ec.europa.eu/digital-single-market/en/policies/shaping-digital-single-market.

fragmentation and barriers to data transfer in order to ease the transfer and exploitation of data. The declared intention is not to prevent the exploitation of personal data, but to ensure that such exploitation is performed in accordance with the data subjects.

However, this approach has a direct impact on business activities. We will highlight some important effects on DBMs.

Risk Management

A first consequence of the GDPR on DBM is the necessity to better control the risks related to personal data protection. Any non-compliant activity has the potential to bankrupt a company. In such a context, DBM must take this major risk into account and should start by assessing the risk to be exposed to GDPR-related sanctions and penalties.

Data Subject Rights Ownership and Control

Another change is related to the legal recognition of data subjects' rights. Data cannot be any more disconnected from their source, the data subjects. DBMs must design their model with the data subjects at the core of the model, including in terms of economic transactions.

Purpose Consistency

The prior informed consent must be specific and a company cannot use the collected data beyond the announced purpose at the time the data subject gave consent. If the company wants to substantially extend the use of the collected data, it should collect a complementary consent. In some cases, such complementary consent may be difficult to obtain. As a consequence, companies will have to better anticipate the evolution of their activities and prepare clear wordings.

Data Transfer to Third Parties

The GDPR defines a third party as a natural or legal person, public authority, agency, or body other than the data subject, controller, processor, and persons who under the direct authority of the controller or processor is authorized to process personal data.[76]

---

[76] Art. 4 clause (10) GDPR.

The general principle of transfer of personal data to a third country or an international organization states that it should be undertaken only when the prerequisites enshrined in Chapter V of the GDPR are met and must ensure a high level of protection of personal data.[77]

As a consequence, companies must clearly map, manage, monitor, and control the way they process and share data. As the scope of their responsibility is expanded by the GDPR, they must adapt their internal organization and processes to internalize these additional duties.

Cross-Border Transfer

Another direct impact is the requirement to control cross-border data transfers toward non-trusted countries. In other words, DBMs must take into account the territoriality of data processing and transfer. It will require that global companies separate and segregate the processing of data coming from European residents from data processes in countries which are not recognized as adequate countries.

5 GDPR Exemptions for Research and Anonymized Data

It makes sense to discuss more specifically two specific cases that can apply to specific DBMs: research data and anonymized data.

Research Data

The GDPR is applicable whenever personal data are processed for scientific research purpose. The GDPR states that the scope of a definition of the processing of personal data purposes must be construed broadly including, inter alia, scientific research in a technological development research area as well as studies conducted in the public interest in the area of public health. Furthermore, in the GDPR application it does not distinguish between publicly and privately funded research, and thus encompasses both equally.[78]

---

[77] Art. 44 GDPR and Recital 6.

[78] Recital 159 GDPR.

The processing of personal data for an accomplishment of the objectives in the scientific research is encouraged and is not obstructed under the GDPR. However, the appropriate safeguards have to be applied while processing personal data to guarantee the rights and freedoms of the data subject.[79] The safeguards are to be aligned with the GDPR and should encompass technical and organizational measures, and specifically should ensure the respect of the data minimization principle. Further, the GDPR provides an example of the application of pseudonymization as one of the recommended safeguarding measures.[80]

Further in this context, the European legislator fosters a conducive approach toward conducting scientific researches by adopting an exemption and by allowing implementation by the EU or member states of legal derogations from the rights of the data subject guaranteed by the GDPR. Whereas the rights of the data subjects may seriously impede the achievement of the specific research purposes or render them impossible to obtain, only then can the derogations (if necessary) be implemented.[81]

Those rights from which the derogations are allowed under the strict conditions stated hereinabove are enumerated *numerus clausus* (the right of access by the data subject,[82] the right to rectification,[83] the right to restriction of processing,[84] and the right to object to the processing of personal data),[85] and are otherwise subject to guarantees in Article 89.1. GDPR. This provision is in line with the European legislator intention that member states are allowed to maintain or introduce national provisions to further specify the application of the rules of the GDPR.[86]

The necessity of processing special categories of data for conducting scientific research nullify its prohibition that is otherwise applicable by

[79] Art. 89 clause (1) GDPR.
[80] Art. 89 clause (1) GDPR.
[81] Art. 89 clause (2) GDPR.
[82] Art. 15 GDPR.
[83] Art. 16 GDPR.
[84] Art. 18 GDPR.
[85] Art. 21 GDPR.
[86] Recital 10 GDPR.

default, and renders it lawful.[87] This exemption, however, is subject to further conditions. It invokes a direct alignment with Article 89(1) GDPR and emphasizes that the processing shall be proportionate to the aim pursued and respect the essence of the right to data protection. This provision echoes the intention of the European legislator that the GDPR does not exclude a specification of the member state laws according to the processing of the special categories of data, and determines more precisely the conditions under which the processing of personal data is lawful.[88]

Anonymized Data
The GDPR states that the principles of data protection do not apply to anonymous information, namely information which does not relate to an identified or identifiable natural person or to personal data rendered anonymous in such a manner that the data subject is not or is no longer identifiable. The GDPR does not therefore concern the processing of such anonymous data, including for research purposes.[89] Anonymization techniques for personal data are defined by Article 29 Data Protection Working Party.[90]

6 Building a New DBM Paradigm

On the basis of our analysis, we can sketch the foundations of a new paradigm for GDPR-compliant DBMs.

Data Subject Involvement
Future DBMs will have to involve the data subjects from day one. Companies that are able to engage with their data subjects in a constructive manner in order to build trust and get their consent will gain a competitive advantage.

[87] Art. 9 clause (2) letter (j) GDPR.
[88] Recital 10 GDPR.
[89] Recital 26 GDPR.
[90] Art. 29 Data Protection Working Party Opinion 05/2014 on Anonymisation Techniques.

Anonymization
In line with the principle of data minimization, the use of anonymization techniques will become more important. Anonymized data may still be highly valuable. A smart exploitation of effective anonymization techniques could become a source of competitive advantage.

Shared Monetization
By recognizing the fundamental ownership and rights of individuals on their data, the GDPR prevents companies from using and trading personal data as they wish. Companies that acknowledge this evolution may take advantage of it by developing new economic models based on a shared monetization and distribution of revenues with the data subjects. It could pave the way to new business models.

Certification
Another factor that is expected to impact future DBMs is the use of certification mechanisms. The GDPR makes 72 references to the notion of certification. Solutions are emerging. The H2020 European research project Privacy Flag has developed a comprehensive certification scheme to assess the compliance of products and services with the GDPR, as well as with complementary national obligations. This certification scheme, named EuroPrivacy (www.europrivacy.org), is intended to be adopted as a global certification scheme to be managed by the European Center for Certification and Privacy in Luxembourg. On one hand, the emergence of certifying third parties may make DBMs more complex. On the other hand, it will enable certified companies to reduce their risks and to benefit from a competitive advantage over their non-certified competitors.

7 Conclusion

As has been illustrated by this chapter, the GDPR is directly impacting DBMs in the EU, as well as beyond its borders. The GDPR brings new legal and financial risks that force companies to evolve and adapt their DBMs. While the GDPR is perceived by some companies as an extra burden, it will certainly constitute a great opportunity for DBM innovation that will benefit to first and fast movers. It will require a more general extension of the traditional model of economic transactions to a parallel model of personal data transactions that are controlled from the source by the anonymization or deletion of the data. Considering that the management of personal data has and will have a cost, the ability to optimize the process of personal data management may become a competitive advantage.

Many years ago, Xerox realized that by minimizing its packaging because of environmental concerns it could save a lot of money and become more competitive. We anticipate that data protection may have a similar impact. Minimizing data processing and data storage may save a lot of hidden costs in terms of maintenance and processes.

Acknowledgement This chapter has been written on the basis of several H2020 research projects, including Privacy Flag and Synchronicity. Both projects have been cofinanced by the European Commission and the Swiss State Secretariat for Education, Research and Innovation. The content of the article is shared on a non-exclusive basis.

9

Prosumers' Digital Business Models for Electric Vehicles: Exploring Microfoundations for a Balanced Policy Approach

Saku J. Mäkinen, Jussi Valta, Kirsi Kotilainen, and Ulla A. Saari

1 Transformation of Energy Markets

The energy system is undergoing a big transformation that comes from at least three sources. First, smart meters and other digital solutions increase the amount of information in the system and create possibilities for new business models (BMs). Second, increasing shares of renewable energy (RE) sources in the energy system require flexible energy resources, including energy storage, alongside them. Third, the introduction of new loads, such as electric vehicles and heat pumps, can create peak demands in the energy system if not managed properly.

This energy transition can be looked at from different perspectives (Meadowcroft 2009). On one hand, an energy transition can be described

S. J. Mäkinen (✉) • J. Valta • K. Kotilainen • U. A. Saari
Laboratory of Industrial and Information Management,
Tampere University of Technology, Tampere, Finland
e-mail: saku.makinen@tut.fi

A. Aagaard (ed.), *Digital Business Models*,
https://doi.org/10.1007/978-3-319-96902-2_9

as the shift from a top-down supply system to a multi-level exchange system (Schleicher-Tappeser 2012). The traditional energy system has five components: energy source, generation, transmission, distribution, and end user (Richter 2012; Rodríguez-Molina et al. 2014). It is characterized by centralized energy production, one-way communication and energy flows, a small number of data and sensors, manual control, and only a few user choices. In contrast, a distributed energy system means small-scale energy generation, two-way real-time communication, and extensive control systems (Zame et al. 2017). On the other hand, energy transition can mean the shift from fossil fuels to clean energy sources. This perspective highlights the shift on the generation side instead of adaptation efforts on the demand side or changes in actors and their roles.

A systemic change such as energy transition can be viewed from different theoretical perspectives. The multi-level perspective (MLP) looks at interlinked changes at niche, regime, and landscape levels from a longitudinal perspective (Geels 2002). The technological innovation systems perspective emphasizes the structures, functions, and inner dynamics of the innovation systems (Hekkert et al. 2007). The strategic niche management perspective is close to the MLP but looks more precisely at how innovations can be shielded, nurtured, and empowered (Smith and Raven 2012). Other important concepts in transition theories are path dependencies, lock-ins, and path creations, which are tightly interlinked with the theories mentioned. However, these perspectives lend little to a scrutiny of transitions at the microlevel.

The drivers for energy market transition come from a combination of interventions on the micro- and macro-levels. The transition management governance theory builds on such a balanced approach (Loorbach 2007). Micro- and macro-level policies address the problem in a coordinated manner with an attempt to balance between a hierarchy and a free-floating market with the right timing for interventions. A balanced approach requires taking into account the provision of knowledge and demand-side activities, providing constituents with the required legislation/regulations and support for the innovation system and the firms operating in it (Edquist 2014).

In the energy transition, the landscape has changed on the macro-level to mitigate climate change. The Paris agreement and other political commitments have mandated governments' intervention in energy markets with such measures as the emission trading system. Other policy objectives of the energy trilemma (i.e. measures for accelerating energy transition, security of supply, and energy equity) are also taken into account by implementing different energy-capacity mechanisms and market deregulation.

These modifications have changed consumer awareness and behavior on the microlevel (Balcombe et al. 2013). Responding to the bottom-up movement, governments have fostered the diffusion of RE technologies by mitigating the biggest barriers to consumers' adoption of RE technology (Painuly 2001). In successful transitions, local regions' own dynamics such as labor skills, culture, and opposition to top-down policies are taken into account (Loorbach 2007). In the case of solar photovoltaic (PV) systems or electric vehicles (EVs), demand has been created by financial subsidies, for example. Subsidies have sometimes proved to be tricky instruments by causing too weak a demand or boom-and-bust cycles in the market. For instance, Spain and Denmark monitored and changed the course of their solar PV markets after high and sudden expenses (IEA-PVPS 2016). The interplay between companies and institutions in this meso–macro link has been shown to be important for the creation of new institutions; for example, advocacy coalitions have legitimized the new technologies in the regime (Jacobsson and Lauber 2006). This has led to the standardization of technologies and procedures, property rights, and market structure and regulation (Scholten and Künneke 2016).

Finally, this trajectory has opened up the energy market to complementary technologies and activities that are needed in integrating the distributed energy resources in the system. Thus far, market structures for properly valuing demand response and flexibility have changed in many countries (SEDC 2017). Incumbents and new entrants in the energy markets, such as aggregators, are incentivized to build creative processes and BMs. Market structure changes are further accompanied by offering data and networking possibilities to the actors in the markets. For instance, home energy management systems (HEMS) can gather information about the whole energy community and in that way optimize the use of local resources (Koirala et al. 2016). Increasing competition coevolves with consumers' preferences and has given consumers the power to steer investments for better efficiency overall. All of this has created a dynamic playing field where the micro-, meso-, and macro-levels of the energy system are closely interlinked and coevolving, and at the same time the evolution of national systems is constrained by lock-ins and path dependencies. In this chapter, we investigate the microlevel transition from consumers to prosumers and seek microfoundations for a balanced policy approach, especially focusing on how EVs might engage prosumers in creating various digital business models (DBMs).

Based on these microfoundations, we explore a balanced approach to the governance of the change in energy systems and sustainable development, taking into account individual prosumer behavior and the institutional environment and its changes (Spaargaren 2011; Liedtke et al. 2013). In essence, the balanced approach requires policy-makers to set an agenda, coordinate change plans, incentivize individuals and corporations to desired actions in plans, and furthermore, induce follow-up measures to reinforce change (Akenji 2014; Liedtke et al. 2013). We concentrate on exploring microlevel DBMs that EV prosumers could have in the future following a similar approach of micro-level measurement as in Saari et al. (2017). In doing so, we explore opportunities to link the micro- and macro-levels (Coleman 1990) in a balanced approach to achieving the sustainability goals for changes in the energy system.

Measuring microlevel phenomena to understand macro-level phenomena has been presented in sociology as a preferred approach instead of focusing purely on macro-level factors and understanding (Coleman 1990; Raub et al. 2011). Prosumer-level DBMs have an impact on the meso- and macro-levels and lead to market change, and possibly to sustainable development if properly guided. At the meso-level prosumers are directly linked to other actors, such as traditional energy market actors, and at the macro-level prosumers' DBMs challenge the institutional role of regulators and structures; the consumer institution in itself is pressured to change to prosumer, and so on. Thus, macro-level changes are outcomes resulting from the interdependence of actors on different levels (Raub et al. 2011).

2 The Evolving EV markets

The EV market is still a fraction of total global car sales, but market shares are increasing rapidly. The two biggest markets are China and the USA. In Europe, the biggest markets are Norway, the UK, France, Germany, the Netherlands, and Sweden (IEA 2017). In Norway, EVs accounted for more than 39% of the market in 2017, which is by far the largest in the world. In 2017, China's EV market grew 71% compared with 2016, and more than 600,000 vehicles were sold. China's market is almost completely closed to foreign brands as non-Chinese car manufacturers reached only 4% of sales. China is also leading the market for electric buses, although sales decreased 23% to 90,000 in 2017 (Dixon 2018). Europe's market in total grew 38% from 2016 to 306,000 registrations in 2017 (Shaham 2018). In the USA, approximately 200,000 EVs were sold in 2017, meaning growth of 26%. The growth of the EV market seems destined to continue, as an increasing number of car manufacturers are introducing EV models and are investing in the technology. The price parity of EVs compared with internal combustion engines (ICEs) is expected to hit in about 2025, but estimates vary.

Political interventions have been the main driver for the diffusion of EVs. Many governments see EVs as a way to reach environmental and energy independence goals. In 2016, 14 countries (including China, Germany, and the UK) set EV targets and even mandates (IEA 2017). These targets are important in the policy strategy as they also form the level and scope for the choice and implementation of policy instruments. In total, these 14 countries set a target of 13 million EVs on their roads by 2020. These countries do not include many potentially major markets for EVs, such as India, which has expressed ambitious plans for 100% EV sales in 2030. Estimates for the total number of EVs on the road by 2025 vary from 40 million to 70 million (IEA 2017). However, the rollout of EVs will vary across countries even inside the European Union (EU). For instance, it is estimated that sales in central and eastern Europe will not increase until 2030.

The increase in the EV market poses opportunities and challenges for car manufacturers, especially the incumbents. To achieve the deployment targets, 60% annual growth in overall EV production is needed (IEA 2017). Until recently, the global market has been dominated by Chinese original equipment manufacturers (OEMs) that accounted for 43% of the global production of EVs in 2016 (Hertzke et al. 2017). Accordingly, several global OEMs have announced targets for bringing new EV and plug-in hybrid EV models to the market. Some manufacturers aim at a certain annual sales figure whereas others target a certain number of models or a certain share of cars in the cumulative sales figures. These figures are currently determined by the emission standards and targets in different countries. For example, in the EU the average emissions standard by 2021 is 95 g/km CO_2 (European Commission 2017).

As some markets aim to thrive as leaders, the charging infrastructure and energy markets will experience the biggest impact. The European Commission target is one charging point per ten EVs. Several countries such as France and Germany are estimated to miss this target even if they manage to reach their EV deployment targets (Electromobility platform 2018). To foster the development and deployment of EV charging infrastructure, governments use, for example, subsidies and public–private partnerships (IEA 2017). The growing demand for charging infrastructure accompanied by low wholesale prices in the energy markets has driven incumbent utilities and oil companies to compete in the EV charging infrastructure market. Incumbents such as Enel, Engie, Total, and Shell, for instance, have invested in EV charger providers and aggregators (Foehringer Merchant 2017).

EV charging can potentially have a major impact on the electric grid at certain locations if charging is not managed smartly. This is highlighted by the fact that the current EV penetration is concentrated in certain areas. Notably, about 40% of the world's EVs are located in only 20 cities worldwide (Hall et al. 2017). However, lead markets also show that the majority of households that own an EV have it as a second car that is used for everyday commuting, whereas ICE cars are driven more often during holidays (IEA 2018). The need for charging infrastructure coevolves with consumer preferences and behavior, which also forces traditional energy supply utilities to be more agile in their investment planning.

Charging of EVs needs to be coordinated so that local grid problems can be avoided (Clement-Nyns et al. 2010). Possible problems for the local grid in the form of voltage deviations, increased need for transformers, electrical losses, and so on will increase as EV penetration increases, and therefore intelligent and coordinated charging is needed (García-Villalobos et al. 2014). Plug-in electric vehicles (PEVs) may also be linked bi-directionally to the electric power system, and then they are referred to as vehicle-to-grid (V2G) solutions. This leads to additional efficiency in the electricity grid, reduces transport emissions, facilitates the use of RE sources in local energy production, and so on. (Sovacool et al. 2018).

However, as PEV penetration increases with decentralized energy, production information and communication technologies also need to be integrated into existing electricity networks to facilitate a two-way flow of information (Kotilainen et al. 2016c). Recent advances in the digitalization of smart meters have enabled the creation of smart grids that can deliver electricity in a controlled way from generation to consumption points (Siano 2014). However, no BMs have yet been developed for the smart grid environment (Niesten and Alkemade 2016), and the prosumers' role in smart grid development is still in its infancy (Kotilainen et al. 2016a).

Therefore, the smart grid infrastructure as a whole facilitates the transition of energy systems to a more efficient and effective innovation ecosystem that integrates transport in a holistic system. Furthermore, smart grid functionalities allow the creation of new services, and new actors are needed to develop new sets of activities and BMs (Niesten and Alkemade 2016). Prosumers' roles are central in the development of DBMs that all the actors in the energy ecosystem need, and the activities in the BMs need to be aligned between the different roles (Kotilainen et al. 2016b). Furthermore, it has been shown that few archetypes of BMs dominate EVs (Bohnsack et al. 2014) mainly owing to path dependencies. As these lock-ins require new activities on the part of policy-makers, as well as other actors (Kotilainen and Saari 2018), DBMs facilitate these changes.

BMs essentially describe how value is created, delivered, and captured by activities (Teece 2010). One way of structuring a BM is according to the BM canvas (BMC), consisting of the value proposition, customer segments, customer relationships, key resources, key activities, key partners, key channels, revenue streams, and cost structure (Osterwalder and Pigneur 2010). These elements describe the needed resources and the activities that need to be aligned with revenue streams and costs, and how the economic entity is planned according to the function. The term DBM refers to a collection of activities in the BMC that are or can be fundamentally changed by changes in digital technologies or functionalities (Veit et al. 2014). A digitalized energy system provides point-to-point possibilities for monitoring and controlling all the devices in the grid, and this facilitates the creation of new services and BMs for all the actors involved (Giordano and Fulli 2012).

Energy consumers are turning into energy prosumers within local energy production systems as EVs are connected to the grid and act as

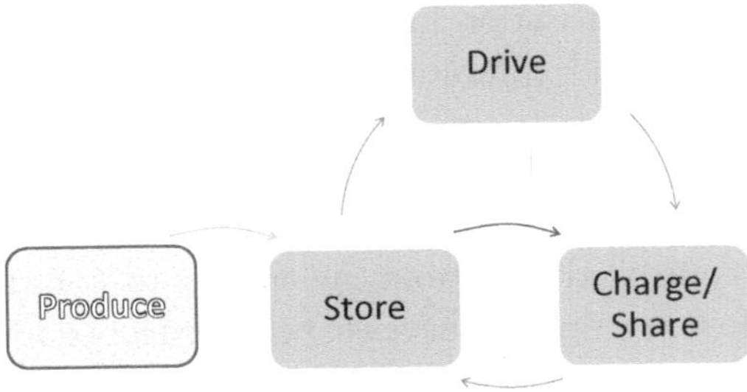

Fig. 9.1 Three use case perspectives of the analysis

energy storage. This transition means that consumers become active actors who need a BM for their activities and transactions in the energy production system. DBMs transform the business processes (Weill and Woerner 2013) of a prosumer in energy production, store, and use. In this chapter, we consider the prosumer DBM from three use case perspectives. Prosumers can use energy to drive, charge, store, and share energy in the location of the EV (see Fig. 9.1). Naturally, there is also the possibility of producing energy (e.g. with solar panels or wind energy), but we leave this side of prosumerism out of the analysis.

3 Exploring the Digital Business Model for Prosumers

This section presents the outcome of a multidisciplinary expert workshop where company representatives and academic researchers brainstormed and ideated DBMs related to prosumers and EVs in a future energy system. The role of a prosumer is still new in the energy sector, and how prosumers as EV users can create, deliver, and capture value businesswise in smart grids remains to be explored. The aim of this study is to provide new innovative ideas for testing later in conjunction with a research project focusing on the concept of social energy and the creation of a prosumer-centric energy ecosystem (ProCem). The result of the workshop is a compilation of the participants' expertise and know-how. To explore potential new prosumer-centric value propositions, the workshop participants sketched BMs according to the key elements included in the BMC (Osterwalder and Pigneur 2010).

First, we briefly describe how workshops can be used as a research method and the approach we used in the workshop to facilitate the discussion and collect input from the participants. Second, we introduce the workshop participants and their areas of expertise. Then we report the results from the three working groups and the BMs that were developed by the participants. Finally, we discuss how the ideas and BMs created in the workshop could be developed further, based on a cross-case analysis of the models.

Workshops can be analyzed from three different perspectives: practice, means, and research methodology (Ørngreen and Levinsen 2017). Workshops can be considered as a means to achieve a goal; for example, strategic prospective workshops (Durance and Godet 2010). Alternatively, workshops can serve as a way to cooperatively develop a solution, a design, or a process for future use (e.g. participatory research; Wakkary 2007; Wiek et al. 2014). Finally, workshops can be utilized as a research methodology to achieve a research target and produce relevant data about the research domain (Ørngreen and Levinsen 2017). The participatory methods applied in workshops support the application of the knowledge and experience of the participants and thus produce valuable results (Öberg and Hernwall 2016). Workshops can be used in research as forums for finding and exploring key elements in complex fields, including processes implemented with information and communications technology (Ørngreen and Levinsen 2017).

Generally, workshops are prepared and planned beforehand so that they achieve a purpose that was decided before the workshop was conducted. Workshops last for a certain limited time, the participants often work in the same field, and the facilitation of the workshop is the responsibility of someone who has experience in the domain. The number of participants is usually small, which permits all the participants the possibility to actively contribute to the discussion and group work (Ørngreen and Levinsen 2017).

A multidisciplinary workshop focusing on new BMs for energy prosumers and EVs was held at the beginning of 2018 at the Tampere University of Technology. The workshop participants included four company representatives from four companies operating in the energy sector and eight representatives from the Tampere University of Technology, including professors, researchers, and doctoral students. Three working groups were formed so that there was at least one company representative and two academic representatives in every group. The workshop lasted three hours altogether, including the initial introduction to the topic and the briefing on the target of the group work, the group work discussions, and the final presentations by the three working groups and the wrap-up of the workshop; each section lasted one hour. Each group was given one EV use case to analyze from the prosumer perspective, and the group's task was to design a BM with a strong prosumer-led value proposition that would fit that particular scenario. The first group focused on driving an EV, the second on scheduled charging, and the third on storing energy and offering it to the energy markets, for example via V2G or vehicle-to-home connections.

Energy storage, such as an EV battery, is the central feature that unites energy prosumers, EV users (who in many cases are the same individual or a member of a household), and the smart energy grid. Prosumers generate energy and store any excess energy in a battery, which can be the battery of an EV. Prosumers may also opt to share energy in a smart grid, energy communities, or even peer to peer (P2P). The EV user drives the vehicle, charges it, and may opt to store and share energy with the power grid.

The working groups were each presented an empty BMC template on which they were asked to note ideas on how prosumers could add value in the different phases and what was required for the implementation in the energy system according to the BMC content elements (Osterwalder and Pigneur 2010). In addition, the groups discussed who could benefit from the prosumers in the energy system and what types of partners, infrastructure, and technology were required to implement the ideas. After the group work, the three groups presented their work to each other and discussed the ideas further. The discussions were audiotaped, and the analysis was conducted by researchers who were present at the workshop.

The company representatives were from four different companies operating in different parts of the energy sector.

- Company A is one of the largest service providers in Finland, and it operates in the Nordic and Baltic countries. Company A offers power network services, telecom network services, industry services, and information management. The company participates in all the different stages of the energy sector lifecycle, offering design, construction, installation, maintenance, and hosting services.
- Company B is a Finnish information technology company that provides digital software services targeted to industrial systems and platforms, including solutions for cross-platform systems, communications systems, and monitoring systems. Company B has created, for example, a software tool and platform for the Internet of Things (IoT) that enables big data analytics. The tool facilitates the creation of IoT applications and BMs that are based on tracking data, for example, on users in the network and their energy consumption.
- Company C is a Finnish electricity distribution and heating company, that is, a distribution system operator (DSO) that manages energy distribution in the smart grid, which allows two-way information and energy flows, invoicing of electricity usage based on real-time consumption, and many possibilities for consumers to track their electricity consumption on a daily or hourly basis. The company cooperates with different industrial operators in Finland so that the operators can feed their surplus energy in the company's network, which improves energy efficiency.
- Company D is a small energy company that is a subsidiary of a heat production company. Recently, the company invested in a smart decentralized energy production system for an industrial area based on a smart grid in central Finland. The target of the company is to produce RE (electricity and heat), for example from large solar panel parks and other sources, such as natural gas.

The academic researchers included two professors (one from Electrical Energy Engineering and one from Automation and Hydraulic Engineering), two researchers (one from Automation and Hydraulic Engineering and one from Industrial and Information Management), and four doctoral students (two from Industrial and Information Management, one from Electrical Energy Engineering, and one from Pervasive Computing).

4 Results

We first report the results individually from the three working groups and then provide a holistic cross-case analysis of the combined BM including all three EV use cases. The EV prosumer is used to describe the user of an EV who may generate energy and store it, drive the vehicle, charge the vehicle, and share its battery as a flexible resource with the smart grid.

Results from Group 1 focused on driving and moving the mobile energy storage unit are mapped according to the BMC content elements.

Value Creation

- *Value proposition.* The ecofriendliness of the parking garage and the possibility of sharing energy with other EV drivers are some of the key benefits of driving for EV users. In addition, when the EV is connected to the smart grid of a shopping mall, the EV helps to reduce the spikes in the energy consumption of, for example, the center's cooling system. A novel concept created in the group work, Bring Your Own Energy (BYOE) describes how the energy provided by EV prosumers can be used for cooling, heating, and producing special experiences. EV prosumers could provide energy at festivals and social events. EV prosumers can also use the EV to optimize their own energy consumption at a holiday cottage. Another way to make use of the EVs is to use them as an extension of the infrastructure by connecting them to an electric ferry, so that the ferry would use the EVs' batteries. Even a truck for transporting EVs could be designed, forming a collective battery, which allows EV prosumers to work during the trip on the truck.
- *Customer segments.* The potential could be extended from EV drivers to other prosumers, stores, shopping malls, and inhabitants in small communities in rural areas.
- *Customer relationships.* Relationships are formed between communities and institutions, and together these form a larger infrastructure and system for EV prosumers.

Value Delivery

- *Key resources.* The EV is a mobile storage unit, and the V2G loadings are tracked as anonymous transactions.
- *Key activities.* The EVs would serve as enablers for community events even in remote areas where there is no power supply. In addition, EVs could be used as power sources for smart grids.
- *Key partners.* Transport companies, shopping malls, stores, festival organizers, and ferry operators would be the main partners in utilizing the EV as a power source.
- *Key channels.* The network for EV prosumers can be provided via the facilitating community, the transport companies that own the trucks, and the ferries that transport the EVs.

Value Capture

- *Revenue streams.* The time EV prosumers save when they can concentrate on their work instead of driving is an indirect source of revenue in the form of savings. In addition, there are savings on the energy price and a reduction in the price of transport.
- *Cost structure.* In the cost calculations, one needs to take into account, in addition to the EV itself, the charging costs and replacement of the EV and the worn-out battery. When the mode of transport is a truck or a ferry, the costs of transforming the equipment for compatibility with the docking stations for EVs must be taken in account. If the EV prosumer belongs to a community, there may be a membership fee as well.

Results from Group 2 focused on scheduled charging and flexibility are mapped according to the BMC content elements.

Value Creation

- *Value proposition.* Charging an EV offers, for example for shopping malls, an energy source that they can control and optimize according to their own usage and thus result in a more stable electrical load. At departure, the EV battery is full.

- *Customer segments.* Shopping malls, EV parking spaces at the workplace, and sports clubs are potential customers that can be connected to EV prosumers.
- *Customer relationships.* The EV prosumer has a close relationship with the aggregator, and a more random relationship with parties that are involved when charging, such as at shopping malls. The relationship can be dedicated in the case in which the EV prosumer has a scheduled parking space arrangement, such as with a sports club. The parking space is reserved beforehand for a certain fixed time period regularly and is available for the EV prosumer then.

Value Delivery

- *Key resources.* The EVs and mobile applications for tracking the charging rate and level are the most important resources.
- *Key activities.* Charging EVs that are parked while the EV owners are running personal errands.
- *Key partners.* Aggregators and HEMS owners and providers are the main partners.
- *Key channels.* Availability of parking spaces with charging capability can be checked and reserved with a mobile application that offers real-time data also on the schedules when the spaces are reserved or free and can be reserved.

Value Capture

- *Cost structure.* The major costs come from the replacement of the worn-out EV battery.
- *Revenue streams.* A regular charging time based on a deal with the property owner enables lower charging costs for the EV prosumer.

Results from Group 3 that focused on the EV battery as a storage unit connected to the power grid are mapped according to the BMC content elements.

Value Creation

- *Value proposition.* The storage capability of EVs adds flexibility to the network, as they can receive surplus electricity and thus also stabilize the network. For example, if a DSO is having problems fulfilling electricity demand, EV prosumers can help with distribution and thus prevent a power outage and a potential fine (if there is damage to electric distribution due to storms and power outages that last for longer than stated in the customer's power purchase agreement).
- *Customer segments.* The DSO, the transmission system operator (TSO), the aggregator or electricity reseller, and individuals (e.g. neighbors) are the main customers.
- *Customer relationships.* There are different kinds of relationships with prosumer to consumer (P2C) and prosumer to business (P2B) channels.

Value Delivery

- *Key resources.* Solar panels, the EV driver, and the energy storage unit are the main resources.
- *Key activities.* Energy acquisition, the reception of orders, and maintenance of the flexibility capability in the network are the main activities. These are enabled by a navigation platform that offers P2C electricity. An automated system could offer P2B electricity.
- *Key partners.* The partners include providers of the platform, producers of EV batteries, and EV producers.
- *Key channels.* A direct relationship exists with the aggregator on the energy market, neighbors, and DSOs. An indirect relationship is formed with, for example, the TSO.

Value Capture

- *Cost structure.* The costs are generated from the equipment, energy acquisition, working hours, service costs, and implementation of the platform.

- *Revenue streams.* In the power purchase agreement, the total is the sum of the subscription and a flat rate cost. The unit used in energy sales could be Kwh × km. The sources of revenue are P2B and P2C contracts, possible road service, and services that have pay-per-use rates.

After the workshop, the researchers conducted a high-level cross-case analysis of the BMC content elements of the three BMs created for the different EV use phases. A cross-case analysis allows a comparison of the commonalities and differences in the elements which is required for further exploration of microfoundations for the balanced policy approach (see Table 9.1).

The most striking similarity across the use cases is that the value proposition is similar in its core: Storage creates value in all use cases. DSOs and TSOs have similar roles in being the channel, but this is not

Table 9.1 A summary of the cross-case analysis of the workshop results

BMC content element	Drive: Mobile energy storage unit (Group 1)	Charge: Scheduled charging and flexibility (Group 2)	Store: Connected storage (Group 3)
Value proposition	sharing energy with other EV drivers BYOE transport of EVs that form a collective battery focus on small communities	control and optimization of the energy source according to own usage more stable electrical load at departure, the EV battery is full	offers flexibility to the network can receive the surplus electricity and thus stabilize the network eliminates bottlenecks in the network
Customer segments	other prosumers stores and shopping malls EV drivers small communities in rural areas	shopping mall EVs at a workplace	DSO TSO aggregator/ electricity reseller neighbor
Customer relationships	community --> institution = infrastructure and system	tight relationship with the aggregator random charging, e.g. at shopping malls dedicated and scheduled parking space arrangements	different kinds of relationships with P2B and P2C customers

(*continued*)

Table 9.1 (continued)

BMC content element	Drive: Mobile energy storage unit (Group 1)	Charge: Scheduled charging and flexibility (Group 2)	Store: Connected storage (Group 3)
Key resources	mobile storage unit anonymous transactions	EV mobile apps	solar panels EV driver energy storage
Key activities	enabler for communities connected to smart grids V2G	charging at certain time keeping storage opportunity open (for quick balancing) V2G	energy acquisition reception of the orders maintenance of the flexibility capability navigation P2C platform automated P2B system V2G
Key partners	transport companies stores festival organizers ferry operator	aggregators HEMS	provider of the platform producer of batteries producer of EVs
Channels	facilitating community trucks ferries DSO TSO	DSO TSO	aggregator/energy market neighbor DSO TSO
Cost structure	charging EV truck, ferry wearing out of the EV and the battery community membership	replacement of the EV battery	equipment energy acquisition working hours service costs platform
Revenue streams	saved time savings in energy price reduction in the price of transport peak avoidance benefit	lower charging costs	power purchase agreements P2P and P2C contracts road services

necessarily pre-determined as the utilization of bi-directional information may be device dependent owing to standardization issues, intellectual property rights agreements, and so on. In addition, the V2G connection mode emerged as an important activity across the use cases, as without this connection the whole digital business case becomes obsolete. This, however, requires multiple activities from many partners.

The value propositions can be viewed very differently depending on the stakeholders, although the proposition itself remains similar across use cases. For example, storage facilitates low-cost charging at surplus production peaks, which is in a sense a multi-sided market where all actors can simultaneously benefit from the consumption of energy, but the value is different for different actors. EV prosumers can have lower prices and the DSO can receive network stability.

Customer relationships exhibited multiple perspectives across use cases. This underlines the differences between the drive, charge, and store use cases. The use cases present multiple avenues for delivering value to different actors in the system. Key partners also vary considerably between use cases. Although DSOs and TSOs have necessary roles, these channels do not determine the nature of prosumers' activities.

The cross-analysis of the BMC results reveals that the value creation elements differ in each case. However, the value capture part has similar elements. For example, the cost structure and concerns related to wearing out the batteries were shared in all cases. The analysis of the Group 3 value creation, value delivery, and value capture shows that the value creation is solid; the utilities are looking for flexibility, and the EV prosumers could offer that as the value proposition. In addition, the needed resources, including key technologies, are becoming available, with some short-term limitations related to V2G availability, and key activities could be implemented in the near future. However, the value capture part is not looking well balanced for EV prosumers as the cost structure is heavy and potential revenue streams are unclear and seem narrow. Based on the current understanding of, for example, the demand response, compensation for households does not promise a rewarding revenue compensation for flexibility. A summary of the cross-case analysis from the value creation–value delivery–value capture perspective is shown in Table 9.2.

Table 9.2 Summary of the value creation-delivery-capture in the use cases

	Group 1: Drive	Group 2: Charge	Group 3: Store
Value creation	Value proposition has potential for further elaboration. Sharing energy with others in parking lots, on special occasions, or with a shopping mall for peak demand reduction can offer value but includes uncertainties More focused segmentation should be done to find potential regularity in driver behavior The relationship requires a lot of trust and has to be institutionalized at least in larger solutions	The EV prosumer can control and optimize the use of energy, the electrical load is more stable, and at departure the EV battery is full. All of these are part of the value proposition Customers include regular EV prosumers at shopping malls and EV owners who park at their workplace or home The relationships vary depending on the customer type—a close relationship with the aggregator but a random relationship with shopping malls	Value proposition (P2B) is strong as the potential customer segments (DSO and an aggregator) see EV flexibility as important for the grid stability, especially peak load balancing. Prosumers would be an important resource for aggregators that could consolidate the offerings for the grid The P2C proposition is novel, and there is no evidence of customer demand for it. However, P2C potentially could offer value
Value delivery	V2G and its servitization are under constant development but are not ready Key partners such as shopping malls and festival organizers have to be engaged in becoming frontrunners The channels do not exist yet	The EV is the main resource required in addition to mobile applications that track the EV's charging status Charging happens while EV prosumers are running personal errands The potential future partners are aggregators and HEMSs The channels do not exist yet	The technology required for connecting EV battery to the grid is ready but not widely available. There are gaps in offering aggregation services or a platform for selling prosumer services Channels are under development
Value capture	The cost structure, including the replacement of a worn-out battery, finding compatible equipment, and possible membership fees, is high Revenue streams include savings from energy prices and time savings but remain low compared with the cost structure	The main costs come from the EV battery wearing out The value comes from savings resulting from lower charging costs	The cost structure is high compared to the potential revenue as compensation for flexibility Battery wear-and-tear concerns have not been addressed

5 Discussion and Conclusions

The DBMs developed in the workshop revealed that EV prosumers added value to the energy network for the value creation part in the BM. However, in value delivery and value capture, major issues prohibiting realization of value remain. In value delivery, the uncertainty comes from customer behavior and the rate at which the use of EVs will diffuse among users. In addition, the development of a technical infrastructure involving incumbents such as DSOs and TSOs and facilitating new entrants in future energy markets is still in its infancy. Another factor complicating the development of DBMs for EVs is that the coverage of EV charging stations in many countries is still very sparse and concentrated in major cities and a few small towns. In addition, there are competing alternative fuel vehicles, such as those based on natural gas. Finally, the value capture seems to be hard to materialize as there are costs from the technical investments and implementation, and the actual amounts of energy offered to the markets would be fairly low, at least in the initial phase, when the number of EVs is still low. The value creation–delivery–capture readiness is summarized in Fig. 9.2.

The role of digitalization is crucial for the implementation of any of the phases where EV prosumers contribute to the energy system. Real-time follow-up of the charging level of a battery and the uploaded amount of energy to and from the grid need to be tracked for each EV prosumer. This can best be implemented with an IoT where each EV is tracked and

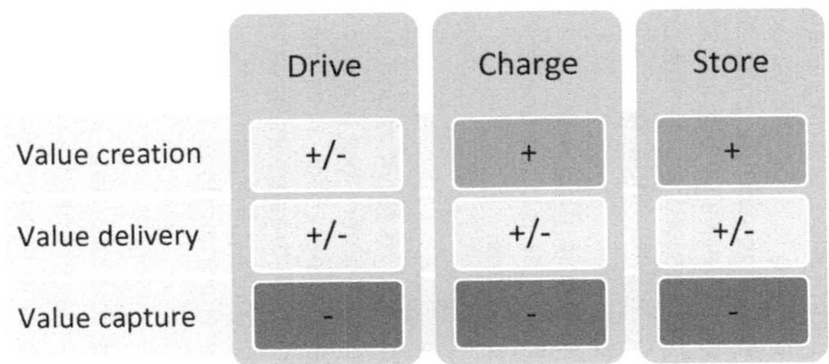

Fig. 9.2 Summary of the current state of the value creation–delivery–capture readiness of EV DBMs for the prosumer

provides data to the prosumer, to the smart grid provider, as well as to the other actors in the network. In smart grids, electricity is produced, distributed, and optimized locally for consumers, and thus is an optimal method for integrating RE resources in communities and facilitating the contribution of EV prosumers to the community network.

Despite the similarities in the use cases, there are significant differences that require a digital platform to unify the user experience across use cases. To build a DBM for EV usage that includes driving, charging, and storage, the results of the group work indicate that there is a need for a digital system that is continually updated and close to real time so that EV users acting as prosumers can monitor and control the energy usage of their EVs. The digitalization of the processes for tracking EV prosumers in a smart grid network could possibly be based on the initial BMs created in the workshop. In addition, automation and artificial intelligence-based monitoring and operation may be needed for the system as a whole to remain stable. Thus, large-scale adoption of EVs and DBMs for EVs would require improving the user experience with easy-to-use applications that unify different services and DBMs for the prosumer with a single interface.

Based on the DBMs from the workshop, we designed a balanced policy framework that would take into consideration the microfoundational change mechanisms and requirements revealed in the analysis above. The goal of the framework (see Fig. 9.3) is not to be a normative guideline but to draw attention to three issues: the process of developing a future sustainable energy system, the multi-level nature of the changes needed, and

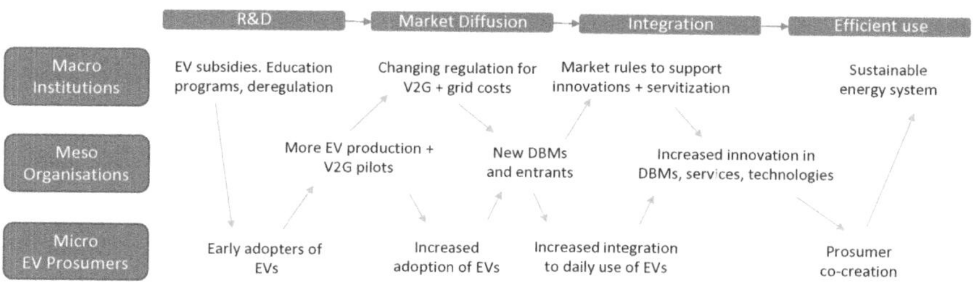

Fig. 9.3 Opportunities for macro-, meso-, and microlevel actions in a balanced policy approach supporting EV DBMs for the energy market transition

causal dependencies between levels and phases. In Fig. 9.3, the phases of the energy system evolution in EVs are depicted as starting with the research and development conducted by meso-level organizations. This leads to the market diffusion phase of EVs as more and more user segments adopt EVs. Furthermore, large-scale adoption is followed by integration of various services and products to provide better and better functionalities for EV prosumers. Finally, efficient use of EVs as part of the energy system leads to the incremental evolution of services and products in the EV innovation ecosystem. Thus, we depict possible routes of institutional evolution from the early technology-driven market with a subsidy-driven policy leading to microfoundations of prosumer behavior, and finally to a sustainable future energy system.

At the microlevel, early adopters of EVs still present rudimentary testing grounds for DBMs as most of the functionalities that EVs might have are still missing, owing to a lack of V2G connections or the overall infrastructure. However, the basic functionality of charging–storing–driving will be built and tested leading to new opportunities in providing new services and products as adoption levels increase and value delivery from EV prosumers becomes possible. Later, EVs will be integrated in daily use for prosumers, and value capture will be facilitated in mass markets. At the same time, meso-level companies will develop EV technologies and related infrastructure, but in the early phases they need external support to increase adoption levels; for example, the chicken and egg problem (no charging–no users–no charging) needs to be solved. Once adoption levels start to increase, more EVs will be produced, and owing to learning curve effects prices will decrease, and the quality and functionality of the EVs will increase. The increased adoption and infrastructure development will lead to new entrants and opportunities for services, such as community-based sharing of energy or demand response DBMs for EVs. Further development of the infrastructure will lead to prosumer engagement in service and product development. Finally, at the macro-level, policy guidance and regulations will evolve from facilitating technology development and the adoption of EVs to facilitating infrastructure development and new meso-level activities, and finally to engaging all the actors in cocreation.

In summary, the whole process can be described as follows. The start of the balanced approach should support EV adoption and infrastructure so that manufacturers' production volumes increase, leading to a decrease in EV prices and an increase in the quality and usability of technologies for mass market adoption. This leads to a need to support grid connections at the institutional policy level, regulation and incentives leading to infrastructure deployment and new organizations entering the system. This is supported by increased EV adoption by mass market segments. Furthermore, V2G and new DBMs of entrants support the integration of EVs in prosumers' daily use. If at this point prosumers' daily use is supported by macro-level policies to encourage further servitization and innovation, new innovations are cocreated at the micro- and meso-levels, leading further to efficient and effective implementation of smart grids at the institutional level.

Naturally, this study has several limitations, offering some potentially fruitful avenues for future research. One limitation of the workshop approach is the intensive and cooperative environment in which the participants interacted. Depending on one's personal level of motivation and interest in participating in that moment, as well as the extraversion or introversion of the participants, they can be either very active or passive, which has also been noted in focus group discussions (Barry and Stewart 1997). However, as each group had a facilitator who kept the discussion going, we attempted to minimize this problem. In addition, as the participants had been in contact previously in several project meetings, even the most timid participants should have had the opportunity to participate in the discussion. Another limitation of a workshop approach may be the uneven presentation from different organizations and the hierarchical structure in the academic world that may hinder open communication and a flow of ideas (Ørngreen and Levinsen 2017). However, in this case, as the participants already knew each other well beforehand and referred to each other by their first names (including the professors), this factor did not have much influence on the open exchange of ideas among the workshop participants. Furthermore, our depiction of a balanced policy approach heavily relies on the heuristics of the authors, and therefore the framework is more of a discussion opening for raising awareness of the possible influence of prosumers' DBMs on the systemic change taking place in energy systems. Our aim is to show that microfoundations as prosumers' DBMs for EVs have significant systemic effects, and these effects should be taken into account when policy issues are considered.

In conclusion, the transformation of energy consumers into prosumers with BMs in mind—that is, transforming consumers into entrepreneurs—is a dramatic behavioral change at the individual level and leads to a multitude of institutional changes at the macro-level. This transformation calls for new institutional arrangements and institutions, such as behavioral guidelines for new organizational forms (energy collectives, etc.) and individual behavioral norms (such as flexible commuting allowed by smart charging, etc.). This transformation may be approached with a balanced policy approach, and for this purpose we have proposed several opportunities for delineating interlevel connections of causalities in order to draw attention to opportunities in the balanced policy approach.

Acknowledgements This work was partly supported by funding from the Academy of Finland (Mechanisms of Technological Change in Business Ecosystems, grant number 279087 and EL-TRAN, grant number 314319), and from the Tekes—the Finnish Funding Agency for Innovation (Social Energy—Prosumer Centric Energy Ecosystem, Dnro 2559/31/2016). Furthermore, the authors gratefully acknowledge the support of the participants of these projects.

References

Akenji, L. 2014. Consumer Scapegoatism and Limits to Green Consumerism. *Journal of Cleaner Production* 63: 13–23.

Balcombe, P., D. Rigby, and A. Azapagic. 2013. Motivations and Barriers Associated with Adopting Microgeneration Energy Technologies in the UK. *Renewable and Sustainable Energy Reviews* 22: 655–666. https://doi.org/10.1016/j.rser.2013.02.012.

Barry, B., and G.L. Stewart. 1997. Composition, Process, and Performance in Self-Managed Groups: The Role of Personality. *Journal of Applied psychology* 82 (1): 62.

Bohnsack, R., J. Pinkse, and A. Kolk. 2014. Business Models for Sustainable Technologies: Exploring Business Model Evolution in the Case of Electric Vehicles. *Research Policy* 43 (2): 284–300.

Clement-Nyns, K., E. Haesen, and J. Driesen. 2010. The Impact of Charging Plug-in Hybrid Electric Vehicles on a Residential Distribution Grid. *IEEE Transactions on Power Systems* 25 (1): 371–380.

Coleman, J. 1990. *Foundations of Social Theory*. Boston: Harvard University Press.

Dixon, T. 2018. China 100% Electric Bus Sales Drop To ~89,546 in 2017. Retrieved March 20, 2018, from https://evobsession.com/china-100-electric-bus-sales-drop-to-89546-in-2017/.

Durance, P., and M. Godet. 2010. Scenario Building: Uses and Abuses. *Technological Forecasting & Social Change* 77 (9): 1488–1492.

Edquist, C. 2014. Striving Towards a Holistic Innovation Policy in European Countries – But Linearity Still Prevails! *Science, Technology, and Innovation Policy Review* 5 (2): 1–19.

Electromobility Platform. 2018. How EU Member States Roll-Out Electric-Mobility: Electric Charging Infrastructure in 2020 and Beyond. Retrieved from https://www.transportenvironment.org/sites/te/files/publications/Emobility Platform AFID analysis.pdf.

European Commission. 2017. *Towards the Broadest Use of Alternative Fuels*. Brussels. Retrieved from https://ec.europa.eu/transparency/regdoc/rep/1/2017/EN/COM-2017-652-F1-EN-MAIN-PART-1.PDF.

Foehringer Merchant, E. 2017. The Next Big Obstacle for Electric Vehicles? Charging Infrastructure. Retrieved March 23, 2018, from https://www.greentechmedia.com/articles/read/the-next-big-obstacle-for-electric-vehicles-charging-infrastructure.

García-Villalobos, J., I. Zamora, J.I. San Martín, F.J. Asensio, and V. Aperribay. 2014. Plug-in Electric Vehicles in Electric Distribution Networks: A Review of Smart Charging Approaches. *Renewable and Sustainable Energy Reviews* 38: 717–731.

Geels, F.W. 2002. Technological Transitions as Evolutionary Reconfiguration Processes: A Multi-Level Perspective and a Case-Study. *Research Policy* 31 (December): 1257–1274. https://doi.org/10.1016/S0048-7333(02)00062-8.

Giordano, V., and G. Fulli. 2012. A Business Case for Smart Grid Technologies: A Systemic Perspective. *Energy Policy* 40: 252–259.

Hall, D., M. Moultak, and N. Lutsey 2017. Electric Vehicle Capitals of the World: Demonstrating the Path to Electric Drive. The International Council on Clean Transportation (ICCT), March. Retrieved from www.theicct.org.

Hekkert, M.P., R.A.A. Suurs, S.O. Negro, S. Kuhlmann, and R.E. Smits. 2007. Functions of Innovation Systems: A New Approach for Analysing Technological Change. *Technological Forecasting and Social Change* 74 (4): 413–432. https://doi.org/10.1016/j.techfore.2006.03.002.

Hertzke, P., N. Müller, and S. Schen. 2017. Dynamics in the Global Electric-Vehicle Market. Retrieved March 23, 2018, from https://www.mckinsey.com/industries/automotive-and-assembly/our-insights/dynamics-in-the-global-electric-vehicle-market.

IEA. 2017. Global EV Outlook 2017 – Two Million and Counting.

———. 2018. Nordic EV Outlook 2018.

IEA-PVPS. 2016. Review and Analysis of PV Self-Consumption Policies.

Jacobsson, S., and V. Lauber. 2006. The Politics and Policy of Energy System Transformation – Explaining the German Diffusion of Renewable Energy Technology. *Energy Policy* 34: 256–276. https://doi.org/10.1016/j.enpol.2004.08.029.

Koirala, B.P., E. Koliou, J. Friege, R.A. Hakvoort, and P.M. Herder. 2016. Energetic Communities for Community Energy: A Review of Key Issues and Trends Shaping Integrated Community Energy Systems. *Renewable and Sustainable Energy Reviews* 56: 722–744. https://doi.org/10.1016/j.rser.2015.11.080.

Kotilainen, K., and U.A. Saari. 2018. Policy Influence on Consumers' Evolution into Prosumers – Empirical Findings from an Exploratory Survey in Europe. *Sustainability* 10 (1): 186.

Kotilainen, K., M. Sommarberg, P. Järventausta, and P. Aalto. 2016a. Prosumer Centric Digital Energy Ecosystem Framework. In *Proceedings of the 8th International Conference on Management of Digital EcoSystems,* 47–51. ACM, November.

Kotilainen, K., P. Järventausta, and P. Aalto. 2016b. Prosumer Centric Co-creation in Smart Grid Innovation Ecosystem. In *Innovative Smart Grid Technologies-Asia (ISGT-Asia), 2016 IEEE,* 884–889. IEEE, November.

Kotilainen, K., S.J. Mäkinen, P. Järvetausta, R. Antti, and J. Markkula. 2016c. The Role of Residential Prosumers Initiating the Energy Innovation Ecosystem to Future Flexible Energy System. In *European Energy Market (EEM), 2016 13th International Conference on the,* 1–5. IEEE, June.

Liedtke, C., J. Buhl, and N. Ameli. 2013. Microfoundations for Sustainable Growth with Eco-Intelligent Product Service-Arrangements. *Sustainability* 5 (3): 1141–1160.

Loorbach, D.A. 2007. Transition Management: New Mode of Governance for Sustainable Development. June 7. Retrieved from http://hdl.handle.net/1765/10200.

Meadowcroft, J. 2009. What About the Politics? Sustainable Development, Transition Management, and Long Term Energy Transitions. *Policy Sciences* 42 (4): 323–340. https://doi.org/10.1007/s11077-009-9097-z.

Niesten, E., and F. Alkemade. 2016. How Is Value Created and Captured in Smart Grids? A Review of the Literature and an Analysis of Pilot Projects. *Renewable and Sustainable Energy Reviews* 53: 629–638.

Öberg, J., and P. Hernwall. 2016. Participatory Design with Teachers: Designing the Workshops. In *Designs for Learning, Proceedings of the 5th International Conference on Designs for Learning,* 269–282. Aalborg: Aalborg University Press.

Ørngreen, R., and K. Levinsen. 2017. Workshops as a Research Methodology. *The Electronic Journal of e-Learning* 15 (1), 70–81. Available online at www.ejel.org.

Osterwalder, A., and Y. Pigneur. 2010. *Business Model Generation: A Handbook for Visionaries, Game Changers, and Challengers.* Hoboken: John Wiley & Sons.

Painuly, J.P. 2001. Barriers to Renewable Energy Penetration; a Framework for Analysis. *Renewable energy* 24: 73–89.

Raub, W., V. Buskens, and M.A. Van Assen. 2011. Micro-Macro Links and Microfoundations in Sociology. *The Journal of Mathematical Sociology* 35 (1–3): 1–25.

Richter, M. 2012. Utilities' Business Models for Renewable Energy: A Review. *Renewable and Sustainable Energy Reviews* 16 (5): 2483–2493. https://doi.org/10.1016/j.rser.2012.01.072.

Rodríguez-Molina, J., M. Martínez-Núñez, J.F. Martínez, and W. Pérez-Aguiar. 2014. Business Models in the Smart Grid: Challenges, Opportunities and Proposals for Prosumer Profitability. *Energies* 7 (9): 6142–6171. https://doi.org/10.3390/en7096142.

Saari, U.A., R.J. Baumgartner, and S.J. Mäkinen. 2017. Eco-Friendly Brands to Drive Sustainable Development: Replication and Extension of the Brand Experience Scale in a Cross-National Context. *Sustainability* 9: 1286. https://doi.org/10.3390/su9071286.

Schleicher-Tappeser, R. 2012. How Renewables Will Change Electricity Markets in the Next Five Years. *Energy Policy* 48: 64–75. https://doi.org/10.1016/j.enpol.2012.04.042.

Scholten, D., and R. Künneke. 2016. Towards the Comprehensive Design of Energy Infrastructures. *Sustainability* (Switzerland) 8 (12). https://doi.org/10.3390/su8121291.

SEDC. 2017. Explicit Demand Response in Europe: Mapping the Markets.

Shaham, Z. 2018. 2017 Electric Car Sales – US, China, & Europe (Month By Month)e. Retrieved March 20, 2018, from https://evobsession.com/2017-electric-car-sales-us-china-europe-month-month/.

Siano, P. 2014. Demand Response and Smart Grids – A Survey. *Renewable and sustainable energy reviews* 30: 461–478.

Smith, A., and R. Raven. 2012. What Is Protective Space? Reconsidering Niches in Transitions to Sustainability. *Research Policy* 41 (6): 1025–1036. https://doi.org/10.1016/j.respol.2011.12.012.

Sovacool, B.K., L. Noel, J. Axsen, and W. Kempton. 2018. The Neglected Social Dimensions to a Vehicle-to-Grid (V2G) Transition: A Critical and Systematic Review. *Environmental Research Letters* 13 (1): 013001.

Spaargaren, G. 2011. Theories of Practices: Agency, Technology, and Culture: Exploring the Relevance of Practice Theories for the Governance of Sustainable Consumption Practices in the New World-Order. *Global Environmental Change* 21 (3): 813–822.

Teece, D.J. 2010. Business Models, Business Strategy and Innovation. *Long Range Planning* 43 (2–3): 172–194.

Veit, D., E. Clemons, A. Benlian, P. Buxmann, T. Hess, D. Kundisch, ..., and M. Spann 2014. Business Models. *Business & Information Systems Engineering* 6 (1): 45–53.

Wakkary, R. 2007. *A Participatory Design Understanding of Interaction Design*. Science of Design Workshop. San Jose: CHI.

Weill, P., and S.L. Woerner. 2013. Optimizing Your Digital Business Model. *MIT Sloan Management Review* 54 (3): 71.

Wiek, A., S. Talwar, M. O'Shea, and J. Robinson. 2014. Toward a Methodological Scheme for Capturing Societal Effects of Participatory Sustainable Research. *Research Evaluation* 23: 1–16.

Zame, K.K., and Christopher A. Brehm, Alex T. Nitica, Christopher L. Richard, G. D. Schweitzer III. 2017. Smart Grid and Energy Storage: Policy Recommendations. *Renewable and Sustainable Energy Reviews.*, July. https://doi.org/10.1016/j.rser.2017.07.011

10

Summary and Concluding Remarks

Annabeth Aagaard

The global growth in digitalization and in the application of digital technologies in business development is creating immense opportunities, but it also raises questions to be answered by research and practitioners. The traditional ways of doing business and of engaging with customers and ecosystems is changing through the use of data and will alter the future of many established platforms, concepts, and models. Through digital business models (DBMs), companies are bridging their businesses into a digital age, using data to guide their existing and totally new business endeavors. The existing structures of companies and the way value is created and captured in businesses is changing with the digital transformation. The vast amounts of data made easily available through, for example, the Internet of Things (IoT) influences (or forces) organizations to change their ways of organizing, managing, collaborating, and engaging with all types of stakeholders and ecosystems in exploring the multiple and multisided digital business opportunities. With this emerges a need for new

A. Aagaard (✉)
Department of Business Development & Technology, Aarhus University, Herning, Denmark
e-mail: aaa@btech.au.dk

A. Aagaard (ed.), *Digital Business Models*,
https://doi.org/10.1007/978-3-319-96902-2_10

theoretical models and empirical understandings of business modeling in today's interconnected and global societies.

Thus, the aim of *Digital Business Models: Driving Transformation and Innovation* is to contribute to the development of new knowledge of the concept: how DBMs can create value; how DBMs are designed, implemented, and managed in digital start-ups and established organizations, with customers, and in an international context; and what the implications are of general data protection emphasizing the privacy, security, trust, and ethics issues of digital business models. In bridging the theoretical understanding of DBMs to empirical findings and case examples, this publication explores how the DBM concept is understood in theory and applied and integrated in practice, as stressed as an insufficiently researched area by several authors. Throughout the chapters of the book, different aspects of DBMs are explained and discussed in further elaboration and exploration of the concept and its applications.

In Chap. 1, the concept and models of DBMs are identified, mapped, and presented. This chapter provides a structured literature review about DBM research and what drives and challenges the design, integration, and management of DBMs in start-ups and in established companies.

Chapter 2 emphasizes IoT as the driver for DBMs. This chapter takes a more technological approach regarding how IoT can be applied, what is available at the moment, how technologies are connected, and how technology drives and challenges companies in pursuing and developing DBMs.

Chapter 3 explores the journey from product to service, while using IoT as a lever for servitization. As such, the IoT provides unique business opportunities for servitization, helping companies go from traditional product development to servitization offerings. This chapter explores business development through the car industry, showing how to go from selling cars to selling mobility and exploring new business models for connected cars. The pervasive use of information technologies in vehicles have transformed cars into a digital living space, while making everyday traveling more efficient, safe, and sustainable. For car manufacturers, this transformation means a shift in current business models and considerations of how to transform from selling cars to selling mobility services.

The focus of Chap. 4 is on the digitalization of value chains and ecosystems as well as novel business models in these domains, emphasizing digital agriculture, manufacturing, and retail. In all these domains, new and interesting concepts are being explored and created, involving multiple organizations, new business model constellations, and interesting partnerships. The chapter explores the main features and compares different models from the perspective of different stakeholders. It emphasizes the business potential of connecting fast-moving consumer goods and the role of a product passport as an important enabler of circular economy. This is done through multiple examples from the practice of leveraging the work on ecosystems done in the context of H2020 TagItSmart project and its commercial activities.

Chapter 5 explores the question of how business value is extracted from operational data through a case study. This case study focuses on emerging values that Big Data and data analytics provide to a growing business organization and explores the process of unlocking these values and the difficulties the organization encounters in identifying and extracting insights from the data they collect during their operations. In this particular case, it is often the clients who drive data initiatives. Most benefits are realized from externally motivated activities and leadership believing in the potential value of Big Data and analytics in terms of adding value to processes. However, at the same time, allocating limited resources between diverse business demands slows the transition toward a more data-driven decision-making paradigm within the firm.

Chapter 6 discusses the impact of DBM innovation on sales channels and organization. As such, digitalization may in many cases lead to disruptions of existing sales channels by making it possible for original equipment manufacturers to shortcut or reshape earlier channels and have direct contact with end customers. This poses challenges to several stakeholders in the business ecosystem, as existing relationships may change from collaboration to different types of competition. Digitalization of business models also frequently implies substantial changes to the sales organization, as sales focused on selling solutions with bundled products and services is often very different from sales dedicated to selling only products, in terms of, for example, incentives and competence requirements. This chapter explores a number of fundamental challenges related to sales channels and organization when introducing DBM innovations, based on case studies from different parts of the Swedish company Husqvarna.

Chapter 7 examines how DBMs are explored in an international context and what makes a DBM internationally scalable. Where the Internet has paved the way for a rapid international expansion for firms such as Google and Facebook, most digital businesses face difficulties in expanding across borders. Based on data and case studies from European Internet firms, this chapter analyzes the determinants for international scalability for firms with DBMs, and contributes with new theoretical insights and practical advice for business managers seeking to internationalize their digital businesses.

Chapter 8 addresses DBMs and general data protection while emphasizing the privacy, security, trust, and ethics issues of DBMs. With the increasing emphasis on data security, companies must consider and establish the proper data protection. The main focus of this chapter is on the establishment of new paradigms and business opportunities related to European GDPR.

Chapter 9 examines prosumers' digital business models for electric vehicles and the microfoundation for a balanced policy approach. The emphasis of the chapter is to explore how prosumers can create, deliver, and capture value with EVs in future energy systems. Focusing on prosumers' digital business models (DBMs), the chapter illustrates the complex interdependencies between various activities and actors needed in the development of an energy system.

Digital Business Models: Driving Transformation and Innovation thus elaborates upon the concept of DBMs as well as widening the scope and the understanding of what DBMs actually are and may become, and how they can help drive digital transformation and innovation in different ways and contexts while creating value and performance through data-driven business development. One clear conclusion from this publication and its literature reviews is that this concept is still at a very early stage and constantly moving at a pace that is hard to keep up with, as the development and adaption of digital technologies increases by the minute. Access to Big Data and improved data analytics provides the optimal foundation for DBM innovation and effective data-driven decision-making for businesses. However, security, privacy, and trust are key challenges that must be addressed and attended to, as interconnectivity between devices and actors opens up the "market of data" to a very wide and often global group of stakeholders. Consequently, the majority of the chapters here have emphasized these challenges by presenting case examples or frameworks of how to overcome some of these managerial and strategic challenges. However, more research is needed in exploring how to effectively and successfully facilitate the digital transformation, organization, integration, and impact across companies, customers, collaborators, and ecosystems.

The majority of existing literature has addressed the use and development of DBMs in established companies. However, the research field and empirical cases of digital start-ups and digital entrepreneurship is growing and underlines the potential in this area, now and in the future. With more companies starting up with digital DNA, business models, and strategy, new frameworks and models will have to emerge too, and new ways of differentiating digitally will be required.

One very timely and relevant research area is the use of data and digitalization in solving the United Nations' sustainable development goals and developing more sustainable solutions and sustainable business models. Through the use of Big Data, businesses can make more sustainable decisions, optimizing their business processes, portfolios, and functions (e.g. production, logistics, and sales) in making smarter, more efficient, less resource-consuming and polluting business choices. In addition, through the interconnectivity between users, businesses, society, and other stakeholders, entire ecosystems can start making more sustainable, socially and environmentally friendly decisions and developments. For the reader who seeks more knowledge on sustainable business models and how data and digitalization can support sustainability, we suggest another Palgrave Macmillan publication, *Sustainable Business Models—Innovation, Implementation and Success* (2018).

Where is digitalization heading? There is no simple answer to this question, as the sky is the limit and we have only seen the first developments in digital business development. Digital technologies such as artificial intelligence, robotics, and blockchains are finding their way into sectors and applications never anticipated. Although large corporations are leading the digital business development, digital start-ups are defining the new paths for the more disruptive digital business model innovation. Yet at the same time, new technologies are emerging. All of this challenges companies—now and particularly in the future—to be more radical in their digital transformation, their use of data, and their DBM innovation to be able to differentiate and compete globally. Thus, new frameworks and models have to be invented in exploring, developing, and deploying more radical DBMs. Moreover, the growing trends of digital entrepreneurs provide new venues for entrepreneurial research and processes as well as for the development of frameworks and models in managing, facilitating, and assessing these digital entrepreneurs and enterprises. As DBM innovation is all about open innovation and interconnectivity across the ecosystems, new types and forms of collaboration across new and multiple stakeholders have to be explored theoretically and in practice.

At the end of the day, digital technologies should not be integrated for the sake of technology or of seeing how far it can go, but for the sake of building better, more efficient, and sustainable societies and businesses. Consequently, governments have to consider the social implications of increased digital transformation and how to avoid the possibility of digitalization creating an A-team and a B-team of countries, citizens, and employees—those with or without (the right) digital skills. If we take digitalization to the ultimate level, do we really want to live in societies where data is the new currency and you are greeted by robots everywhere and have artificial intelligence installed in every device you encounter? New research is therefore requested on how digital technologies and DBMs should be applied in a sustainable, digital transformation that not only leaves people and societies more efficient, but also happier and more sustainable.

Index[1]

[1] Note: Page numbers followed by 'n' refer to notes.

A. Aagaard (ed.), *Digital Business Models*,
https://doi.org/10.1007/978-3-319-96902-2

The manufacturer's authorised representative in the EU is Springer Nature Customer Service Centre GmbH, Europaplatz 3, 69115 Heidelberg, Germany. If you have any concerns regarding our products, please contact ProductSafety@springernature.com

Printed and bound by CPI Group (UK) Ltd, Croydon, CR0 4YY
22/09/2026
02221067-0008